S0-AJD-131

MARGINAL-COST PRIC

CONTROL

MARGINAL - COST PRICE - OUTPUT CONTROL

A CRITICAL HISTORY AND
RESTATEMENT OF THE THEORY
BY
BURNHAM PUTNAM BECKWITH

NEW YORK
COLUMBIA UNIVERSITY PRESS
1955

38677

338.52
B 397

LIBRARY OF CONGRESS CATALOG CARD NUMBER: 54-11665

COPYRIGHT 1955, COLUMBIA UNIVERSITY PRESS, NEW YORK

PUBLISHED IN GREAT BRITAIN, CANADA, INDIA, AND PAKISTAN
BY GEOFFREY CUMBERLEGE, OXFORD UNIVERSITY PRESS
LONDON, TORONTO, BOMBAY, AND KARACHI

MANUFACTURED IN THE UNITED STATES OF AMERICA

ACKNOWLEDGMENTS

ACKNOWLEDGMENTS are due to the following publishers for permission to quote from the listed works under copyright. To the Oxford University Press, Inc., for quotations from J. E. Meade, *An Introduction to Economic Analysis and Policy* (1938); from H. D. Dickinson, *Economics of Socialism* (1939); and from I. M. D. Little, *A Critique of Welfare Economics* (1950). To the Macmillan Company for quotations from Alfred Marshall, *Principles of Economics,* 8th edition (1948); from Joan Robinson, *The Economics of Imperfect Competition* (1933); and from Abba P. Lerner, *The Economics of Control* (1944). To Routledge and Kegan Paul, Ltd., for quotations from E. F. M. Durbin, *Problems of Economic Planning* (1949).

BURNHAM PUTNAM BECKWITH

Pasadena, California
July, 1954

CONTENTS

MARGINAL-COST PRICE-OUTPUT CONTROL

I

INTRODUCTION

THE SUBJECT of this book is the theory that price and/or output is ideal when price equals marginal cost. We call our restatement of this idea the theory of marginal-cost price-output control. By earlier writers it has usually been called the theory of marginal-cost pricing or, less often, the theory of incremental-cost pricing. Both of these names are misleading because the function of the theory is to guide the control of *output*.

In its earliest (1936) form the new theory was stated as a theory of output control, namely, as the theory that output should be increased or decreased until price equals marginal cost, and it has since been periodically restated in this form. Many writers, however, have ignored this version of the theory and claimed merely that price should equal marginal cost, without explaining whether this result should be achieved by means of price or output control. No one has ever explained when it is better to control directly price rather than output or, vice versa. This is one of the contributions of this study, but we shall not further anticipate it here. What we wish to stress now is that there are two separate methods of achieving an ideal output: marginal-cost price control and marginal-cost output control. The term marginal-cost pricing has sometimes been used to mean one, sometimes the other, and sometimes both. Those who use it rarely explain which of these three meanings they have in mind. In our restatement of the theory of marginal-cost pricing, we have tried to make clear that it includes both price and output control. *We have restated it as the theory that either price or output should be directly controlled so as to make price equal marginal cost, and we have ex-*

plained when it is best to control price and when it is best to control output directly. We call this the theory of marginal-cost *price-output* control to further stress that it includes both direct price control and direct output control.

If we had to choose between the terms price control and output control, we would prefer the latter, for the purpose of price control is output control. Prices are merely means of controlling production and consumption; they are not ends in themselves.

Whatever the form in which it is stated, the theory of marginal-cost price-output control is a fairly new one, dating back only to 1936, though it was foreshadowed earlier. We believe it is the most significant contribution to economic theory since the introduction of marginal analysis. It is still largely ignored, however, and there is a great need for a careful restatement and defense of it.

ISOLATING THE PROBLEM OF IDEAL OUTPUT

The analysis of economic problems may be simplified by disentangling them from each other and considering each one separately and by assuming certain conditions. In this study we shall rely chiefly on the former method. The use of arbitrary simplifying assumptions too often results in conclusions which are inapplicable in the real world. On the other hand, the isolation of a single problem from other problems not only simplifies its analysis but results in a solution whose application is practical.

The use of partial rather than general analysis is one, but only one, method of disentangling economic problems from each other. It separates the problem of fixing a particular price or output from the problem of fixing other prices and outputs. In practice all prices and outputs must be individually determined. There is no feasible method of simultaneous general determination. *Hence, general analysis has no practical value, unless it be that it suggests methods of partial analysis and individual price-output control.*

It is unnecessary to list all of the economic problems which we shall not try to solve in this study. We shall only mention those which are most closely related to the problem of ideal output or which other writers have argued must be solved by a theory of ideal output.

First, aside from a few incidental remarks, we shall not try to solve the many problems involved in improving the accuracy with which marginal money costs measure marginal real costs. The better these problems are solved, the more desirable will be the results of marginal-cost price-output control, but they are separate problems which deserve separate analysis.

Secondly, we shall not discuss the interesting problem of how to make the consumers' price offers a more accurate measure of marginal utility to him. The ideal solution of this problem might require special education, taxes, and subsidies, but such reforms could be considered and adopted independently of marginal-cost price-output control and would be desirable whether or not ideal price-output control is adopted.

Thirdly, we shall ignore the problem of minimizing the real cost of producing desired outputs, the problem of the ideal combination of productive agents, because this also is a distinct problem which should be treated separately. Price should equal marginal cost whether or not the factors are perfectly combined, and improvement in the combination of the agents in production is needed whether or not price equals marginal cost. Moreover, each of these goals can be pursued more efficiently when they are treated as separate ends than when they are treated as parts of the same end. A decision to increase or decrease output because price or marginal cost has fallen or risen is a different kind of decision than one to combine the factors in a different way in order to reduce average costs. These decisions are usually made at different times and for different reasons. The fact that a single decision can affect both the volume of output and the ratios of factor combination does not prove that all decisions should achieve both ideal output and ideal factor combination.

Fourthly, we shall not discuss, except incidentally, the problem of the ideal distribution of income. This is an entirely distinct problem which in our opinion can be solved in an ideal way regardless of the method of price-output control. The fact that a change in the price or output of a single good affects the distribution of income does not prove that the problem of ideal price and/or output and the problem of ideal income distribution must be considered and solved together. Every economic change affects all prices, outputs, and other economic quantities, but simultaneous determination of all quantities is obviously impossible.

Finally, we believe that *it is of the utmost importance to separate the short-run problem of ideal output with existing capital from the long-run problem of ideal investment in new fixed capital.* This vital distinction has been almost completely ignored by writers on marginal-cost price-output control. While they are rarely explicit, nearly all of the supporters of such control seem to think that the theory of marginal-cost control solves both the price-output and the investment problems.

THE RELATIONSHIP OF MARGINAL-COST PRICE-OUTPUT
THEORY TO ORTHODOX PRICE THEORY

From 1880 to 1930, orthodox price theory was largely a theory of price determination under perfect competition. Most orthodox economists considered this theory to be both prescriptive [1] and descriptive, but actually it was neither. It did not even roughly describe price determination in practice, and it did not correctly prescribe how prices should be fixed.

The first response to the realization of these defects of orthodox value theory was the development of the new and deservedly influential theories of monopolistic and/or imperfect competition. These theories provide a description of actual price formation far superior to the descriptive theory of pricing under perfect competition. They also prescribe how private profits can be maximized.

The second response was the development of a new prescriptive theory, the theory of marginal-cost price-output control, which, though first stated only a few years after the theory of monopolistic competition, remains relatively unknown. It differs from the traditional theory of price and output under perfect competition not only in being more explicitly prescriptive but in applying to the real world of imperfect competition. The old orthodox theory assumes that all firms produce one product only, that all have increasing costs, that all capital is perfectly liquid, that each firm is so small that its actions have no effect on its costs or prices, etc. The new theory makes none of these assumptions and can be applied to prices and outputs in the real world.

[1] "At least from the time of the physiocrats and Adam Smith there has never been absent from the main body of economic literature the feeling that in some sense perfect competition represented an optimal situation." P. A. Samuelson, *Foundations of Economic Analysis* (Cambridge, Mass., 1948), p. 203.

The new theory, however, does not contradict the old one. If perfect competition did exist, prices equal to marginal costs would be ideal prices, as traditional value theory implies. But this is only one very trivial application of the new and more general theory that prices should equal marginal costs under both competition and monopoly. It is trivial because perfect competition has never existed and never will.

Some economists claim that under perfect competition prices do and/or should equal average as well as marginal costs. This claim is illogical, for average cost never equals marginal cost, even under perfect competition. It is based upon the fallacy that rent is a cost rather than a surplus. Under perfect competition price equals the sum of average cost and average rent per unit, not average cost alone. This confusion of average cost with average outlay is found in the reasoning of all who advocate so-called average-cost pricing instead of marginal-cost pricing.[2] They really want prices which cover average costs and yield a surplus, not prices which equal average costs. They are interested in preserving surpluses and profits, not in achieving optimum prices.

A few words may be in order concerning the relationship of marginal-cost price-output theory to Marxian price theory. The Marxian theory that prices are, or should be, determined by average socially necessary labor time is as unsound as the Capitalist theory that prices do or should equal average cost. Both ignore the many virtues of marginal analysis. However, since average labor costs are always below average outlay, the application of the Marxian dogma would result in prices closer to the optimum than would so-called average-cost pricing in the great majority of cases, i.e., whenever average outlay is above short-run marginal cost.

THE GREAT IMPORTANCE OF MARGINAL-COST PRICE-OUTPUT THEORY

We believe that the theory of marginal-cost price-output control is the most important contribution to economic theory since the introduction of marginal analysis, of which it is the natural result, because it prescribes how prices and outputs should be fixed. Prescriptive eco-

---

[2] For a discussion of the terminological problems created by this distinction, see the note on Terminology (pp. 21–22).

nomics is far more important than descriptive economics. Description is not an end itself; it is useful only when it aids the development of prescriptive theories which help men to satisfy their wants. Moreover, the problem of ideal price or output is the heart of economic theory. Since the theory of marginal-cost price-output control is a prescriptive theory of price and output, it is certain to become the central integrating doctrine of economics if it is valid.

Orthodox price theorists have been reluctant to develop a valid prescriptive price theory because they believe that the state should not control prices. Capitalist states have, nevertheless, steadily assumed new price-regulating functions, and the political power of advocates of public ownership has steadily increased. The result is that even in the relatively conservative United States we have hundreds of boards, commissions, and agencies which regulate the prices charged by private firms or directly fix the prices charged by public enterprises. Yet these authorities get little help in their work from orthodox price theory. The theory of price determination under perfect competition is inapplicable to the real world of imperfect competition, and the theory of imperfect competition does not prescribe how prices should be regulated. The continued use of the rule that regulated prices should cover so-called average cost is based chiefly upon legal rather than economic theory. The law prohibits confiscation of private property, and the courts have held that this means that regulated prices must cover average outlay. Hence, the theory of utility-rate regulation given in most textbooks on public utility economics has degenerated into a summary of court decisions and lawyers' arguments concerning the interpretation of the law. Few public utility economists explain that the theory of what prices are legal is entirely different from the theory of what prices are economically ideal. Moreover, for the reasons previously given, the general price theory stated in nearly all books on the principles of economics cannot be applied to public utility rates and is now rarely so applied. When a chapter on public utility regulation is included, the author abandons economic for legal analysis of the price problem without calling the students' attention to this radical shift. Consequently, students get the impression that general price theory cannot be applied to problems of rate regulation and/or that lawyers know more than economists about price theory.

A valid prescriptive theory is needed not only to aid state authorities to regulate or fix prices, but also to enable economists to determine how far unregulated prices and outputs are above or below the ideal level. It is impossible to evaluate the present economic system, or any proposed major or minor economic reform, unless we have valid criteria to use in judging the resulting prices and outputs. Almost every new law has significant effects upon the price and output of some economic good. How can we judge the economic merits of these laws unless we know whether their effects upon prices and outputs are desirable? Only a valid prescriptive theory of price and output, i.e., only the theory of marginal-cost price-output control, can provide these essential criteria.

This theory is also significant because its growing acceptance will strengthen the case for public ownership of utilities and other industries whose marginal costs are usually well below their average outlay. It not only provides the first valid rule for controlling the output of such industries, but also makes clear that large gains would result from sound price-output control and that these gains can be fully achieved only under state ownership. The critics of marginal-cost control seem to have been much more aware of this implication than its advocates.

The new price-output theory will be more useful under Socialism than under Capitalism. Hence, it will attract more and more attention as Socialism becomes more popular. But this does not mean that the theory is only of minor importance under Capitalism. The theory of marginal-cost control will eventually become the heart of orthodox Capitalist economic theory as it has already become the heart of Socialist economic theory. Whether or not Capitalist economists approve of the application of marginal-cost control outside the field of railroads and public utilities, they will increasingly find it logical to begin every general discussion of price-output problems with the statement of marginal-cost price-output theory as an ideal criterion by which alone all existing prices and outputs, and all proposed price and output policies, can be evaluated.

The practical significance of this theory depends upon how often marginal costs are below so-called average costs. There has been little if any non-Marxian objection to raising prices to the level of marginal costs when such costs are above average outlay. Marginal-cost price-output control would not have any practical effect if marginal costs were above average outlay at all times. On the other hand, the larger the number of cases in which marginal costs are below average outlay, the greater would be the effect of the application of marginal-cost

theory. We shall argue later (pp. 201–3) that marginal costs are below average outlay in 80 to 90 percent of actual cases.

THE NEGLECT OF MARGINAL-COST PRICE-OUTPUT
THEORY AND SOME REASONS FOR IT

To one familiar with the idea of marginal-cost price-output control
it seems to follow almost obviously from the use of marginal analysis.
The natural tendency of marginal analysis to suggest marginal-cost
control is clearly shown in Alfred Marshall's early (1890) statement of
his acceptance of the marginal approach:

Under the guidance of Cournot, . . . I was led to attach great importance
to the fact that our observations of nature, in the moral as in the physical
world, relate not so much to aggregate quantities, as to increments of quantities, and that in particular the demand for a thing is a continuous function, of which the *marginal increment* is, in stable equilibrium, *balanced
against the corresponding increment of its cost of production.*[3] (Italics
added.)

Nevertheless, Marshall failed to say that, in order to determine an
ideal price, one should balance the marginal increment in benefit,
measured by price, against "the corresponding increment of its cost
of production." And nearly all other users of marginal analysis have
had the same peculiar blind spot. While a number of economists have
suggested the new theory since 1936, 99 percent of orthodox users of
marginal analysis still ignore or deny the need for a marginal balance
between price, the best available measure of marginal benefit, and
marginal money cost, the best available measure of marginal real cost.

Perhaps the greatest problem of any future historian of value and
price theory will be to explain, (1) why economists failed to perceive
that marginal price should equal marginal cost for almost one hundred years after they began to apply marginal analysis to value and
price problems, and (2) why the theory was so long ignored by the
vast majority of economists after it had been clearly stated.

We suggest the following reasons as worthy of consideration. Probably the chief reason for the long failure of marginal-utility economists
to state the theory that price should equal marginal cost was their
belief that price does equal marginal cost, if not in all cases, at least

3 Alfred Marshall, *Principles of Economics,* 8th ed. (New York, 1948), p. x.

in the great majority of cases. Most of them believed that the theory of perfect competition provides a rough description of the real world. Since price equals marginal costs under perfect competition, they believed that this is also usually true in the real world. In other words, they ignored or minimized the widespread existence of surplus capacity, imperfect and/or monopolistic competition, and monopoly.

There are, of course, economists who fully recognize the universality of imperfect and/or monopolistic competition, though few textbooks which consistently adopt this point of view are available. Nearly all of these men have implicitly or explicitly assumed that price theory should be purely *descriptive*. Since they see that the theory of price determination under perfect competition does not describe our world, they have abandoned the idea that economists should state a theory of ideal prices. They have stated new descriptive theories of price determination under monopoly and imperfect and/or monopolistic competition, but have not developed any theory of *ideal* prices under these conditions.

To justify this failure, some of them have argued that science is incapable of prescribing personal or social conduct. This argument is basically religious or philosophic and, hence, unscientific. It implies that "ethical" problems should be reserved for the priest and the philosopher. Most economists are also Christians, and therefore are influenced by the religious dogma that the scientific method should be applied only to problems not reserved to their religion. Economists who have progressed beyond the religious stage of intellectual development are mostly followers of some philosophic system which teaches that moral problems should be reserved for philosophers. Thus very few economists hold that science should deal with ethical or welfare problems. The fact that religious and philosophic economists have nevertheless often used economic theories to justify or criticize social policies means that these economists have been inconsistent, not that they have abandoned their basic Christian or philosophic beliefs.

The sole function of science is to aid men to solve practical problems, and all such problems are problems of personal or group conduct. In our opinion, the final ends of all personal conduct are provided by man's inherited desires or drives (his instincts), and therefore all problems of conduct are scientific problems, problems which deal with the most efficient means of satisfying *given* ends. There is no need for ethics to provide men with ends, for they are born with them. Moreover, students of ethics have never been able to agree upon any other ends. This is because they are trying to solve a meaningless problem. The problem of what end is ethical is meaningless since no method of verifying any solution of it is conceivable.

While some economists argue that price theory ought to be purely descriptive because a prescriptive theory would require an ethical foundation or itself be ethical and therefore unscientific, *many more economists have stated a descriptive price theory and then tried to apply it to the solution of social problems.* This is a serious error. In order to solve price-output problems, we must have a theory of ideal price and/or output. For instance, the fact that prices are now determined by the intersection of demand and supply curves (a truth by definition) does not justify the conclusion that the state should fix prices at this level. To justify this action, one must prove that such prices would result in a socially ideal output. This point is so obvious it should not require restatement here; yet many of the ablest contemporary economists have assumed that descriptive value theory can be used to determine ideal prices.

Underlying all of the above reasons for the long failure to apply marginal analysis to prescriptive price theory is the basic reason that orthodox economists consciously or unconsciously wish or feel compelled to apologize for the performance of Capitalism and to ignore or attack potential arguments in favor of Socialism. Recognition of the obvious fact that prices ought to equal marginal cost has been slow to develop because this ideal can be more fully and more easily achieved under Socialism than under Capitalism. Indeed, many economists seem to believe that the new price theory has no significant applications under Capitalism. In this study, we shall try to show that in addition to being the only valid general price theory of a Socialist economy, it also has very important applications under Capitalism. It is true, however, that the possibility of applying this price theory more fully under Socialism than under Capitalism is a significant new argument for Socialism.

TOTAL ANALYSIS VERSUS MARGINAL ANALYSIS

The organization of this book is based upon the belief that a critical review of previous statements of a theory will help readers to grasp and appreciate a revised restatement of it. At the same time, we realize that the reader will be better prepared to follow our criticism of earlier writers after he has read our restatement of the theory in question. The ideal solution is to read the entire book and then to reread the critical history. However, we shall try to help the reader in his first reading of our criticism of earlier writers by outlining at this point certain key ideas of our revised statement. This is all the more justifiable since these ideas are among the chief contributions of our book and therefore deserve more than one statement.

We consider it of vital importance to draw a clear and sharp distinction between total and marginal analysis. This is the basic idea upon which rest both our criticism of earlier writers on marginal-cost price-output control and our argument that such control is superior to average-cost control.

Total analysis adds up the total gains and outlays of producing a quantity of goods and compares the resulting totals in order to judge the economic wisdom of producing the goods in question. The totals compared include intramarginal as well as marginal gains and outlays. The intramarginal gains should include consumers' surplus, and the intramarginal outlays should include economic rent.

Total analysis is useful in weighing any economic decision which would increase the output of a good by many units. Such decisions include decisions to start a new business, to keep a business in operation, to close down a business or a plant, to start or stop producing a new good, to make a fixed investment, to buy a patent, to purchase a business or plant, to sign a rental contract, and so forth. The essence of such decisions is that they involve lumpy changes in output continuing over a considerable period of time. Thus a fixed investment permits a significant increase in output over the life of the new capital good.

Marginal analysis compares marginal money gains and costs for a single marginal unit of output, assuming no increase in fixed capital. The money gain may be the marginal social gain (the selling price) or the marginal gain to the producer (marginal revenue, the increment in total revenue). The money cost may be the marginal social cost (cost at the intensive margin) or the marginal cost to the producer (the increment in his total variable costs) . Marginal analysis never requires the measurement and use of consumers' surplus, land rent, quasi-rent, or any other intramarginal surplus because they are never included in marginal gains or costs.

Marginal analysis is applicable to the problem of whether to raise or lower the output of a given good by one unit and to the closely related if not identical problem of whether to raise or lower prices in order to change this output by one unit. In other words, marginal analysis should be used to solve price-output control problems, assuming no change in fixed plant capacity. It should not be used to solve any of the problems listed above as suitable for total analysis.

The problem of whether to raise or lower output by one unit may be approached from either the private or the social point of view. Private profit seekers should balance marginal revenue against marginal cost (defined as increment in total cost) as suggested by the theory of imperfect and/or monopolistic competition. Public welfare seekers should balance market price against marginal cost (defined as cost at the margin) as prescribed by the theory of marginal-cost price-output control. In both cases, marginal analysis is applicable, but the results are different because the quantities balanced at the margin are different.

It should be noted that neither total nor marginal analysis ever uses a long-run marginal-cost curve. Indeed, in our opinion, long-run marginal cost is a self-contradictory concept. The term *long-run* contradicts the term *marginal.* Also, if we examine the various quantities called long-run marginal cost, we find that they include both fixed and variable costs. As we have noted, decisions creating fixed cost should be based upon total, not marginal, analysis. Moreover, there is no agreed way of allocating fixed costs to individual units of output. Hence, an estimate of long-run marginal cost is always arbitrary and undemonstrable, and the differences between various estimates may be very great.

It is true that in the long run nearly all fixed costs become variable, but this does not mean that eventually it becomes practical to allocate them to individual units of output. Mathematically, the full cost of a new hydroelectric plant can be allocated to the first unit of power produced in it, but this is of no practical use since price should never be that high. And when one tries to allocate the cost to many different units of output, many equally valid methods are available. Hence, long-run marginal cost is indeterminable.

Moreover, even if some method of allocating fixed cost to individual units of output could be agreed upon, the resulting "long-run marginal cost" should never be used. Total analysis uses total cost; marginal analysis uses current cost at the margin. No other kind of analysis is suitable for prescribing either investment or price-output decisions.

It was long customary to divide price theory into two parts, short-run price determination and long-run price determination. Our distinction between marginal analysis and total analysis is inconsistent with this traditional division. It implies that all price theory is short-run theory, and that long-run problems are problems requiring total analysis. The solution of every long-run problem affects prices indirectly, as do all economic decisions, but only by changing the factors considered in short-run price determination. Every actual price should be a short-run price determined by short-run marginal analysis. There should be no long-run prices determined independently by long-run analysis.

The concept of long-run price is extremely vague if not meaningless. At times it seems to be a price assumed to be stable over a long period, though such stability is always harmful. At other times it seems to be an average of short-run prices, but whether it is a weighted or unweighted average, a mean, a mode, or an arithmetic average is never specified. At still other times it seems to be used to mean the goal towards which short-run prices tend to move in the long run. It may also mean a price determined by the intersection of an arbitrary long-run average-outlay curve and a long-run demand curve. Finally, it might mean the arithmetic average obtained by dividing total income by total output, which is not an average of actual short-run prices.

In the long run, price and output are influenced by lumpy changes in land use, fixed investment, product design, production methods, etc., changes which should be guided by total analysis, as well as by other changes affecting current variable costs. Hence, the effort to apply marginal analysis to long-run price-output theory is misguided. The long-run price-output problem must be broken up into its parts, so that each part can be approached by the method of analysis which is suitable to it. It cannot be solved as a single problem by either marginal or total analysis.

Although long-run price-output analysis is thus based upon a vital error—the failure to grasp the distinction between the functions of marginal and total analysis—it has received more honor and attention than short-run price-output analysis. Economists seem to think that it is more useful to solve long-run problems than to solve short-run problems.

Orthodox price theorists have been inconsistent in their treatment of economic rent. Sometimes they claim that it is price-determining and sometimes that it is not. This contradiction results from the fact that they have two price theories, one for the short run and one for the long run. Rent does not enter into the short-run marginal cost, but it does enter into both long-run average cost and long-run marginal cost. By abandoning long-run price theory, we eliminate the case in which rent is alleged to determine price and regain a consistent Ricardian treatment of rent as non-price-determining.

It has been claimed that marginal-cost price-output control would result in harmful continuing deficits. Surpluses and deficits are the difference between total cost and total income. They can be estimated by total analysis. They are relevant therefore to the control of fixed investment but not to the direct control of price or output. These latter are ideal when price equals cost at the margin, regardless of whether this results in surpluses or deficits. When the resulting surpluses and deficits are shown to be harmful by total analysis, they can be eliminated by suitable control over investment in fixed capital. In other words, our distinction between marginal and total analysis implies that any temporary surpluses or deficits due to the application of marginal analysis can be eliminated by the application of total analysis. Continuing deficits are therefore not a result of ideal price-output control.

Our distinction between marginal and total analysis is essential to a definition of marginal cost suitable for marginal analysis. We have already defined marginal cost briefly in explaining marginal analysis, but some additional remarks on this vital point, discussed more fully in Chapter VII, may help the reader to follow our criticism of other writers.

DEFINITION OF MARGINAL COST

In our history of the theory of marginal-cost price-output control, we shall show that few writers on this theory have defined marginal cost. Moreover, they have used the term in at least four senses:

1. As the increment in variable costs and rents due to the production

of the marginal unit (A curve showing marginal costs in this sense can be derived from a short-run average-cost curve.)

2. As the increment in long-run costs and rents (whose curve can be derived from a long-run average-cost curve)

3. As the sum of the costs and rents of additional variable factors used to produce the marginal unit without plant expansion

4. As the sum of the costs and rents of all additional variable and fixed (long-run) factors so used when plant is expanded

Definition Number 1 is useful in explaining how the prices and outputs of reproducible goods produced by unregulated private firms are determined. This is the definition which should be used by writers on price-output control under imperfect and/or monopolistic competition.

Definitions Numbers 2 and 4 are varieties of long-run marginal cost and are subject to our previous criticism of this concept. Therefore, they should not be used either to describe actual price-output determination or to prescribe ideal price-output control.

Belief in the existence and determinability of marginal cost in sense Number 2 is due in part to the ease with which a curve apparently showing increment-in-cost for each unit of output can be derived from a smooth long-run average-outlay (so-called average-cost) curve, in the same way that a short-run increment-in-cost curve can be derived from a short-run average-outlay curve. But this analogy is misleading. A short-run average-outlay curve does not include any additional fixed costs, and therefore all the additional costs represented by it can be allocated to individual marginal units of output. A long-run average-outlay curve includes lumpy fixed costs which cannot be allocated in this way. The mere fact that a so-called long-run marginal-cost curve can be mathematically derived from a smooth long-run average-outlay curve is completely irrelevant.

The custom of deriving a marginal-cost (increment-in-cost) curve from a long-run average-outlay curve is due in part to the misleading practice of drawing *smooth* long-run average-outlay curves. If realistic, such curves are never smooth, they are full of scallops. When scallops are smoothed out, the resulting curve does not show actual average cost and rent per unit, but an average of average outlay for different batches of output. Obviously the increment in cost for a single marginal unit of output cannot be derived from a curve showing averages of average cost and rent. But any effort to derive a marginal-cost curve from a properly scalloped long-run average-cost curve (we cannot recall seeing such an effort) would show that marginal cost defined as increment in long-run average cost and rent is often far above long-run average outlay (when new fixed plant is first used) and that the long-run marginal-cost curve repeatedly intersects the long-run average-outlay curve before average costs reach their minimum. Thus the intersection of these curves cannot uniquely determine either an equilibrium or an optimum price or output.

In our restatement of the theory of marginal-cost price-output control, we shall argue that for the purposes of this theory marginal cost should be defined in a way which would make it fall under definition Number 3 above but that it should be defined more narrowly. We shall define marginal cost as the sum of all *socially necessary* variable money costs incurred to produce the marginal unit at the intensive margin. This excludes variable advertising costs and other nonessential variable costs from marginal costs because, while often profitable, they are optional and are not essential to the production of any individual marginal unit.

It is worthy of emphasis that when marginal cost is used in senses Numbers 3 and 4, the marginal-cost curve cannot be derived from a so-called average-cost curve and does not intersect the latter at its lowest point. Cost at the margin is usually below the increment in total cost and rent, which alone can be derived from an average-outlay curve, because it does not include the additions to the prices paid for the factors already employed. Moreover, the exclusion of optional variable costs like advertising from cost at the margin, which we propose, would increase the difference between the cost at the margin and the increment in total cost and rent. Therefore, conventional theories about the relationship of marginal-cost (increment-in-total-cost) curves to so-called average-cost curves cannot be used to explain the relationship of marginal-cost (cost-at-margin) curves to such average-cost curves.

Since we define marginal cost as a short-run cost, it is the cost of a single unit at a given moment. In some cases, however, the best way to estimate this marginal cost is to determine the average marginal cost of a number of marginal units and assume that marginal cost equals average marginal cost. This does not mean that marginal cost is an average of the marginal costs of a batch of units, but only that these quantities may sometimes be almost equal.

ORGANIZATION AND HIGHLIGHTS

The remainder of our study is divided into two parts: (1) a critical history of the theory of marginal-cost price-output control, and (2) a restatement and detailed elaboration of both the pure and applied forms of this theory.

Only one previous writer, Nancy Ruggles, has offered a history of this theory, and that is quite short (about fourteen pages) and quite different in its conclusions. Perhaps the most novel feature of our history is its review of neglected pioneers who first anticipated some of the basic ideas in the new theory (Chap. IX). After covering these men, we shall devote separate chapters to Marshall's tax-subsidy proposal, the first statements of the new marginal-cost theory by Socialist economists (1936–39), its application to railroad and utility rate theory (1938–47), and the discussion of the new doctrine as a general price theory (1942–50). Altogether, we shall review individually the contributions of about fifty writers on marginal-cost price-output control. Our bibliography contains references to ten additional writers whom we have not discussed because they referred to the theory too briefly to deserve comment or too late for our review. In other words, our coverage is almost complete down to 1951, the year in which our history was completed.

We shall begin Part Two, our restatement of the theory of marginal-cost price-output control, with a chapter (VII) in which the pure theory of such control is stated. The most novel and significant features of this chapter are the isolation of the price-output problem from the fixed-investment problem and the redefinition of marginal cost, both of which have been outlined above, and the statement of eight major corollaries of the basic principle of marginal-cost control.

In Chapter VIII, we shall digress from our main line of thought to state briefly the pure theory of ideal investment in fixed capital in order to emphasize the vital distinction between the problem of price-output control and that of investment control. Perhaps the chief feature of this chapter is the argument that continuing deficits would be a result of ideal investment policies rather than of ideal price-output policies.

In Chapter IX, we shall briefly consider the best methods of financing the temporary deficits which might result from ideal price-output control and the continuing deficits which would result from a combination of such control with ideal investment in fixed capital.

In Chapter X, we shall discuss at length the application of the pure theory of marginal-cost price-output control to specific cases. We shall concentrate on those cases where such application would have the greatest effect upon prices and output. We shall also discuss separately the application of each of the eight corollaries. Many of the applications of marginal-cost theory proposed in this chapter have never been discussed before.

Our final chapter (XI) deals briefly with the general effects of ideal price-output and investment control upon the economic system as a whole. We shall consider the effects upon the location of industry, the scale of production, the relative growth of different industries, national income, the price level, business fluctuations, and so forth.

Even though this is the first book-length study of the marginal-cost price-output theory, we have been compelled to deal briefly and superficially with many topics because of space limits. We hope that this study will stimulate other writers to discuss some of these points more thoroughly.

A NOTE ON TERMINOLOGY

ECONOMISTS have long denied or obscured the vital distinction between costs and surpluses by including surpluses in average costs. We have periodically inserted the adjective *so-called* before *average cost* in order to remind readers of the fact that average cost includes surpluses. We have also used the term *average outlay* instead of *average cost* at times because the latter includes surpluses. We have not been consistent in either practice, however.

Our primary purpose in this book is to restate and elaborate the theory of marginal-cost price-output control, not to suggest a new terminology, and we fear that even our partial use of the term *average outlay* may distract the attention of some readers from our main line of analysis.

The suggested use of *average outlay* in place of *average cost* is only one of the terminological reforms required in order to distinguish consistently between surplus and cost. Strictly speaking, *cost* should only be used to describe cost, never to describe surplus. *Outlay* may not be the best term to describe quantities including both surpluses and costs, but some new term—expense, expenditure, outgo, etc.—should be agreed upon and used consistently to describe such quantities.

Since *cost* should not be used to describe quantities including surplus, the terms *increasing cost, constant cost,* and *decreasing cost* should be abandoned and replaced by *increasing outlay, constant outlay,* and *decreasing outlay,* or some other agreed terms. Increasing, constant, and decreasing costs include rent, quasi rent, and other surpluses because they describe long-run conditions. Even short-run marginal cost may include such surpluses as a result of contracts (see p. 181 below).

To apply this suggested new terminology to our book, we would have to replace terms like *fixed cost, average cost, decreasing cost, increasing cost,* etc., with strange new terms in literally hundreds of places. We fear that this would confuse our readers more than it would enlighten them. Most of our book, moreover, is a critical history of doctrine, and here especially it is desirable to use the terms used by previous writers. We have already complicated this history by substituting *marginal-cost price control, marginal-cost output control, marginal-cost control,* and *marginal-cost price-output control* for various meanings of *marginal-cost pricing.*

In Chapter VII we argue that average costs are in practice determined in many different ways, no one of which can be proven superior to the others. This raises a question as to what is meant when the term *average cost* is used in our study. The answer is that, outside of our historical chapters, we have tried to use it only in statements which would be correct regardless of how average cost is determined. Since decreasing and increasing costs are average costs, this applies to these terms also.

PART ONE

A CRITICAL HISTORY

OF THE THEORY OF

MARGINAL-COST PRICE-OUTPUT

CONTROL

II

THE FIRST FORESHADOWINGS OF
MARGINAL-COST PRICE-OUTPUT THEORY
1885 TO 1923

INTRODUCTION

WITH THIS CHAPTER we begin our critical history of the theory of marginal-cost price-output control. This chapter and the next describe developments before the first clear statement of this theory in 1936. The succeeding four chapters deal with the criticism and elaboration of this theory from 1936 to 1950. Our primary purpose in this study is to achieve an improved statement of the pure and applied theory of marginal-cost price-output control, not to present a comprehensive and definitive history of the theory. We believe, however, that a critical history of the new price theory will help the reader to grasp its meaning and significance.

The scope of this history has been largely restricted to literature in the English language. The present chapter is an exception to this rule, but all the foreign literature here discussed has been cited by English-speaking economists. We have made no attempt to undertake an independent study of price-output theory in foreign languages because of: (1) the difficulty of covering the literature in other languages; (2) our belief that there has been little if any discussion of marginal-cost price-output theory in foreign languages, based in part upon the absence of Anglo-American references to such discussions; and (3) the negligible influence of continental writers on the development of this theory by British and American economists.

LAUNHARDT

So far as we are aware, the first writer to adumbrate the theory of marginal-cost price-output control was a neglected German economist, Wilhelm Launhardt. He applied the new theory only to railroad rates, but in so doing he anticipated English-speaking economists by over fifty years. Launhardt's discussion is also notable because in it he made use of the concept of consumers' surplus before Marshall.

We begin our remarks on Launhardt with a review of the discussion of railroad rates in his *Mathematische Begrundung der Volkswirtschaftslehre* (1885) as that is the earliest book of his we have been able to secure.[1] Launhardt devoted four pages of this work (201–5) to a discussion of socially desirable railroad freight rates (*des volkswirtschaftlich besten Frachtsatzes*). His discussion is half mathematical, but we shall summarize it in verbal form. He began by noting that a reduction in freight rates below the perfect price discrimination level makes possible a saving to consumers on each unit shipped. The average amount of this saving is about half the difference between the highest prices any shipper would be willing to pay for the first unit shipped and the actual price charged. Thus we can calculate the total savings to consumers (consumers' surplus) made possible by any given price. An ideal price is one which maximizes the sum of such savings and the profit to the railroads. A price equal to current or direct costs (*Betriebskosten, Selbstkosten*) is the only price which maximizes the total social gain (*gesammte volkswirtschafliche Gewinn*). This price results in losses and therefore railroads should never be privately owned. Taxpayers would probably refuse to permit taxes high enough to allow railroad rates to be reduced to the ideal level, but the state should reduce rates as close to this level as politics allow.

The chief defects in this brilliant foreshadowing of marginal-cost price-output theory are: (1) that it is not stated as a general price theory but is applied to one industry only, and (2) that Launhardt did not have a very clear idea of marginal cost. His *Betriebskosten* seems to include all costs except interest on and amortization of capital (see p.

[1] Launhardt's work was called to my attention by a footnote of Schumpeter's in his article on Pareto in the *Quarterly Journal of Economics*, LXIII (May, 1949), 147–73. Schumpeter has attributed the same ideas as appear here to Launhardt's "earlier writings."

109). Nevertheless, his theory of ideal railroad rates is far superior to those of Marshall and Pigou.

Launhardt restated the same basic ideas in greater detail in his *Theorie der Tarifbildung der Eisenbahnen* (1890). The first half of this eighty-four-page monograph is devoted to the theory of ideal rates, and contains rough estimates of the cost and benefit of applying his rate theory to freight traffic on the German railroad system in his day. He thought the gain in consumers' surplus from reducing German freight rates to the current cost level would be between 87 and 124 million marks, and that the increase in the physical volume of freight traffic would be 35 to 60 percent. He estimated the resulting financial loss to the railroads at 500 million marks a year, 2½ percent of the German national income at that time. He also asserted that the ratio of current costs to total costs is lower for passenger traffic than for freight traffic, which suggests that the adoption of ideal passenger fares would have proportionately greater effects upon the volume of passenger traffic.

In view of the fact that many American economists were trained in Germany, it seems odd that American writers on railroad rate theories have ignored Launhardt's early suggestion of marginal-cost pricing for railroads. For instance, it was not mentioned by D. P. Locklin in his historical review of railroad rate theory.[2]

WICKSELL

In his *Finanztheoretische Untersuchungen* (1896) and in his other writings, Knut Wicksell took over Launhardt's theory of ideal railroad rates, elaborated it, and applied it to all state-owned enterprise. Wicksell did not call attention to Launhardt's priority, but he referred to other points in Launhardt's books and was therefore probably familiar with his treatment of the new price-output theory. Wicksell did, however, call attention to Marshall's tax-subsidy proposal, which is much inferior to Launhardt's suggestion as a foreshadowing of the theory of marginal-cost control.

Wicksell's own contribution was completely ignored by English and American writers until 1951 when two articles in American economic

[2] D. P. Locklin, "The Literature on Railway Rate Theory," *Quarterly Journal of Economics*, XLVII (Feb., 1933).

journals (by C. G. Uhr [3] and J. M. Buchanan [4]) revealed Wicksell's brilliant pioneering to the English-speaking world. We have not been able to study Wicksell's writings, and shall rely on these articles for our review of him. First we quote the relevant passage from Uhr's article:

His program involved first a substantial expansion of the public sector of the economy, . . . Expansion of the public sector was in part to take the form of public ownership and operation of "natural" monopolies (public utilities) and also of "artificial" ones. . . . Once acquired, Wicksell insisted they should be publicly operated to give consumers the full benefit of their realizable "economies of scale." This was to be achieved by a combination of taxes and a technique of pricing their output according to marginal unit cost. Their prices were to be reduced by trial and error, and their output and sales expanded according to elasticity of demand, up to an equilibrium point where the sales value of output increment sold after the last price reduction (i.e., output increment times new lower price) exactly equals the increment in total cost of producing the extra output. Since marginal unit cost and price would in most such cases be less than average total unit cost on the corresponding total product, the resulting deficit should be met from taxation.

It is not certain that he would have applied this method universally, for he was aware that complications would arise in all but the simplest cases, but he did not stop to work them out. . . . he thought it irrational for governments deliberately to operate public enterprises for profit. . . . To his mind the *raison d'être* for public enterprises was to obtain a better allocation and utilization of the nation's resources. (pp. 834–35)

We turn now to Buchanan's "condensed running paraphrase" of Wicksell's argument, which throws additional light on Wicksell's outstanding achievement:

Wicksell begins . . . by pointing out that there are, in many instances, good reasons that public enterprises should be partly financed by some method other than the charging of fees or . . . prices. . . . One distinguishing feature of most public undertakings is the fact that the general (*allgemeinen*) costs of operation are very high relative to the marginal costs (*Einheitkosten* or *Mehrkosten fur einzelne Leistung*). The latter are usually insignificant and sometimes scarcely present at all. He refers to streets, canals, harbors as examples. As for railroads, he says that the yearly in-

3 C. G. Uhr, "Knut Wicksell—A Centennial Evaluation," *American Economic Review*, XLI (Dec., 1951), 829–61. This account is much shorter than Buchanan's but is based upon all of Wicksell's writings, including *Socialiststaten och nutidssamhallet* (1905); see pp. 12–21.

4 James M. Buchanan, "Knut Wicksell on Marginal Cost Pricing," *Southern Economic Journal*, XVIII (Oct., 1951), 173–78. This account is based solely on Wicksell's *Finanztheoretische Untersuchungen* (1896).

crease of a million passengers has little influence on the annual operating costs and still less on the interest on the initial investment.

Wicksell further points out that if such enterprises are required to charge fees sufficient to cover full costs, then the . . . fees will be much greater than . . . marginal costs. . . . Only those who are willing to pay this high fee will demand the service, and a great portion of the real demand . . . will be left unsatisfied. Some fuller utilization might be achieved by a system of differential fees or rates . . . but there exists another method which is certainly theoretically superior to this, and which warrants more practical consideration than hitherto has been given it. This method is that of charging fees equal to the marginal costs . . . and making up the deficit by tax revenues. In the cases where the marginal costs are so low that the expenses of collecting fees outweigh the revenues, then the service should be provided gratuitously and the whole cost paid out of tax revenues. This system would result in a tremendous increase in the use of the service and would be advantageous both to the individual beneficiaries and to society as a whole.

This method of financing is precluded for private enterprises because producers and consumers are separate, but is ideally suited for the state. It provides, therefore, an important and scarcely mentioned argument for state operation of such public enterprises as public transport. (p. 174)

One of the most noteworthy ideas here is the use of marginal-cost control theory as an argument for free provision of certain economic goods. This important idea is rare even in the most recent literature on ideal price-output control.

Buchanan went on to explain that Wicksell rejected marginal-cost control whenever it injures some individuals, or when they think it does. This amounts, of course, to a repudiation of the theory of marginal-cost control, for such control would always harm someone, and even if it did not, there would always be some who think it would harm them. The great fallacy in Wicksell's treatment of ideal price-output theory, therefore, is his nihilistic assumption that desirable economic policies must benefit everyone. This in turn is due to the unjustifiable belief that interpersonal comparison of utility is impossible. Buchanan, however, stressed these features of Wicksell's treatment as evidence of its *superiority* over many later statements of the theory.

There is some excuse for the neglect of Wicksell's version of marginal-cost price-output theory by English-speaking economists, most of whom read German with difficulty and have trouble finding copies of German books, but there is much less excuse for the neglect of both

Launhardt and Wicksell by German economists like Mises, Halm, and Hayek who wrote at length on the problems of ideal pricing under Socialism. The chief thesis of these writers—that rational economic calculation is impossible under Socialism—had already been roughly anticipated and answered by Wicksell, yet they neglected him and insisted that the problem he solved, or tried to solve, had been ignored. As a result, they have been praised for being the first to raise the problem of ideal price-output control under Socialism, even by some Socialists.[5]

PARETO

A number of economists—among them Schumpeter, Bergson and Henderson—have given the chief credit for developing the theory of marginal-cost price control to Pareto, or to Pareto and his disciple Baronne. Only Schumpeter offered a citation to support his statement. We shall quote it and discuss it in a moment.

First, however, it is worthy of emphasis that in his discussion of value or price theory Pareto devoted virtually his whole attention to a descriptive analysis of equilibrium in a static state under conditions of perfect competition (which assumes, among other things, the absence of decreasing costs and surplus capacity). He did not attempt to state a general prescriptive theory of price determination for the real world.

It is also noteworthy that Pareto did not use the concept of cost at the margin or marginal cost in his description of price determination under perfect competition. Instead of using conventional demand and cost curves, he developed a quite different apparatus—that of indifference curves—to further his analysis. This may have been a contribution to the description of price determination in the imaginary world of perfect competition, but it does not aid the formulation of practical prescriptive rules of price determination in the real world of imperfect competition. More specifically, it does not suggest the inclusion in such rules of the term *marginal-cost* or any equivalent, without which the theory of marginal-cost control cannot be stated.

Nevertheless, Pareto did make certain brief remarks which vaguely suggest the idea of marginal-cost control. These remarks occur in

[5] On this subject see also pp. 56–78 below.

digressions on the subject of pricing under Socialism. We quote below the most explicit of them, the one cited by Schumpeter:

58. The Collectivist state, better than free competition, seems to be able to bring the point of equilibrium to the line of complete transformations. Indeed, it is difficult for a private company to follow precisely in its sales the line of complete transformation. To do that, it must require its customers to pay the overhead costs (*depenses general*) first, and then sell them goods at current costs (*prix de cout*), the overhead costs having been deducted. Except in special cases, it is difficult to see how that could be done. The socialist state, on the contrary, can impose the overhead costs of production as a tax on the consumers of its merchandise, and can then sell at prices equal to current costs: it can consequently follow the line of complete transformation.[6]

At the time Pareto wrote, that was a brilliant new insight, but it is far too brief and vague to be considered a statement of the theory of marginal-cost price-output control.

In his article "The Ministry of Production in the Socialist State" (1908),[7] Pareto's disciple, E. Baronne, argued that Socialist prices should equal "costs," without mentioning what kind of costs he had in mind. He must have meant so-called average costs, however, for he concluded that "the economic quantities of the collectivist equilibrium [prices and outputs] . . . will be the same as those in the individualist equilibrium" (p. 274). Baronne was so sure of himself on this point that he described the opposite opinion as "fantastic" (p. 289), which suggests he did not realize that his master, Pareto, disagreed with him. This supports our conclusion that Pareto's anticipation of the theory of marginal-cost price-output control is vague and superficial.

LINDAHL

In his 1919 doctoral thesis, *Die Gerechtigkeit der Besteurung* (1919), written under Wicksell's supervision, Erik Lindahl devoted five pages (158–63) to a sympathetic restatement of Wicksell's theory of marginal-cost control. Lindahl used it to justify both price discrimination and marginal-cost price control by public utilities. He noted

[6] V. Pareto, *Manual d'Economie Politique* (Paris, 1906). Quoted from second edition (1927), pp. 363–64.
[7] Reprinted in F. A. von Hayek (ed.), *Collectivist Economic Planning* (London, 1935), to which our page references apply.

that the case for applying the theory to roads, bridges, tunnels, etc., is especially strong. Moreover, he claimed that the general principle of marginal-cost price control is valid whenever the problem of distributing overhead costs (*Kollectivkosten*) among consumers arises. He credited Wicksell with being the first to state the new theory clearly.[8] Lindahl's treatment of the new theory is far superior to Pareto's.

CLARK

While Pigou and other critics were discussing Marshall's tax-subsidy plan, the subject of our next chapter, without even raising the question of how high the proposed taxes and subsidies should be, an American economist, John M. Clark, solved the problem of ideal price and output but immediately rejected his solution as impractical under Capitalism. Apparently he did not realize either the novelty or the significance of his new theory. There is no reference to it either in his table of contents or in his ten-page appendix. He not only failed to stress the novelty of his theory, but neglected to point out that it solved the problem of optimum price and output far better than the Marshall-Pigou tax-subsidy proposal. Hence, his contribution to the solution of this problem was ignored by other economists.

Clark thought of the idea of marginal-cost price-output control because he undertook a detailed analysis of the effects of overhead costs upon price, published as *The Economics of Overhead Costs* in 1923. Overhead costs are closely related to nonmarginal costs, and an analysis of overhead costs naturally leads to a consideration of the nature and significance of marginal costs, called differential costs by Clark. Unfortunately, his able study is largely a description of the nature and importance of overhead costs, rather than an effort to state a new price or output theory based upon the admitted importance of such costs, but it contains some shrewd remarks on the failure of orthodox value theory to recognize the significance of overhead costs, and repeatedly implies the benefits of marginal-cost price-output control. His book makes clear the importance of overhead costs and their neglect by neoclassical value theorists. For instance, he noted that orthodox value theory assumes a one-product firm without overhead costs, a situation

---

[8] Lindahl's comment on marginal-cost pricing was called to my attention by C. G. Uhr.

most closely approached under the domestic system of handicraft production, and asserted that:

From the slowness with which economic science has assimilated the facts of overhead expense, one is almost tempted to conclude that its prevalent ideas on expenses of production date back to the domestic system *and are not really appropriate to any later stage of industrial development.* (p. 2; italics added)

A few pages later, Clark pointed out how the fact that railroads have an unusually high proportion of overhead costs led to the development of a special railroad rate theory, unrelated to orthodox value theory, and remarked:

The thing that seems more in need of explanation is why economists should have thought that other industries were different from railroads or why they should have thought that they explained the prices of single goods by showing that they tended under competition to cover the expenses of production. (p. 10)

Many other stimulating remarks of this sort might be quoted from this brilliant study.

Clark came closest to stating the theory of marginal-cost price-output control in his two formulations of the "paradox of overhead costs," one of which occurs near the beginning and the other near the end of his study. In the first he said:

If any business that would pay its own particular costs is refused because it will not pay its share of overhead, there is a loss. Yet prices must be charged which will cover the overhead, so long as industry depends on private enterprise. There is only one answer to this dilemma—discrimination. . . . However, this is only a partial answer to the question, and creates more problems than it solves. (p. 23)

His second formulation of this dilemma was more detailed, and differed chiefly in failing to recommend discrimination.

The interest of the community at large calls for the production of any goods which are worth more than the differential cost of producing them. The private interest of industry requires prices to be high enough to cover the residual or constant expenses of production. As a result, prices are frequently high enough to shut off the production and sale of goods which are economically worth producing, for the community. (p. 448)

Neither of these quotations contains the explicit statement that prices should equal marginal or differential costs, or that output is at an ideal level when prices equal such costs, but both theories are clearly implied.

One of the chief defects of this book is the use of the term "overhead costs," a vague and inappropriate term. Some overhead costs are marginal costs and some are not. The vital distinction is not between overhead and direct costs but between nonmarginal and marginal costs. Clark approached this distinction most closely in his distinction between differential and residual costs, but he defined differential costs as the aggregate addition to total costs, not as costs at the margin (pp. 49–50).

Much more serious is the fact that he probably was thinking of long-run rather than short-run differential cost. He failed to discuss this vital point in connection with either of the above quotations or in his definition of differential cost, but elsewhere he implied that ideal railroad rates equal long-run rather than short-run variable cost (p. 45) and he stated that differential cost includes interest (p. 49).

After his second statement of the paradox of overhead costs, Clark went on to explain that ideal prices are possible only under Socialism.

The only system which would be perfectly free to put prices down to differential costs would be a system of public industry with command of the taxing power and the courage to cover most of the constant costs of production by the use of direct taxes. Indirect taxes, falling on output, would merely present the same difficulty in another form . . . and direct taxes, to the *enormous* amount required for the purpose, would be *out of the question* (pp. 448–49; italics added)

Here we have a hint as to the real reason Capitalist economists so long ignored marginal-cost price-output theory. It casts doubt upon the social desirability of Capitalist prices, and implies that only under Socialism can prices be properly determined.[9]

The claim that "direct taxes, to the enormous amount required for the purpose, would be out of the question," indicates bias, for Clark had little knowledge of how high these direct taxes would have to be or of the ability of a Socialist state to levy direct taxes, and he ignored the possibility that land rent, interest, newly created money, and

---

[9] Clark fully realized the subversive trend of his analysis. He devoted a section of Chapter II to the question, "Is the Argument Dangerously Radical?" (pp. 30–31), a question irrelevant to the truth of a scientific theory but of vital importance to American professors. He tried to defend himself by pointing out that "the majority do not think the Socialist organization could succeed" and by claiming that his ideas would be of more use in reforming Capitalism than in building Socialism.

other new sources of income would be available to a Socialist state. Oddly enough, he suggested in the next paragraph that the problem is not hopeless even under Capitalism because "when demand is active, it exceeds normal productive capacity, and prices can be put high enough to make up the necessary average return, without shutting off any production which the social interest requires."

A special merit of Clark's book is that he pointed out that the rewards of the factors must be less than their marginal productivity as long as prices are above differential costs (pp. 467–70). Thus, he noted that, "wages must nearly always be less than marginal product so long as business is run on old-fashioned business principles" (p. 474). This exploitation of labor is distinct from and additional to that due to monopoly. Clark even explained that existing piece rates usually "do not give the fast worker his full differential worth as compared to the slower worker on the same job" (p. 478).

On the whole, Clark's adumbration of the theory of marginal-cost price-output control was an outstanding achievement. This makes it especially unfortunate that his contribution was completely ignored, but Clark himself deserves much of the blame for this, since he considered the new theory of little value and did nothing to call attention to his contribution.

III

MARSHALL'S TAX-SUBSIDY

PROPOSAL

INTRODUCTION

THE THEORY of marginal-cost price-output control was foreshadowed by continental economists much more accurately and much earlier than by English-speaking economists. Nevertheless, the theory was first clearly stated, actively supported, and extensively discussed by English-speaking economists, beginning about 1936. Their discussion of the new theory appears to have been entirely unrelated to the work of Launhardt, Wicksell, and J. M. Clark.

So far as we know, the contribution of these three men was never mentioned by any English-speaking writers in their discussion of marginal-cost theory. Pareto also was ignored until the theory had been repeatedly stated in English. Instead of being based upon the brilliant anticipations of these authors the subsequent formulation and development of the new theory in English seems to have developed out of a long discussion of Marshall's suggestion that ideal output might be approached more closely by means of taxes on certain industries and subsidies to others. This proposal is not nearly as close to marginal-cost price-output theory as the adumbrations discussed above, but it provoked a discussion which probably led J. E. Meade and Abba P. Lerner to their own pioneer statements of the new theory. Therefore, we shall devote this chapter to a review of the history of Marshall's suggestion.

MARSHALL

Alfred Marshall believed that the science of economics is merely a *description* of some of the factors which a Christian guided by theology should consider before reaching decisions on economic policies. In the preface to the first edition (1889) of his *Principles of Economics,* he said:

It is held that the Laws of Economics are statements of tendencies expressed in the indicative mood, and not ethical precepts in the imperative. Economic laws and reasonings in fact are merely a part of the material which Conscience and Common Sense have to turn to account in solving practical problems, and in laying down rules which may be a guide in life.[1]

In addition to being a Christian, Marshall was firmly convinced that Capitalism is the best of all economic systems, and because he was both a Christian and a Capitalist,[2] his *Principles of Economics* is devoted almost entirely to a *description* of economic phenomena under Capitalism rather than to a *prescription* of how economic problems should be solved or how the economic system should be reformed. The same is true, of course, of most economic treatises by orthodox economists. However, Marshall could not refrain completely from policy suggestions.

Marshall's discussion of pricing illustrates both points. His chapters on price theory are purely descriptive and contain no reference to the problem of ideal price or output. At the close of his description of Capitalist pricing, however, he criticized the then best known prescriptive price-output theory, "the doctrine of maximum satisfaction," which holds that competitive outputs are ideal outputs. He claimed that under competition prices are too high in industries subject to increasing returns and too low in industries subject to decreasing returns. His proof was admirably simple and lucid. He pointed out that in the former industries an increase in output beyond the equilibrium point would result in losses to producers, but that these losses may

---

[1] Alfred Marshall, *Principles of Economics,* 8th ed. (New York, 1948), p. vi. All references are to the eighth edition, in which the treatment is substantially as in the first edition (1889).

[2] In this work *Capitalist,* with a capital "c," is used for a supporter of Capitalism. We shall capitalize *Capitalism* to distinguish it from *capitalism,* an economic system using large amounts of capital. We capitalize *Socialist* and *Socialism* to place them on the same basis as *Capitalist* and *Capitalism.*

be much less than the money value of the increase in consumers' surplus.

In the case then of commodities with regard to which the law of increasing returns acts at all sharply, the direct expense of a bounty sufficient to call forth a greatly increased supply at a much lower price, would be much less than the consequent increase of consumers' surplus. And if a general agreement could be obtained among consumers, terms might be arranged which would make such action amply remunerative to the producers, at the same time that they left a large balance of advantage to the consumers.

One simple plan would be the levying of a tax by the community on their own incomes, or on the production of goods which obey the law of diminishing return and devoting the tax to a bounty on the production of those goods with regard to which the law of increasing returns acts sharply. (pp. 472–73)

Marshall had previously stated that returns may increase because of both internal and external economies (p. 460). He did not consider internal economies inconsistent with competition, but tried to reconcile their coexistence by means of his confusing concept of the representative firm and its life cycle.

The above quotation contains the entire positive statement of Marshall's proposal. He did not proceed to indicate how numerous or important such increasing-return industries are, or whether his theory would aid in the determination of public utility and railroad rates. Instead, apparently fearful of the unorthodox implications of his theory, he immediately qualified it so as to minimize its significance.

But before deciding on such a course they would have to take account of considerations, which are not within the scope of the general theory now before us, but are yet of great practical importance. They would have to reckon up the direct and indirect costs of collecting a tax and administering a bounty; the difficulty of securing that the burdens of the tax and the benefits of the bounty were equitably distributed; the openings for fraud and corruption; and the danger that in the trade which had got a bounty and in other trades which hoped to get one, people would divert their energies from managing their own businesses to managing those persons who control the bounties.

Besides these semi-ethical questions there will arise others of a strictly economic nature, relating to the effects which any particular tax or bounty may exert on the interests of landlords, urban or agricultural, who own land adapted for the production of the commodity in question. These are questions which must not be overlooked; but they differ so much in their detail that they cannot fully be discussed here. (pp. 473–74)

Marshall's attempt to complicate the problem with ethical considerations is entirely consistent with his basic point of view, but it is unsuccessful here because the "semi-ethical questions" which he raised are obviously purely economic questions on which theologians cannot throw any light.

In spite of his eagerness to limit and qualify his basic proposal, Marshall overlooked the most serious defect in his theory—namely, its failure to explain how much output should be increased or decreased in each industry. Hence, his proposal had no practical value, even if stated more boldly.

Marshall failed to distinguish the problem of ideal price-output control with existing fixed capital from that of ideal investment in new fixed capital. By using consumers' surplus, he rejected marginal analysis, the only method of analysis suitable for the solution of the pricing problem, and adopted total analysis, which is suitable for the solution of the problem of ideal investment. Moreover, Marshall used only long-run demand and supply curves in his analysis. These are useless for the determination of ideal price. *As a result, his tax-subsidy proposal is more an adumbration of the theory of ideal investment than of the theory of ideal price.*

Apparently Marshall intended his tax-subsidy proposal to apply only to competitive industries. This is not explicitly stated but is suggested by the fact that he discussed ideal price and output under monoply in a separate chapter, which followed immediately that containing his tax-subsidy proposal but contained no reference to it.

More significant, however, is the fact that this neglected discussion came perhaps closer to suggesting the principle of marginal-cost price-output control than had his tax-subsidy proposal. It contains a definition of the net benefit from the production of any good which implies that this benefit can be maximized by extending output to the point which would make price equal to marginal cost.

If the consumers' surplus which arises from the sale of the commodity at any price, is added to the monopoly revenue derived from it, the sum of the two is the money measure of the net benefits accruing from the sale of the commodity to producers and consumers together, or as we may say the *total benefit* of its sale. And if the monopolist regards a gain to the consumers as of equal importance with an equal gain to himself, his aim will be to produce just that amount of the commodity which will make this total benefit a maximum. (p. 487)

This seems to contradict Marshall's tax-subsidy proposal, for it defines optimum output without any reference to the previously demonstrated fact that optimum output in decreasing-cost industries is well below the point at which a monopoly profit can be earned. Actually the new definition of optimum output under monopoly can be reconciled with his tax-subsidy theory in the case of decreasing-cost industries by treating a monopoly loss as a negative monopoly profit, but it cannot be reconciled with this theory in the case of increasing-cost industries because the definition of total benefit is incorrect.

This definition is bad because: (1) it fails to include land rent and quasi rent, pure surpluses which are always a part of the net benefit from production, and (2) it fails to include the producers' surplus which accrues to workers and savers because the marginal disutility is above the average disutility of their labor and thrift. The second defect in the definition has no practical importance, at least in the present case, because such producers' surpluses cannot be measured and may properly be ignored in determining optimum output. However the failure to include land rent in total benefit has serious effects. If Marshall's definition were correct, the total benefit produced by an increasing-cost monopoly could be considerably increased by raising price above marginal cost, for, up to a point, this would raise monopoly profit, at the expense of rent, more than it would lower consumers' surplus. He ought to have said that total benefit is the sum of consumers' surplus, monopoly revenue, and producers' surplus but that part of producers' surplus must be ignored because it cannot be measured.

In a long footnote to the above quotation Marshall tried to show how the precise price and output which maximize total benefit may be determined by the use of curves showing aggregate costs, profits, etc. He assumed decreasing costs, so that the chief defect in his definition of total benefit does not become apparent, but the alleged ideal price shown in his graph is nevertheless obviously wrong, because it does not equal marginal cost.

The basic mistake in Marshall's treatment of ideal price and output under monopoly was his decision to use aggregate rather than marginal curves as his tools of analysis. In the preface to the first edition of his *Principles* he had expressed great admiration for the marginal method of analysis introduced by Cournot and Von Thunen, but he failed to apply the method to the problem of ideal price and output.

In his discussion of monopoly price Marshall stressed again the importance of giving due weight to the real benefit represented by consumers' surplus and again rejected the popular idea that an enterprise must cover its own costs to prove its value to society (pp. 489–93). These are perhaps the most constructive ideas in his entire discussion of ideal price and output.

Commentators on Marshall seem to have ignored his suggestion that a monopoly maximizes welfare when it maximizes the sum of consumers' surplus and monopoly revenue, but they were greatly intrigued by his tax-subsidy proposal. We shall now review the prolonged discussion of this scheme.

PIGOU

Arthur C. Pigou played a key role in the long discussion of the tax-subsidy proposal. Marshall's original statement of the theory in 1889 was followed by twenty-three years of significant silence. So far as we are aware, no one discussed his proposal during that time, presumably because it was considered too radical. Pigou deserves the credit for rescuing Marshall's stimulating idea from oblivion. Beginning in 1912, Pigou restated and defended the tax-subsidy proposal repeatedly over a period of twenty years. As a result of his role in reviving and defending Marshall's proposal, students of marginal-cost price-output theory have varied all the way from full attribution of this theory to Pigou to complete denial that he ever stated it. We believe the latter is the correct view, but there is evidence that the idea of marginal-cost control first crystallized in the minds of economists like Meade and Learner as a result of reading Pigou's restatement of Marshall's tax-subsidy proposal.

In sharp contrast to Marshall, who was almost solely interested in describing economic phenomena, Pigou set out, in *Work and Welfare* (1913) and in *The Economics of Welfare* (1920–32), to prescribe how to maximize welfare, which he defined as real income. Marshall's remarks on ideal output were an illogical digression from his main task, but Pigou set out deliberately to deal with such problems.

Marshall had used his concept of consumers' surplus to analyze the effect of taxes and bounties on industries with increasing and decreasing costs. He measured and compared lumps of welfare to solve the problem of approaching more closely to ideal output and price in particular cases. Pigou ignored the use of consumers' surplus, probably because he grasped the advantage of marginal analysis. He approached the problem of ideal output and price in individual cases by stating a general rule, which, in its final form, says that each factor should be allocated among different uses so as to equalize its marginal *social* productivity in all uses.[3]

This rule is not false but it has no practical value. In the first place, there is no available means of measuring marginal social productivity, which is quite different from both the price of the marginal unit and the marginal addition to total revenue. Neither price nor marginal revenue includes the significant non-monetary gains which often result from production and are a part of marginal social productivity. Pigou ought to have said that the factors should be allocated so as to equalize marginal factor cost and market price, for both of these quantities are determinable. He could then have treated the many problems involved in correcting factor costs and market prices to make them measure real costs and benefits more accurately as the separate problems they are. This breaks down the grand problem of how to achieve optimum allocation, outputs, and prices into its natural parts. Pigou attempted to solve the whole problem with a single rule, and his rule is therefore useless.

Moreover, Pigou made a mistake in approaching the output problem from the standpoint of allocation. There is no one in charge of allocating any factor under Capitalism, and there should be no one under Socialism. Rules as to the allocation of factors are therefore directed to no one. Production is actually controlled by managers who combine small quantities of the factors in order to produce goods. What is needed is a rule which will guide these men in the combination of factors. The rule that prices should equal marginal costs is directed to such men and can be applied by them. The rule that factors should be allocated so as to equalize their marginal productivity in all uses is not directed to them, and could not be applied by them.

After stating the general rule that the factors should be allocated in such a way as to equalize their marginal social productivity in all uses, Pigou asserted that, when marginal private productivity equals marginal social productivity, private firms have an adequate incentive to achieve ideal output. State interference is necessary only in those

3 Pigou, *Economics of Welfare*, 4th ed. (London, 1948), p. 136.

cases where marginal private productivity differs from marginal social productivity, and Pigou believed that such cases are the exception rather than the rule. The case of industries with increasing or decreasing costs is one of these exceptions.

Unlike Marshall, Pigou was not content to deal only with industries having increasing or decreasing *money* costs. He introduced the concepts of "increasing and decreasing costs from the standpoint of the community," i.e., increasing or decreasing *real* costs, including those not represented by money costs. This not only complicated his discussion but added more indeterminable quantities to his analysis.

Pigou attempted to prove that marginal social productivity is below marginal private productivity in industries having increasing costs from the standpoint of the community and above it in industries having decreasing costs from this standpoint, but his efforts in this direction are involved and obscure. On the basis of these propositions— propositions which concern unknown quantities—Pigou concluded that there is "a presumption in favor of state bounties to industries in which conditions of decreasing supply price *simpliciter* are operating, and of state taxes upon industries in which conditions of increasing supply price from the standpoint of the community are operating" (p. 224).

In the appendix to the fourth edition of *The Economics of Welfare* (1932), Pigou stated another theory of ideal output. He said that output is ideal when price equals the "money value of the resources engaged in producing a marginal unit of output; in other words, it will be the output that makes demand price and marginal supply price *to the community* equal" (pp. 803–4). This is the closest he ever came to stating the theory of marginal-cost pricing. However, marginal supply price to the community, the estimated money value of all real costs, is another indeterminable quantity. It is not marginal money cost to the firm. Moreover, if Pigou considered this theory of ideal output valid, why did he not explain that it made his exposition of the tax-subsidy proposal superfluous? A theory which explains precisely how much output should be produced in each industry certainly renders obsolete Marshall's suggestion that output should be raised by an indefinite amount in certain industries and lowered by an indefinite amount in other industries. The fact that Pigou stated the tax-subsidy proposal in detail in the main text of his fourth edition of *The Economics of Welfare* and vaguely foreshadowed the new theory of ideal output control only as an afterthought in the appendix suggests that he did not understand the relationship between these theories, or that he did not have much confidence in his theory of ideal output.

In discussing his appendix theory of ideal output, Pigou occasionally defined marginal supply price in such a way as to suggest the actual increment in money cost rather than the increment in the estimated money value of all real costs. For instance, an ambiguous phrase like "the difference made to the total money expenses of the community by adding a small increment of output" (p. 805) is meant to include money expenses not borne by the producer, and actually unknown to and immeasurable by him, but some readers seem to have interpreted such phrases to mean marginal cost in the sense of increment in the producers' money cost.

The above criticism of Pigou applies to the fourth and last edition (1932) of *The Economics of Welfare*. In *Wealth and Welfare* (1912), he had defined marginal supply price as supply price *to the industry*, not to the community (pp. 173–79). This quantity may be determinable, but it is not nearly as easily determinable as is marginal supply price to the firm.

Unfortunately, after defining marginal supply price to the industry as the actual increment in total cost, Pigou hopelessly confused its meaning by claiming that marginal supply price is always above the supply price in increasing-cost industries operating under simple competition (p. 174). He seems to have believed that in such cases the marginal supply curve includes increases in the rent on intramarginal output while the supply curve does not. This error was noted by Allyn Young in his 1913 review of *Wealth and Welfare* [4] and by F. H. Knight in a 1924 article, "Some Fallacies in the Interpretation of Social Cost," [5] but neither Young nor Knight offered a better theory of ideal output. Much of the later criticism too of Pigou's defense of the tax-subsidy proposal centered on this early error of his.

We have noted only the major defects in Pigou's elaboration of Marshall's proposal. There are minor ones as well. He stressed the importance of external economies so much that most critics have assumed he ignored internal economies. He assumed that decreasing-cost industries are compatible with simple competition. He argued

---

[4] *Quarterly Journal of Economics,* XXVII (Aug., 1913), 683.
[5] *Ibid.,* XXXVIII, 583–85.

that increasing costs from the standpoint of the community are im-
probable if not impossible (pp. 221–23). Some of these minor errors
were noted by his critics.

We have found it difficult to summarize Pigou's treatment of ideal
output and the tax-subsidy proposal because his discussion is full of
new terms, because his analysis is unnecessarily complicated, because
he repeatedly revised his discussion without improving it, and because
his statements and definitions are often ambiguous. On the whole,
we think that he weakened rather than strengthened the case for Marshall's tax-subsidy proposal.

One final piece of evidence showing that Pigou had not grasped
the idea of marginal-cost price-output control as late as 1937 deserves
mention. In that year he published *Socialism versus Capitalism,* in
which he discussed the problem of pricing under Socialism, the form
of economy most favorable to marginal-cost control. Pigou not only
asserted that Socialist prices should equal so-called average costs but
did not even mention the theory that they should equal marginal costs
(pp. 109–15), although several writers had supported this alternative
in the years between 1932 and 1937.

ROBERTSON

In an article called "Those Empty Boxes" in the *Economic Journal*
for March, 1924, D. H. Robertson undertook a detailed critique of
Pigou's "most momentous conclusion . . . that under conditions of
free competition production in 'increasing cost' industries is carried
further, and in 'decreasing cost' industries less far than the true interests of society require" (p. 17). Apparently he saw obscurely the conclusion to which the Marshall-Pigou analysis pointed:

Professor Pigou's analysis leads us to suppose that, in the social interest, p
(price) should be such that the additional units of output specifically at-
tributable to the addition of the nth unit of running resources should sell
for a price which adequately remunerates that nth unit of running resources. (p. 21)

. . . .

The logical outcome seems to be that the State, if it takes over an industry
of this type [decreasing costs], is entitled to neglect altogether, in determining its price and output policy, the costs of the fixed capital embarked, pay-

ing for them presumably, out of taxation, and pushing production to such a point that price covers only the special costs of the nth unit of output. (p. 22)

Here we have a much better adumbration of the theory of marginal-cost control than is to be found in Pigou's books. It was stimulated by Pigou's early treatment of the tax-subsidy proposal, in which he used marginal supply price to mean the increment in total *money* cost. It is noteworthy that Robertson's statement suggests the theory of optimum price with existing fixed capital rather than the theory of optimum investment in fixed capital. After this brilliant start, however, Robertson devoted the rest of his article to a vain attempt to refute both his suggestion of marginal-cost control and the tax-subsidy proposal. "If my view is correct," he asserted, "the State . . . ought to so regulate output that aggregate receipts cover aggregate costs" (p. 22).

He flatly denied that the marginal unit of output "is in any significant sense the net product" of the marginal unit of variable resources (p. 21). His chief argument for this odd conclusion was that a denial of it supported the theory that price should equal marginal cost, which he considered so manifestly absurd as to require no refutation, an attitude which we shall soon see was shared by Pigou.

Does it [Pigou's thesis] not lead directly to the conclusion that it [a decreasing-cost industry] should claim to be subsidised to the extent of the whole burden of the charges of the fixed original plant? And can this conclusion possibly be sound?

Robertson seems to have assumed permanent excess capacity in all decreasing-cost industries. Otherwise the deficit would not equal "the whole burden" of the fixed costs.

In this article Robertson attempted a humorous style, referring to Pigou as Goliath and himself as David. This seems to have irritated Pigou, whose reply was curt and unenlightening. He ignored Robertson's chief contribution, the idea that the Marshall-Pigou analysis of ideal output leads toward the conclusion that price should equal marginal costs, and sharply criticized Robertson's unjustified claim that this would involve deficits equal to the whole burden of the fixed plant.

The suggestion that they [the Marshall-Pigou proposals] imply a policy of subsidising nationalised enterprises to the extent of the whole burden of the fixed original plant, is, of course, a grotesque misunderstanding. It is arrived at, so far as I can see, partly by confusing long and short-period conditions and partly by applying to production generally, propositions that are only applicable to quantities of production less than the quantity which the minimum practicable plant could provide. (pp. 30–31)

There is some merit in this criticism of Robertson's most extreme statement, but Pigou failed to recognize the novelty and significance of Robertson's adumbration of the theory of marginal-cost pricing. On the whole, the "grotesque misunderstanding" was as much Pigou's as Robertson's.

SHOVE

The discussion of the tax-subsidy proposal was continued by G. F. Shove in an abstruse nine-page article, "Varying Costs and Marginal Net Products," in the *Economic Journal* for June, 1928. Shove criticized Pigou's 1924 version of this proposal on the ground that it neglects the effect of changes in output upon land rent. More specifically, he asserted that in decreasing-cost industries the expansion of output may reduce land rent enough to offset the resulting increase in consumers' surplus. Hence, the mere fact of decreasing costs does not prove the need for an expansion of output. Rather, this depends "not on its effect upon the cost of the marginal unit but on its effect on the costs of the rest of the output" (p. 263). This argument implies that Pigou had defined decreasing costs to mean that cost at the margin is declining, whereas he actually used it to mean that average cost is declining.[6] Since a decline in "the costs of the rest of the output" would reduce average costs, there is no contradiction between Shove's point and Pigou's theory. And if there were, it could be ended by changing Pigou's definition of decreasing costs.

Shove anticipated this reply to his criticism and tried to answer it by claiming that Pigou included rent in average costs, and that when this is done average cost equals marginal cost (p. 264). But this is true only in increasing-cost industries, not in decreasing-cost industries, and so is irrelevant to the issue of whether Pigou was correct in concluding that output should be increased in decreasing-cost industries.

On the basis of such reasoning, Shove concluded that Pigou's proposal "collapses" when stated in an unqualified form. He thought, however, that "in the form in which it was first enunciated by Marshall the doctrine remains unshaken" (p. 265). He supported the latter

[6] Pigou, *Economics of Welfare*, 4th ed., p. 216.

view by claiming that Marshall's version was correct because Marshall had seen that it was unsound. He thought that Marshall had rejected his own proposal because "he had in mind considerations of the kind advanced above." There is indeed some evidence both that Marshall did seriously question his own proposal after stating it and that he did so in part for reasons similar to those advanced by Shove. We have already stressed the timidity and unnecessary qualifications with which Marshall stated his proposal. Most commentators, however, have assumed that he did not reject it.

Although Shove thought he had refuted Pigou's proposal, he proposed a similar tax-subsidy scheme for dealing with external economies and dis-economies.

> In most industries the addition to aggregate costs (here called final trade cost) is *less* than the cost, to its producer, of the least favourably conditioned unit of the larger output (marginal cost); for, as a rule, the external economies of large-scale production . . . are, for the industry as a whole, greater than external diseconomies . . . so that the production of the additional unit will, on balance, improve the facilities for the rest of the output. . . .
>
> Now, if competition is perfect, resources will tend to be distributed between different industries so as to make marginal cost equal to the value of a unit of product in each industry. But, since the ratio of marginal to final trade cost is different in different industries, this means that the ratio of final trade cost to the value of a unit of product varies from one industry to another. And the national dividend would, obviously, be increased by transferring resources from industries where this latter ratio is small (where net external economies are small or negative) to those where it is large. . . .
>
> It may be argued that an industry which shows increasing (marginal) returns is more likely to belong to the second group than to the first; but it is by no means certain to do so. Nor is there any certainty that an industry showing diminishing returns will belong to the first group. (pp. 265–66)

Shove stated his intention to discuss this obscure proposal in more detail in a separate article, but never did so. However, R. F. Kahn assumed this task, and, consequently, we shall reserve our criticism until our discussion of his article.

FRASER AND ROBINSON

The surprisingly prolonged attack upon the tax-subsidy proposal was continued by L. M. Fraser in "Taxation and Returns," an article in the *Review of Economic Studies* for October, 1933. Fraser devoted the first half of his article to the valid, but not new, point that Pigou's early argument for taxes on increasing-cost industries was unsound. He failed to admit, however, that, in spite of the faults in Pigou's reasoning, his conclusions that (1) output is above the ideal level in increasing-cost industries and that (2) taxation of such industries to support bounties for decreasing-cost industries would increase welfare are both sound.

Fraser devoted the second half of his article to the effects on other industries of the payment of bounties to one industry. He began by assuming, unnecessarily, that some indirect taxation is required to pay bounties, and asked, "On what type of commodity will it fall with the least loss?" He criticized and rejected the "generally accepted view that, conditions on the supply side being equal, taxation for revenue should always fall on commodities with an inelastic demand" (p. 53), and concluded that "it is more important to select for taxation commodities which have *equal,* rather than commodities which have inelastic, demand schedules" (p. 56). This conclusion seems irrelevant and invalid. All excise taxes are harmful unless they correct marginal money costs or reduce the consumption of harmful goods.

Fraser believed that taxes to finance bounties should fall on industry.

We saw that there might be a case for giving a bounty to industries showing decreasing costs. If that is true, it will follow that taxation for revenue should fall if possible on industries which do *not* show decreasing costs. (p.57)

In fact, however, poll taxes, income taxes, inheritance taxes, and other taxes are much preferable to taxes on increasing-cost industries.

In his conclusion Fraser did not say that the Marshall-Pigou tax-subsidy proposal was unsound, though this is the impression most readers probably get. He said only that "bounties and transferences *of the kind I have been considering in this article"* (italics added) cannot add to the national welfare. Since he confined his discussion to the least appropriate taxes, the conclusion seems plausible, but actually it is not valid even for the unsuitable taxes he discussed, provided they are not raised too high. The only fatal defect in Marshall's tax-subsidy proposal is that it does not explain how high taxes and subsidies should be. Fraser missed this obvious defect completely.

Some of the faults in Fraser's reasoning were noted by Joan Robinson in an able four-page reply, "Mr. Fraser on Taxation and Returns," in the next issue of the *Review of Economic Studies*. In addition to pointing out that Fraser had devoted "at least half of the article" to "flogging a dead horse" in criticizing Pigou's early effort to prove that output is above the optimum in increasing-cost industries, she noted other errors in his reasoning and concluded that "Pigou's argument is quite untouched by Mr. Fraser's criticism. Indeed . . . [it] appears to be completely unanswerable" (p. 139).

Much more significant than her criticism of Fraser is the fact that Mrs. Robinson went on to adumbrate the theory of marginal-cost price-output control.

The whole problem really boils down to the familiar difficulty that when any concern is running at falling average cost it is impossible to fix a price which both enables it to cover its costs and enables consumers to buy the output whose marginal cost to the firm is equal to marginal utility to them. This difficulty can be removed by subsidising the firm. *If the firm receives the difference between its marginal and average cost as a subsidy it is able to charge a price equal to marginal cost . . . and at the same time cover its total expenses. The socially desirable output is then produced.* Whether, on general grounds, such subsidies are desirable, or feasible, is another story. (p. 140; italics added)

If this difficulty was "familiar" to English economists, the present author has been unable to find any evidence of it, and Mrs. Robinson cited none. She was referring primarily to Pigou and Marshall, but, as we have shown, these writers never recommended or discussed "a price equal to marginal cost." [7]

Mrs. Robinson also foreshadowed the theory of marginal-cost control very briefly in her discussion of price discrimination in *The Economics of Imperfect Competition*, published in 1933 but probably written before her criticism of Fraser.

From the point of view of society . . . it is impossible to say whether price discrimination is desirable or not. *It is obviously wasteful, . . . if any commodity fails to be produced up to the point where its marginal utility (shown by its demand price) is equal to its marginal cost.* But under simple monopoly . . . output is . . . undesirably small. From one point of view, therefore, price discrimination must be held to be superior to simple monopoly in all those cases in which it leads to an increase in output. . . . But

[7] In a letter to me Mrs. Robinson has stated her position more vigorously. She has urged me *not* to treat her as a pioneer in the development of the theory of marginal-cost pricing because "this doctrine has been the central theme of orthodox economics for the last 100 years." The thesis of this book is that this ought to have been true, unfortunately was not true, but will be true of the next 100 years.

against this advantage must be set the fact that price discrimination leads to a maldistribution of resources as between different uses. (p. 206; italics added)

Here we have an anticipation of the marginal-cost rule in a context which suggests a failure to understand it. The argument that price discrimination leads to a greater maldistribution of resources than simple monopoly is unsound and contradicts the earlier claim that discrimination is beneficial if it increases output until price equals marginal cost.

When price discrimination increases output, it must increase the total allocation of resources to the industry in question. Hence, it must decrease the previously existing maldistribution of resources among industries. The remaining maldistribution does not prove that price discrimination is less desirable than simple monopoly but only that price discrimination is less desirable than marginal-cost price-output control.

Mrs. Robinson used the term *marginal cost* to mean the increment in total long-run costs and rent, including all fixed costs (pp. 47–48, 133–42). In other words, the cost of building a new factory is a part of marginal cost. She used the terms *intensive marginal cost* and *cost at the margin* to describe an increment in total outlay (including fixed capital costs) which does not include any rent (pp. 121–22). When she wished to refer to the value of the additional variable factors used to produce the marginal unit of output, she used the term *marginal prime cost* (p. 152n). She never said that price should equal marginal prime cost.

It is noteworthy that Mrs. Robinson's use of *marginal cost* to mean long-run marginal cost not only marred her adumbration of the theory of marginal-cost pricing but invalidated her basic theory of long-run pricing under imperfect competition, the theory that price is determined by the intersection of the long-run marginal-revenue and marginal-cost curves. The concept of long-run marginal cost implies that marginal analysis can be applied to large indivisible fixed investments, and/or that there is a way, and only *one* way, in which the fixed costs of a multi-product plant can be allocated to each unit of each product. Neither assumption is justified.

Further evidence that Mrs. Robinson failed to grasp the theory of marginal-cost price-output control is to be found in her discussion of the "exploitation of labor," which she defined as the payment of a wage less than the value of the marginal physical product of labor (p. 283). All such exploitation, she claimed, is due to monopoly profits or to monopolistic profits. She ignored, and implicitly denied, the vital fact (noted by J. M. Clark in 1923) that, whenever marginal costs are below average costs, wages are less than the marginal value productivity of labor, regardless of whether profits are being earned. The only way to eliminate exploitation of labor, as she defined it, is to reduce all prices to the level of marginal costs. Her statement that "the only remedy for exploitation is to control prices in such a way as to obtain the competitive output (the output at which price is equal to average cost) from the monopolist" (p. 284) is therefore in error.

To summarize, Mrs. Robinson virtually put an end to the long and fruitless controversy over Marshall's tax-subsidy proposal, but she did not understand the significance of her role. She twice adumbrated the theory of marginal-cost price-output control, but she repeatedly misinterpreted or contradicted the theory and failed to mention it in the most appropriate place, her chapter on the "Control of Monopoly Price." For these reasons, we have not credited the first statement of the new theory to her.

KAHN

Seven years after the appearance of Shove's article, R. F. Kahn restated and elaborated Shove's criticism of Pigou and Shove's final suggestion that taxes and subsidies should be used to make price proportional to some measure of real cost at the margin. He did this in a thirty-five-page article, "Some Notes on Ideal Output," in the *Economic Journal* for March, 1935.

Kahn began by re-examining Pigou's last version of the tax-subsidy proposal. He claimed that the Pigovian analysis was based upon an assumption of competition, which implies the absence of internal economies. Pigou's theory means, he said, that output should be increased in all decreasing-cost industries, whereas in fact output should be increased only if external economies are above the average level, as Shove had argued. He thought that Pigou's mistake resulted from his assumption that few industries have decreasing costs under competition. Kahn claimed that his new rule did not contradict Pigou's but was a more general statement of it, one which is valid whether few or most industries have decreasing costs.

To illustrate this point, Kahn assumed an extreme case in which all industries have decreasing costs. He thought that Pigou's scheme could not be applied to this case, presumably because he believed subsidies must be financed by taxes on increasing-cost industries, and tried to develop one which could. He proposed that all industries be ranked by the degree to which they are subject to external economies, that subsidies then be used to expand output in industries with more than the average degree of such economies, and that taxes be used to contract output in other industries. The goal is a situation in which marginal private product would be proportional to marginal social product in all industries (pp. 5–7).

His next step was to admit a limited amount of imperfect competition to his assumed case, enough to permit internal economies in subsidiary industries only and to study the effect of this change in assumptions. He remarked, incidentally, that "external economies must usually take their ultimate origin in the internal economies of some subsidiary industry" (p. 11). He then noted Mrs. Robinson's contribution:

The complicated system of taxes and bounties outlined above would have the effect . . . of bringing the output of each subsidiary firm to its socially desirable level. . . . "But it would be simpler," says Mrs. Robinson, "to give the subsidy direct to the railway so that the . . . [price charged for transport] was made equal to marginal cost to the railway." By this simple device, the ideal distribution of resources can be attained with very little trouble. . . . and it is not very difficult to make a rough estimate of the subsidy required to equate marginal cost and price. (pp. 12–13)

The astonishing thing about Kahn's article is that after this restatement of Mrs. Robinson's penetrating suggestion he proceeded to ignore it. He did not criticize it or offer any reasons for rejecting it. Instead, he proposed another impractical tax-subsidy scheme, revised to apply to conditions of imperfect competition.

The third and final step in Kahn's abstruse analysis was to further relax the assumption of perfect competition. He now assumed imperfect competition in selling and perfect competition in buying. He defined imperfect competition as a condition in which demand for the individual firm is not perfectly elastic, and stated that the degree of imperfect competition is measured by the inverse of the elasticity of demand. He also assumed the absence of price discrimination and external economies not due to internal economies elsewhere. Apparently he thought his first tax-subsidy scheme was the best method of dealing with such economies in achieving ideal output.

Kahn proposed that, under these conditions, all industries should be ranked according to their degree of imperfection of competition and that the output of each industry should be expanded or contracted, presumably by the use of subsidies and taxes, according to its position on this list (p. 21). Presumably, too, he thought this scheme to be applicable to the real world. To us it seems vague and impractical. Industries employing one hundred men are to be given the same weight as those employing one hundred thousand. And what is an industry? But these are minor difficulties compared with that of measuring "the degree of imperfection of competition." And, assuming this is known, how high should the tax or subsidy be? Kahn offered no solution for this problem. Like Marshall and Pigou he merely concluded that output should be raised or lowered by an unstated amount.

Kahn's proposal is also impractical because it deals with industries rather than the individual products of each firm. The problem of ideal output in a concrete case is always the problem of one good produced by one firm. Since there are millions of goods, it would be impossible to rank them in a single list by any criterion.

Kahn's tax-subsidy scheme has been largely ignored by later writers. Subsequent development of the theory of ideal output followed the line suggested by Mrs. Robinson rather than that suggested by Shove and Kahn.

CONCLUSION

The main conclusions of this discussion of Marshall's tax-subsidy proposal are: (1) the proposal is more a result of total than of marginal analysis; (2) it deals with long-period rather than short-period problems and, hence, suggests a theory of ideal investment rather than a theory of ideal price or output in the short run; (3) it does not explain how much output or investment in decreasing-cost industries should be increased but merely suggests the advantage of *more* output or investment; and (4) it was, nevertheless, a stimulating idea, which provoked a long controversy and suggested short-run marginal analysis of the problem of ideal price and output to some economists. Both D. H. Robertson and Joan Robinson foreshadowed the theory of marginal-cost price-output control in their discussion of the tax-subsidy plan.

Discussion of the Marshall-Pigou tax-subsidy proposal did not end with Kahn's 1935 article. A criticism of it was published by Howard S. Ellis and William Fellner in the *American Economic Review* for September, 1943. The proposal was a dead issue by that time, however, having been replaced by the new theory of marginal-cost price-output control. Therefore, we shall not comment on this article.

IV

THE FIRST STATEMENTS OF THE THEORY OF MARGINAL-COST CONTROL— SOCIALIST PRICE-OUTPUT THEORY

1933 TO 1939

INTRODUCTION

WE TURN NOW both to a later stage and to a different current of thought in the development of the idea of marginal-cost price-output control. We have been describing the long and relatively futile discussion by Capitalist economists of Marshall's tax-subsidy scheme for approaching ideal output more closely under Capitalism. We shall next describe the development, largely by Socialist economists, of a new non-Marxian theory of ideal price and output under Socialism, the theory of marginal-cost control. It is these economists who are chiefly responsible for the first clear statements of the new theory and for its elaboration and slowly growing acceptance. It early became evident that the theory of ideal price and output is almost the same for Socialism and Capitalism, the chief difference being that it is easier to apply the theory under Socialism. Thus, the only sound theory of ideal price and output under Capitalism was created largely by Socialists.

This chapter deals with the general theory of marginal-cost price-output control. We shall discuss its application to railroad and public utility prices in the next chapter.

It is remarkable that Socialist economists did not formulate the theory of marginal-cost control until 1936, years after the Socialist party had won office in most European countries. Following the bad advice of Marx and Engels, Socialist writers virtually ignored the economic problems which must develop from any effort to establish and manage a Socialist economy until the Russian and German revolutions brought them face to face with these problems. Thereafter, the Soviet leaders did their best to solve daily problems without appearing to violate any basic Marxian dogma. They found that one easy way to do this was to deal with each new problem individually and to refrain from any effort to state new non-Marxian generalizations. Hence, the Soviet theory of ideal output is a mere description of the channels of communication through which planning proposals are transmitted and of the agencies by and to which they are transmitted. It contains no real price or output theory.

In western Europe, on the other hand, the treatment of Socialist price-output theory followed a different path after the First World War. Although the German revolution of 1918 did not lead to the establishment of Socialism, it did bring the Socialist party into office, and this stimulated the first serious efforts by Socialists to solve the economic problems of a Socialist economy. Between 1920 and 1933, at least a dozen German and Austrian economists, including Heimann, Landauer, Lederer, Polanyi, Klein, and Tisch, discussed these problems, but, so far as this author is aware, none of them stated the theory of marginal-cost price-output control. The statement and application to Socialism of this vital new theory was the work of English economists, writing after the rise of Hitler had put an end to the constructive discussion of Socialism in Germany and after the Labour party had twice been in office in Great Britain. In both countries the serious discussion of Socialist price and output theory began only after the Socialists had come to office.

DICKINSON

We begin our review of the Socialist development of marginal-cost price-output theory with comments on H. D. Dickinson, not because he actually was the first to state the new theory, but because: (1) he has been given credit for so doing; [1] (2) he was a pioneer in the application of marginal analysis to the economic problems of a Socialist economy; and (3) he illustrates the transition from Marshall's tax-subsidy scheme to the theory of marginal-cost control.

In a brilliant article on "Price Formation in a Socialist Community," in the *Economic Journal* for June, 1933, he attempted to apply Pigou's version of Marshall's tax-subsidy scheme to a Socialist economy.

Socialist costing could take into account the difference between supply price and marginal supply-price. Once the supply schedule for a given commodity had been drawn up, it would be possible to calculate its schedule of marginal supply prices. To the sum of costs . . . small additions would be made in the case of goods produced under Increasing Costs; from the sum of costs deductions would be made in the case of goods produced under Diminishing Costs. The additions would go into, the deductions come out of, a special fund that might be called the Marginal Cost Equalisation Fund. The balance of this fund would be added to (or come out of, if a net deficit) the general income of the community. (p. 246)

Here we have repeated again many of the faults in Pigou's version of Marshall's scheme. Taxes are to be imposed on industries of increasing cost, although their prices are already equal to marginal cost, and bounties are to be paid to decreasing-cost industries, but no statement is made as to how large these taxes and bounties should be. It is impossible to achieve prices equal to marginal costs by imposing excise taxes on increasing-cost industries. Such taxes would raise prices above marginal costs by the amount of the tax, and would have to be very high to permit the ideal reduction of prices in untaxed industries, assuming an optimum volume of investment in fixed assets in these industries.

Dickinson took one vital step forward. By naming his equalization fund the "Marginal Cost Equalisation Fund," he implied that ideal prices are prices equal to marginal costs. However, he repeatedly failed to state explicitly that prices should equal marginal costs. Thus he asserted that price should equal "cost" (p. 240), that goods should be imported if their price is below domestic "cost" (p. 248), etc., without ever specifying whether he meant average or marginal cost.

[1] Nancy Ruggles has claimed that Dickinson "did introduce the use of marginal cost as the pricing criterion." "The Welfare Basis of the Marginal Cost Pricing Principle," *Review of Economic Studies*, XVII (1949–50), 43. She also implied that his article provoked an important discussion of the validity of his theory that prices should equal marginal cost. We believe that Dickinson did not state this theory and that the resulting Dobb-Lerner controversy dealt with a different issue, the issue of whether rational calculation is possible and desirable under Socialism.

Furthermore, he contradicted the theory of marginal-cost control when he asserted that in order to be prepared for "gains and losses due to unforeseen fluctuations of demand . . . it would be best to price goods at a small margin above [average?] cost . . ." (p. 246). Unforeseen gains and losses are not marginal costs and should not affect prices. Moreover, they would cancel out if the price level were stabilized.

A more basic criticism of Dickinson's price theory is that he did not propose to have prices determined in markets, where the demand and cost curves of individual goods could be ascertained, thus permitting prices to be made equal to marginal costs by proper control of prices and/or outputs. Rather, he favored at this time the impractical idea that central planning officials should use Paretian equations to determine prices and outputs independently of any markets. Marginal-cost control assumes the existence of prices and markets. It is a method of achieving partial rather than general optimums, and is inconsistent with central planning of output.

HAYEK

Another early but vague hint that prices might be made equal to marginal costs under Socialism was given by F. A. von Hayek in *Collectivist Economic Planning* (1935). He made the suggestion only to attack it, and therefore wasted no time on its merits. His first hint ran as follows:

8. The Criterion of Marginal Costs
It will probably be objected that these strictures may be true of capitalist monopolies aiming at maximum profits, but that they would certainly not be true of the integrated industries in a socialist state whose managers would have instructions to charge prices which just covered costs . . . Does the instruction that they should aim at prices which will just cover their (marginal) cost really provide a clear criterion of action? (p. 226)

Hayek began his effort to prove that prices should not equal "(marginal) cost" by assuming that marginal cost means long-run marginal cost. Since this is a meaningless idea, he had no difficulty in proving this version of the theory unsound. He merely pointed out that fixed costs cannot be allocated to individual units of output (pp. 227–28). To the obvious reply that Socialist trusts could disregard fixed costs he answered that under Socialism as under Capitalism every industry ought to cover its own total cost in order to permit a "rational disposition of resources" (pp. 228–29). Both Marshall and Pigou had explicitly condemned this view, but Hayek did not note or answer their arguments. In Chapter VIII, we shall offer a theory of investment which prescribes that rational disposition of resources among fixed investments in industries operating at a loss which Hayek claimed to be impossible.

In spite of its defects, Hayek's foreshadowing of the idea of marginal-cost control is significant. It suggests that the idea was already being verbally discussed by Socialist economists in England.

MEADE

In our opinion the first economist to state the theory of marginal-cost output control was J. E. Meade. In his brilliant and lucid *An Introduction to Economic Policy and Analysis* (1936), Meade included a chapter on "Public Management and Planning of Industry" in which he argued that the output of state enterprises should be increased until prices equal marginal costs.

The general principles of pricing, which must be observed in order to equate the rewards of the hired factors to the value of their marginal products, can be expressed by three simple rules.

1. Those in charge of a public corporation should always expand their employment of factors and increase production so long as the price offered for the product is in excess of the current market prices of the factors which would be necessary to produce another unit of the commodity.

2. They should substitute one factor for another . . . to produce the same output if the current price of the factor to be thrown out . . . is greater than the current price of that amount of the other factor which is just sufficient to take its place.

3. A central body . . . should insure that prices are charged for the hired factors which would equate, and just equate, the demand for and supply of each. . . . In the case of industries in which the total demand is too small to enable a single plant to be run at full capacity, the marginal cost will be below the average cost, so that if the product is sold at a price equal to its marginal cost it will be selling at a loss.[2]

Such losses, Meade continued, could be easily borne by a Socialist government, as in most cases they would merely mean a reduction in

[2] J. E. Meade, *An Introduction to Economic Policy and Analysis,* pp. 205–8. All citations are to the U.S. (1938) edition.

the interest and rent income paid to the state. In some other cases the state would have to subsidize the industry out of taxes or out of income from other public corporations.

In Meade's statement of the theory of marginal-cost control one defect is that he never mentioned the theory of marginal-cost price control. He failed to realize that his *output* theory cannot be applied to services (see pp. 197–99 below).

Another major defect is that Meade failed to distinguish between the problem of ideal price-output control and the problem of ideal investment in fixed capital. He used marginal cost to mean long-run marginal cost, including the costs of fixed capital (pp. 142–44). Hence, he thought that marginal-cost output control would cause continuing deficits in decreasing-cost industries (p. 289).

In spite of these faults, Meade's statement of the new output theory is much more accurate and complete than that of any of his predecessors. For instance, he said price should equal the "current market prices of the factors which would be necessary to produce another unit." This is a significant advance over earlier suggestions that price should equal marginal cost defined as the increment in total cost.

Unfortunately, Meade did not call attention to the ambiguity of the term marginal cost, nor did he explicitly state that in this chapter he was using the term solely to mean the sum of "the current market prices of the factors which would be necessary to produce another unit of the commodity." Hence, when he referred to "a price equal to its marginal cost" (p. 208), some readers may have interpreted marginal cost to mean increment in total cost, for Meade did use marginal cost in this sense elsewhere in this book (see p. 107 and Chart I).

Anticipating his critics, Meade pointed out that it is easier to determine market prices and costs at the margin than to determine marginal revenue and marginal increment in total costs.

The manager of a public corporation should produce more so long as the price of a factor is less than the value of its marginal product. He will know the price of the factor and the price at which his product is selling, and has therefore only to assess the marginal product of each factor. The manager of an industry run to maximise profits must attempt to produce more so long as the addition to his costs due to employing more of a factor is less than the addition to his receipts due to employing more of that factor. He also will know the price of the factors and the price at which the product is selling, but he has to judge not only the marginal product of each factor, but also the extent to which he will cause a rise in the price of each factor by employing more of it, and the extent to which he will cause a fall in the price of the product by selling more of it. (pp. 209–10)

Meade also made it clear that the theory that factors should be so allocated as to equalize their price and their marginal productivity implies that the prices of their products should equal marginal costs (p. 204). Orthodox economists had long supported the former theory without explaining that it implied the latter.

Since Meade failed to distinguish between the problem of ideal output and the problem of ideal investment in fixed capital, thinking apparently that his theory of marginal-cost output control solved both problems, he reasoned that the sum of rent, interest, and other non-wage income would just equal the deficits due to marginal-cost output control when population is at the optimum level (pp. 289–90). It is true, as he noted, that wages absorb the entire national income under this condition, so that other kinds of income must just equal any deficits, but these deficits include the deficits due to ideal investment as well as the deficits due to ideal price-output control. Still, it was a notable contribution to explain why the deficits due to ideal economic control just equal all non-wage income, assuming an optimum population. He thought that such large deficits make Socialism a prerequisite of ideal economic control (pp. 289–90) .

Meade explained that price should equal marginal cost "both in internal and in international trade" (p. 376). Moreover, he noted that if an infant industry deserves tariff protection, this should be granted only until its marginal cost has fallen to the level of the prices of competing imports. Thereafter, subsidies are preferable to a protective tariff (pp. 375–76).

Meade was also the first economist to sense the implications of marginal-cost theory for tax theory, in particular the strong support which it gives to poll taxes. After noting the defects of other types of taxes, he concluded:

The choice would have to be made between poll taxes and income taxes. The former would have the advantage that they would enable a man to be remunerated for extra hours of work according to his marginal productivity, which is an advantage from the point of view of securing the *individual* optimum balance between work and leisure. (p. 290)

In the preface (dated April, 1936) to the first edition of his book, Meade modestly asserted that "there is nothing original in this work, which is a transcription of the work of many authors." He added that

"Chapter VIII of Part II [Public Management and Planning of Industry] has gained much from articles by Mr. M. Dobb, Mr. H. D. Dickinson, and Mr. A. P. Lerner in the *Economic Journal* and the *Review of Economic Studies*." But Meade actually went far beyond these sources. He was one of the three or four pioneers who independently developed the theory of marginal-cost output control, and he was the first to publish it.[3] Moreover, he left no doubt concerning his approval of the new theory. As we shall see, he restated it several times in the next fourteen years. On the whole, his role in the creation and popularization of the new price-output theory has been outstanding.

SWEEZY

In the same year, 1936, that Meade published his pioneer statement, an American economist, Allan Sweezy, suggested briefly the bare idea that it might be desirable for prices to equal marginal costs in decreasing-cost industries under Socialism. In a short essay, "The Economist in a Socialist Economy," in *Explorations in Economics* (1936), he said that "the economists' formula should be that output should be extended to the point where price equals marginal prime cost" (p. 424). This hint is not explained or developed in the main text, but in a footnote to another sentence on the same page, he added:

If long-run average cost were declining with increased scale of output, price, according to Prof. Pigou's well-known thesis, should be equated to marginal cost, which in this case would be *below* average cost, and the difference made up through subsidy. To what extent this would be practicable could only be determined after thorough exploration of the problem in an actual socialist economy.

We have already argued that Pigou did not say that prices should equal marginal costs. Sweezy's brief mention of the idea of marginal-cost pricing is notable only because it is much superior to Pigou's discussion and is one of the first references to the new idea. It is much closer to Mrs. Robinson's anticipation of the new theory than to Pigou's. Sweezy cited Chapter X of her book as well as Pigou's *Economics of Welfare*.

[3] Thus Mrs. Ruggles's brief summary of Meade's role is misleading. "From Meade's point of view," she wrote, "the principle of marginal cost pricing was by this time [1936] no longer a controversial question, but rather something to be explained in a popular manner." "The Welfare Basis," *Review of Economic Studies*, XVII (1949–50), 46.

DURBIN

Another Socialist economist who mentioned the idea of marginal-cost output control in 1936 was E. F. M. Durbin. In December, 1936, his article, "Economic Calculus in a Planned Economy," appeared in the *Economic Journal*.[4] This was primarily devoted to an able demonstration of the feasibility of rational economic calculation under Socialism, but the author briefly stated and rejected the idea of marginal-cost control. His treatment of Socialist price-output problems was much inferior to Meade's, which he apparently had not seen.

Durbin began his discussion of ideal price and output under Socialism by describing three approaches to the problem.

It is the most familiar truism of the theory of value that perfect competition—including perfect foresight—would secure the right adjustment of production to the preferences of consumers [?]. This basic doctrine has been advanced in three separate . . . forms . . . of very different value for resolving the problems of a Planned Economy.

(a) The first of them is the traditional Marshallian apparatus of Supply and Demand Curves. In its present form the doctrine asserts that the problem of selection is resolved when . . . marginal revenue is equal to both marginal costs and average costs.

(b) The second form . . . is the solution by way of marginal products. The problem is resolved when the products at the margin for interchangeable factors in different employments are equal in value. . . .

(c) Then there are the equational systems . . . stating that when competition is perfect . . . the system of price . . . [is] determinate . . . also that these prices will resolve the problem of rational choice. (pp. 141–42)

Durbin said Dickinson had supported the use of equations to determine prices under Socialism, and he considered this method impractical. He favored the method of equalizing marginal product in all uses, but pointed out that it is difficult to determine marginal products and that the problem of ideal price under Socialism is therefore, "only roughly solved" by this method (p. 144). Hence, he discussed the applicability of English *cost* analysis to this problem. Most of this discussion is on the possibility of using *average* costs as a price-output criterion—Durbin seems to have been unaware that average-cost control is inconsistent with the principle of equalizing marginal products

[4] This article was reprinted in Durbin's *Problems of Economic Planning* (London, 1949), to which our page references apply.

—but he stated and attempted to refute the idea that output should be increased until price equals marginal cost.

Since it is not under the necessity of maximising profit, it could instruct the firm to carry production to the point at which *price* covered marginal cost. As long as the plant is regarded as a technical fixture equivalent to land (bygones being bygones) this is the theoretically desirable course. In all cases the execution of this policy would mean carrying production beyond the point where marginal revenue was equal to marginal cost. Maximum profit would never be made. Indeed, the general direction given to the production units might quite often involve them in incurring large losses. Since, however, losses in one direction would always be offset by equal profits elsewhere as long as total expenditure were constant, the policy would not be impracticable for a Central Authority owning all industries, . . . (p.150)

The final statement concerning the equality of profits and losses is, of course, untrue, as Meade had shown.

One merit of this brief statement of the idea of marginal-cost output control is that it contains the qualifying clause, "as long as the plant is regarded as a technical fixture equivalent to land." This vaguely suggests the whole vital distinction between marginal analysis and optimum price theory on the one hand and total analysis and optimum fixed investment theory on the other. Unfortunately, Durbin did not state and elaborate this distinction.

After his brief statement of the idea of marginal-cost output control, Durbin tried to refute it. He argued that: (a) no clear distinction between marginal prime costs and maintenance costs is possible, and (b) that average-cost output control has the "great practical advantage of simplicity" since it would "enable the management to meet changes in market conditions independently, and without the complex system of taxes and bounties" required by marginal-cost control (p. 151).

To illustrate his first point, Durbin raised the problem of whether the costs of maintaining a railroad line are marginal costs or not. This is, indeed, a nice accounting problem, but one which has been repeatedly solved. Railroads have long measured marginal costs and used them in fixing rates. Moreover, the problem must be solved by every manager who desires to use the factors efficiently. Marginal cost must be determined and compared with the marginal value product of each agent in each use in order to decide how much of each agent to use. The incidental problem of distinguishing between current costs and maintenance, moreover, must be solved in order to determine so-called average costs, and it has never been considered a crushing argument against attempts to measure average costs.

The argument that average-cost control is simpler because it permits more independence to management and does not require taxes and subsidies has more merit. We doubt that marginal-cost control would necessarily reduce the freedom of managers to adjust their prices and outputs to changed conditions—marginal-cost theory requires such changes—but it would certainly involve special taxes and subsidies. The vital question, however, is whether the cost of such measures would exceed the gain from them. Durbin threw no light on this question.

Perhaps the chief defect in Durbin's discussion of marginal-cost control is that he ignored the question of whether output should be controlled so as to make price equal marginal costs when or if this is feasible. He overlooked this basic question and began his analysis by arguing that it is not feasible to make prices equal marginal cost. But this is irrelevant if it is not desirable to achieve an output which makes price equal marginal costs. At the time he was writing, no one had clearly stated and demonstrated that output should be such as to make price equal marginal rather than average costs.

Durbin discussed marginal-cost control again in 1949. We shall comment on this discussion later. His 1936 article was criticized by Lerner in an article which we shall shortly review.

LANGE AND LERNER

Oscar Lange, another Socialist who discussed Socialist pricing in 1936, recommended average-cost instead of marginal-cost control. In an article, "On the Economic Theory of Socialism," In the October, 1936, issue of the *Review of Economic Studies* he proposed two basic rules to guide the activities of the executives of Socialist monopolies, one of which requires efforts to minimize average cost and the other of which requires "an equality of average cost and the price of the product" (p. 62).

Lange's article provoked a brief reply, "A Note on Socialist Economics," in which Lerner ably criticized the use of average costs as a price criterion and asserted that Socialist prices should be proportional to marginal costs. Lerner began his criticism of Lange's price theory by pointing out that an optimum price is not an equilibrium price.

Methodologically my objection is that Dr. Lange takes the state of competitive equilibrium as his *end* while in reality it is only a means to the end. He fails to go behind perfect competitive equilibrium and to aim at what is really wanted.

Lerner developed this key distinction at some length, and used it to support his major point that prices should be *proportional* to marginal costs. We quote below the concluding portion of this discussion.

In competitive equilibrium prices are equal and therefore, also proportional to both average and marginal cost. But it is the proportionality of price to marginal cost that is significant for the optimum distribution of resources, for that condition alone is necessary and sufficient to ensure that no resources that could be used to satisfy a greater need (or marginal utility as measured by demand) are used to satisfy a lesser need. In all cases where the complete system of perfectly competitive equilibrium cannot be attained—and that means always—it is important that the proportionality of marginal cost to price shall be sought after and not some other condition whose only merit is that it is to be found together with the desired condition in the competitive equilibrium. (p. 75)

This emphasis on seeking a social optimum rather than a competitive equilibrium or its equivalent is still much needed, but the conclusion that prices should be *proportional* to marginal price is much inferior to Meade's clear statement that output should be increased until price *equals* marginal cost (see p. 89 below).

In the next sentence Lerner implied that prices equal to marginal costs would result in deficits when excess capacity exists.

Thus, if for any reason there is an excess of equipment for the production of any good so that the production of the output which makes price equal to marginal cost makes price less than the average cost, it would be social waste to restrict output to that which makes price equal to average cost.

Earlier writers had claimed a close relationship between decreasing costs and the losses due to marginal-cost pricing. Actually, new investment is always required to make costs decrease in a decreasing-cost industry. And if demand exceeds capacity, marginal-cost control does not result in losses in these industries. Lerner did not make these points, but his emphasis upon *surplus capacity* rather than *decreasing costs* was a step in the right direction.

In the next issue of the *Review of Economic Studies* (February, 1937), Lange replied:

5. Mr. Lerner's criticism of my including the equality of price to average cost . . . is justified in so far as an inconsistency has crept into my exposition. . . . I failed to distinguish clearly enough between what is a directive rule, a guiding principle for the managers of production plants to be followed in *any* situation, from what is a result of an equilibrium position already reached. Let me, therefore, restate my position briefly. For the managers of existing plants, the [Lerner] rule holds to produce the output which equalises marginal cost to the price of the product. . . . But this rule is not sufficient to determine the output of the whole industry, for additional plants may be built. . . . A second rule is . . . necessary. . . . This . . . is that the output of the whole industry ought to be such as to equalise the price of the product to average cost. (pp. 143–44)

This reply is unsatisfactory. We can find no evidence in his earlier article that Lange understood that output is ideal when price equals marginal cost. He tried to salvage his average-cost rule by applying it to "the whole industry," but the rule that output is ideal when price equals marginal cost applies to the whole industry as well as to each firm in it. However, when he noted that the Lerner Rule holds only for the managers of "existing plants," while a new rule was needed for the "whole industry, for additional plants may be built," he vaguely suggested the need for a clear distinction between the problem of optimum price with existing plant and the problem of optimum investment in new fixed plant.

In restating Lerner's Rule in the last quotation, Lange said that price should be "equal," instead of proportional, to marginal cost, but he did not offer any explanation for this revision.

LERNER

Eight months after his brief criticism of Lange's discussion of ideal output under Socialism, Lerner elaborated his views in "Statics and Dynamics in Socialist Economics," published in the *Economic Journal* for June, 1937. At this time Lerner was a Socialist and was writing a general treatise on the economic theory of a Socialist economy, a work which he eventually revised drastically and published as *The Economics of Control*. He had followed the discussion of rational calculation and output control under Socialism, but apparently had missed Meade's book. In his second discussion of marginal-cost theory, he ignored Meade but criticized Durbin, Hayek, and Dickinson for their failure to apply this theory to a Socialist economy. He noted again that this failure may be due to "approaching the problems of socialist economics . . . from the consideration of competitive equilibrium, instead of going direct to the more fundamental principle of marginal opportunity cost" (p. 253). He also commented on Durbin's treatment of the three alternative methods for solving Socialist price-output problems: (1) supply and demand analysis, (2) marginal analysis, and (3) solution by simultaneous equations.

Although a reasonable account of modern economic theory by any of the three methods of exposition will contain the identical doctrine, the technique of economic administration suggested by them may well be quite different. When Mr. Durbin, therefore, rejects the . . . equational method on account of its lack of usefulness or realism, he must be taken as referring to a technique of economic administration suggested by it rather than to the system of economic analysis itself. . . .
It is natural that just that form of analysis which best elucidates the nature of competitive equilibrium should be the least useful in suggesting a practical technique of economic administration that will bring about such an equilibrium position. The ideal of the former is the inclusion of all the relevant conditions, and in this the general analysis of the equational method far surpasses the particular analysis of the first two methods. . . . But the ideal of the latter is that any officer shall have only a manageable number of things to consider. For this the incomplete or partial analyses are more useful. (p. 254)

This brilliant distinction between method of analysis and implied method of administration, ignored by Durbin and Dickinson, reveals the key role of partial analysis in justifying and guiding actual pricing policies.

Lerner claimed that marginal analysis implies a policy of equalizing marginal revenue and marginal cost, that supply-and-demand analysis suggests a policy of equalizing price and average cost, and that general analysis suggests no practical policy whatever. More important, neither one of the implied policies would achieve the desired end because they are rules for achieving competitive equilibrium. Instead of aiming at such an equilibrium, we must "aim *directly* at our real object, *the most economic utilization of resources.*" This means that prices must be set so that "whenever a shillingsworth less of any good is produced the resources set free are just enough to produce a shillingsworth of any other good" (p. 256). However, in the above long quotation, Lerner implied that Socialist trusts should strive to "bring about such an equilibrium position." This was probably a slip of the tongue.

Lerner noted that, when producers bid against each other to secure factors needed to increase output, they may raise the price of the factors, thus causing an addition to their total costs greater than the cost of the specific factors needed to produce the additional marginal units. Hence, producers should increase their output, not until price equals the addition to total cost, but until price becomes equal to cost at the margin.

> The use of every factor is to be extended up to the point where the marginal physical product multiplied by its price is equal to the price of the factor. Or, in other words, up to the point where the price of the product is equal to the physical quantity of any factor needed to produce the marginal unit of output multiplied by the price of the factor. *This value,* which has to be equated to the price of the product, *we shall call the marginal cost.*
>
> If this principle is universally observed, there can be no loss due to the wrong use of economic resources. *The guiding principle that we seek is none other than the equation of price and marginal cost.* (p. 257; italics added)

Lerner proceeded to give a detailed criticism of Durbin's arguments against marginal-cost control. He asserted that Durbin confused existing nontransferable fixed plant with readily transferable abstract capital. He claimed that Durbin had rejected marginal-cost control because it involves deficits, "a gratuitous assumption," although at another point he (Durbin) said that losses and profits would balance each other. He answered Durbin's charge that marginal product is hard to estimate in advance by claiming that this calls for improved methods of estimating, not for a different rule which requires no foresight.

After replying to these specific objections to marginal-cost output control, Lerner restated and ably criticized the alternative rule supported by Durbin. As we have already criticized Durbin, we shall not comment on this part.

Lerner's next topic was the "relationship between short-period and long-period problems."

> The problem of transition from short to long-period considerations disappears as soon as we recognize that every act of replacement has to be considered, like any other act of investment, in the light of our general principles. Any marginal item must be undertaken if it is anticipated that

the price of the service it will provide, discounted . . . , is greater than the cost incurred. Short-period decisions differ from long-period only by the length of time elapsing from the moment of deciding to make the investment to the moment (or period) of the emergence of the product.

. . . .

> It should be noted that depreciation quotas and supplementary costs are not mentioned, so that the pseudo-problems connected with the difficulty of distinguishing prime from supplementary costs dissolve into thin air. The only costs that are relevant are costs the incurrence of which is in question. They are therefore all *prime*. Supplementary costs are for us nothing but a useless carryover from capitalistic bookkeeping practices. (p. 264)

Here we have an explicit refusal to distinguish between the short-run problem of optimum price with existing fixed capital and the long-run problem of optimum investment in fixed capital.

Lerner rejected Durbin's argument that marginal-cost pricing could not be applied to fares on passenger trains because such costs vary widely from passenger to passenger, depending upon whether an extra car or train must be run.

> To allow people to ride in empty seats is a different service from providing another train, and both are different from the service of building another railroad line. In the first service, price is certainly above marginal cost, and it may often be so for the second, while for the third it is very unlikely. But this appears to present a difficulty only if the three services are gratuitously assumed to be identical.

This reasoning is dubious. The service is the same in all three cases. It is not inconsistent with marginal-cost pricing to change the price for a service when the marginal cost of providing it changes.

In summary, Lerner's 1937 article on "Statics and Dynamics in Socialist Economics" stated, supported, and demonstrated the theory of marginal-cost output control in a way far superior to that of any previous writer except Meade, of whose work Lerner may have been unaware. Moreover, it supplemented Meade's statement in a very useful way, notably in its explicit demonstration of the theory and its criticism of alternative approaches to the problem of price-output control. But it lacks certain notable merits of Meade's statement, such as Meade's explanation of the relationship between total deficits and the sum of rent and interest and his recommendation of poll taxes. Taken together, the statements of Meade and Lerner provide an able presentation of most of the basic elements of marginal-cost output control theory, the principal fault being the failure to distinguish between the problems of optimum price and optimum investment. To these two men belongs the chief credit for the first publication of the theory of marginal-cost *output* control.

DOBB

As the leading Cambridge Marxist, Maurice Dobb participated actively in the discussion of ideal output under Socialism almost from the beginning. He played a critical rather than a constructive role, one characterized as "economic sabotage" by Lerner. He was so devoutly Marxist that he was unable to accept either orthodox value theory or marginal-cost theory.

In his book, *Political Economy and Capitalism* (1937), Dobb denied that the same economic laws apply under both Socialism and Capitalism (pp. 275–76), as maintained by Pareto, Cassel, Dickinson, and Lerner, but he tried nevertheless to apply Marx's theory of value under Capitalism, the labor theory of value, to Socialism. Although there are stimulating remarks in his discussion of the economics of Socialism, his obvious purpose is to use any available argument to attack neoclassical economic theory and its application to a Socialist economy.

Dobb first discussed marginal-cost output control in a chapter on "Economic Law in A Socialist Economy" in this book. Since he favored planning of production by central authorities and opposed the use of a price system to allocate factors and control output, he naturally thought that "the way in which costs were calculated for purposes of accounting would, therefore, seem to be of no importance" (p. 307). He claimed, however, that marginal-cost pricing resembles the Marxian labor theory of value in that it teaches disregard of rent and interest as cost constituents at certain times—i.e., when output is below capacity.

Dobb criticized marginal-cost control in a two-page footnote (pp. 309–10) to the comments noted above. He pointed out that an extra passenger on a half-empty train or an additional guest in a half-empty hotel occasions scarcely any marginal costs and concluded that "the full and logical application of the principle, therefore, is hardly consistent with a price system at all, at least with any system of uniform and stable prices." This implies that hotel rates should be stable throughout the season regardless of whether demand is twice as large or half as large as the supply of hotel rooms.

Dobb thought it impossible to distinguish between marginal and non-marginal costs. "Any dividing line that is drawn must . . . be an arbitrary one." "The most satisfactory compromise" would be to have prices equal to labor costs, he added, without indicating whether he meant average or marginal labor costs. But as Marx meant average labor costs, Dobb probably meant average labor costs. Thus, in the case of the half-empty hotel, Dobb would presumably have rates go up as vacancy rates increase, for average labor costs per guest vary inversely with the number of hotel guests.

Dobb also discussed marginal-cost control in "A Note on Saving and Investment in a Socialist Economy" in the December, 1939, issue of the *Economic Journal*. His reasoning here is obscure. He set out to demonstrate that, "the principle of equating price with marginal cost . . . may well run counter to the maintenance of full employment, and in certain circumstances will be impossible of application" (p. 713). He argued that with full employment an increase in the rate of investment must raise prices above marginal costs because the increased investment could only be financed out of profits. Since profits must be included in prices, this means that prices must be determined by costs plus profits, not by marginal costs (pp. 719–22). However, the mere statement of this theory in a simple form makes its defects evident, for investment may be financed by taxes on consumers as well as by profits.

Dobb argued that any increase in the rate of investment under full employment must reduce sales of consumers' goods, create idle capacity, and thus reduce marginal costs. We disagree. National income normally increases by 2 to 3 percent a year in the United States and if the increase in investment did not exceed 2 or 3 percent of the national income, there would be no reason for an absolute decrease in the sale of consumers' goods.

LANGE

In 1938, Lange's two 1936–37 articles, entitled "On the Economic Theory of Socialism," were reprinted, with articles by other men, in a book of the same name edited by B. E. Lippincott. For this reprinting Lange revised his articles to include a statement of the theory of marginal-cost output control under Socialism.

The decisions of the managers are no longer guided by the aim of maximizing profit. Instead, certain rules are imposed on them.

One rule must impose the choice of the combination of factors which minimizes the average cost of production. This rule leads to the factors being combined in such proportion that the marginal productivity of that amount of each factor which is worth a unit of money is the same for all factors. . . . A second rule determines the scale of output by stating that output has to be fixed so that marginal cost is equal to the price of the product. This rule is addressed to . . . managers of plants and thus determines the scale of output of each plant and, together with the first rule, its demand for factors of production.

The total output of an industry has yet to be determined. This is done by addressing the second rule also to the managers of a whole industry. . . . The marginal cost incurred by an industry . . . may include the cost of building new plants or enlarging old ones. . . . Since in practice such marginal cost is not a continuous function of output we have to compare the cost of each *indivisible input* with the receipts expected from the additional output thus secured. (pp. 75–77)

. . . .

The reasons for adopting the two rules mentioned are obvious. Since prices are indices of terms on which alternatives are offered, that method of production which will minimize average cost will also minimize the alternatives sacrificed. . . . The second rule is a necessary consequence of following consumers' preferences. (pp. 78–79)

The claim that the first rule makes the "marginal productivity" of a dollar's worth of each factor "the same for all factors" is in error. Marginal-cost price-output control is also necessary. Under so-called average-cost control, the marginal productivity of each factor is different in every firm which charges a price above its marginal cost.

In Lange's statement of his second rule, we have again the unsound distinction between marginal-cost output control in individual plants and such control in entire industries, which, however, vaguely suggests a sound distinction between output control and investment control. Unfortunately, Lange never made the latter distinction.

In a footnote, Lange explained that his second rule would result in the same volume of production as perfect competition in industries with constant costs, but that in other industries it would increase output and cause losses or would decrease output and cause profits. "These profits and losses correspond to the taxes and bounties proposed by Professor Pigou" (p. 78n). This reasoning is faulty. Competition is inconsistent with decreasing costs, and it is impossible to compare output in decreasing-cost industries under competition with output under marginal-cost control. Moreover, there are no constant-cost industries, and, if there were, their output would be changed by a new control system which would affect every cost differently. Finally, no profits would be created in increasing-cost industries by the use of Lange's second rule.

Lange believed that marginal-cost control is possible and desirable even if no freedom of choice in consumption or in selection of jobs exists. He thought that the planning authorities in such an economy could prepare arbitrary demand curves and that producers could be told to vary their output until marginal cost became equal to some point on these demand curves (pp. 90–95). He did not explain how marginal labor costs could measure marginal disutility if labor is arbitrarily assigned to jobs. He concluded, however, that he had demonstrated "the economic consistency and workability of a socialist economy with free choice neither in consumption nor in occupation, but directed rather by a preference scale imposed by the bureaucrats in the Central Planning Board" (p. 95). In fact, planners could not draw hundreds of arbitrary demand curves for each of the millions of individual goods—a separate demand curve would be required each day or week for each market—and if they could, such curves would not even roughly measure marginal social utility. Moreover, costs would not reflect social disutility because of the absence of free choice of jobs. Prices based on such preference curves and costs would consequently be useless in maximizing welfare.

Lange did not recommend economic planning. He explicitly stated that he disapproved of it, asserting that "such a system" would scarcely be tolerated by any civilized people" (p. 95). This is a notable advance over orthodox Socialist theory. Yet he seems to have believed such a system to be compatible with marginal-cost output control and rational economic calculation.

In spite of such defects, Lange's revised discussion of ideal output is far superior to that by Pigou, to whom he attributed his basic idea. This attribution is especially questionable because, although Lange was familiar with Pigou when he first wrote this article, he had then argued that price should equal average cost. Only after Lerner's pointed criticism of this conclusion did Lange adopt the idea of marginal-cost control, and then his discussion of it was seriously marred by remnants of the Pigovian analysis. He seems to have been unaware of Meade's discussion of ideal output under Socialism.

HOFF

We turn briefly to the comments of a Norwegian economist, T. J. B. Hoff, on the 1936–37 statements of marginal-cost output control by English Socialist economists. In 1938 he published a treatise in Norwegian, *Economic Calculation in the Socialist Society* (republished in English in 1949), which includes an eight-page chapter on Socialist pricing entitled "Other Solutions, Marginal Costs as Criteria" (pp. 144–52).

The first four pages of this chapter are devoted to a summary and criticism of Durbin's 1936 article, "Economic Calculus in a Planned Economy," but there is no mention of the theory of marginal-cost output control or of the fact that Durbin rejected this theory. Hoff's criticism is directed chiefly at the idea that rational pricing and economic calculation are possible under Socialism.

The last four pages are devoted to Lerner's 1937 criticism of Durbin's and Dickinson's views on Socialist pricing. Like Lange and Lerner, Hoff was apparently unaware of Meade's earlier statement of marginal-cost price-output theory. After two pages of preliminary discussion, in which he mistakenly concluded that at one point Lerner favored the determination "of the importance of products" by a "central authority" (p. 149), Hoff came to the subject of marginal-cost price-output control. He criticized Lerner because: (1) he did not explain how factor prices should be determined and (2) he used prices to measure costs to determine other prices, which is "circular reasoning" (p. 151).

Neither of these criticisms is sound. Lerner had actually explained that the factors should be priced so as to equalize the supply of and demand for them, and the argument that all pricing is unsound because it involves circular reasoning is too weak to deserve comment. Moreover, Hoff himself, had implicitly contradicted his second criticism at an earlier point where he asserted that: "With both markets and prices the problem [of ideal pricing] ceases to be a problem. The question is: How are these to be obtained? Of that Dr. Lerner has nothing to say" (p. 147).

Hoff's real objection to marginal-cost control under Socialism is that he did not believe prices could be determined without markets and thought markets incompatible with Socialism. This argument applies equally to average-cost control under Socialism. He really failed to discuss the question of whether marginal-cost control is preferable to average-cost control. His statement that with markets and cost prices there are no pricing problems suggests, indeed, that he never saw this problem.

DICKINSON

When Dickinson revised and enlarged his discussion of Socialist pricing for his *Economics of Socialism* (1939), he gave a more explicit statement of the theory of ideal output suggested in his 1933 article.

(2) *Average Cost or Marginal Cost?* One point that must be considered is whether . . . average cost or marginal cost should be the basis of price determination. Where goods are produced under conditions of increasing costs, average cost is too low, and marginal cost seems to be indicated. Where diminishing cost is the rule, marginal cost gives a price that does not enable all the costs of production to be covered. Professor Pigou suggests that the social interest would be best served by pricing all commodities according to their marginal cost, subsidizing the production of diminishing-cost goods out of taxes on increasing-cost goods. (p. 105)

In the pages immediately following this passage, Dickinson noted that the subsidies to decreasing-cost industries could be covered by land rent under Socialism, and still later he implied that interest and other non-wage income could be used for the same purpose (p. 136). He never criticized or rejected the proposal of taxes on increasing-cost industries, but he suggested much better sources of revenue to cover the subsidies in question. This is an advance over his 1933 adumbration of marginal-cost control. However, he seems to have been unaware of Meade's theory that such subsidies would just equal total rent and interest when population is at the optimum level.

In the above quotation Dickinson did not endorse the theory he mistakenly ascribed to Pigou. He maintained a neutral attitude towards it whenever he stated or referred to it. But when he came to discuss specific pricing problems, such as the fixing of railroad and public utility rates, he was compelled to take a stand, and he recommended prices well above marginal costs.[5] We shall cover this point in the next chapter.

Dickinson was the first to use the term "negative rent" to describe a deficit due to cost control (p. 106). He thought that negative rent would be much more common than positive rent if marginal-cost price control were adopted. He attributed this to the prevalence of decreasing costs. In other words, he confused the results of marginal-cost price-output control with the results of optimum investment control.

CONCLUSION

On the basis of the facts disclosed in this chapter, we conclude that two Socialist economists, Meade and Lerner, were the first to state the theory of marginal-cost output control with reasonable completeness and clarity, that they actively championed the new theory, and that by 1939 it had a firm hold on English Socialist economists. It was still, however, unknown to the vast majority of Socialists, and was rejected by the few Marxian economists who were aware of it.

In 1939 the new theory was still in a very early stage of development, even among Socialists. No distinction between the theories of ideal output and ideal investment in fixed capital had been drawn. No one had yet stated the theory of marginal-cost price control and explained when price control is preferable to output control. The numerous applications of marginal-cost theory to the control of private monopolies, especially railroads and public utilities, had been ignored. No one had yet discussed in any detail the practical problems involved in measuring marginal costs, though there had been some general discussion of whether it is easier to measure marginal or average costs.

In her brief history of marginal-cost theory, Mrs. Ruggles concluded that "by 1938 . . . the basis of the argument [for this theory] had shifted from the assumption of equal marginal utilities of income to the claim that interpersonal comparisons need not be made" (p. 46). We have now reviewed the history of this theory through 1937 and have found nothing to support this conclusion. None of the English-

---

[5] In a 1950 letter to me Dickinson wrote: "I still think (as I did when I wrote the *Economics of Socialism*) that price should be based on marginal or average cost, whichever is higher." Hayek was in error when he stated that Dickinson had supported *marginal-cost* pricing in this book (see Hayek's review article in *Econometrica*, VII (1940), 138.

speaking proponents of the theory whom we have discussed—and Mrs.
Ruggles mentioned no others—based it upon the assumption that interpersonal comparisons of utility are invalid. We shall examine in
the next chapter the first proponent of marginal-cost control of whom
this claim might be made with some reason, namely Hotelling, but we
shall find the claim is doubtful even there.

V

THE APPLICATION OF
MARGINAL-COST PRICE-OUTPUT THEORY
TO RAILROAD AND PUBLIC UTILITY
RATE THEORY, 1938 TO 1947

INTRODUCTION

IN THE PREVIOUS CHAPTER, we reviewed the first statements of the theory of marginal-cost *output* control. In this chapter, we shall review the first statements of the theory of marginal-cost *price* control. The former theory is not applicable to railroad and utility rates, while the latter is. Unfortunately, none of the writers reviewed in this chapter grasped this point. They refrained from claiming that the output of each railroad or utility should be increased until price equals marginal cost, but they never explained why they did so.

Railroad and public utility managers have long known that they could increase their profits by practicing rate discrimination, but discrimination has been unpopular with consumers. Hence, railroad and public utility economists have tried to justify rate discrimination.[1] They found it easy to defend this practice by developing arguments which point toward marginal-cost pricing. In the railroad industry short-run marginal costs are usually only one third of average costs because surplus capacity is prevalent. Thus, it is obviously desirable to haul additional freight which can pay more than one third of aver-

---

[1] "The theory of railroad rates originated very largely as an explanation and justification of the principle of charging what the traffic would bear." D. P. Locklin, "Literature on Railway Rate Theory," *Quarterly Journal of Economics*, XLVII (Feb., 1933), 172.

age costs. Moreover, since shippers can be classified according to prod-uct and route and then charged different rates, it is possible to haul additional freight at low discriminatory rates without reducing rates on freight already being hauled. However, it is unprofitable to reduce rates on any class of additional traffic below the level necessary to secure it. Hence, different railroad rates were fixed for each class of additional freight, and in time freight rate structures became enor-mously complicated. But it was easy to show that this elaborate struc-ture of discriminatory rates, (1) increased the use of existing capital facilities and thus lowered average costs; (2) justified additional facilities, which reduced average costs because railroad transport is a decreasing-cost industry; and (3) often permitted rate reductions for old as well as new shippers.

This customary apology did not reconcile price discrimination with neo-classical value theory. Orthodox value theorists taught that, under competition, price is, and presumably should be, uniform for all units of a given good in a single market, and that, even in the case of differ-ent goods, prices are the same if costs are equal. The orthodox theory of monopoly price assumes that prices of the same good are uniform to all buyers in the same market at the same time. Thus there was, and still is, a direct contradiction between railroad and utility rate theory on the one hand and general value theory on the other.

One of the first and most influential economists to note and attempt to end this contradiction was F. W. Taussig. In 1891 he argued that since railroads have large overhead costs, railroad services to different shippers are joint products which have joint costs. In other words, he argued that the relationship of the service of transporting a carload of hats to that of transporting a carload of shoes is like the relationship of cotton fibre to cotton seed. If hauling a carload of shoes and hauling a carload of hats are distinct but joint services, there is no more reason for charging the same price for hauling these different carloads than for charging the same price for cotton and cotton seed. The defect in this analogy is that cotton and cotton seed must be produced together while it is not necessary to haul a carload of hats in order to haul a carload of shoes. Unfortunately, the need for a theory to reconcile rate discrimination with orthodox price theory has caused most rail-road and public utility theorists to overlook this defect.

This defect has been noted by critics of the joint-cost theory of rail-road rates, among whom Pigou was a leader, but there is another objection which has been overlooked. Joint products have joint marginal costs which are above or below their joint average costs. Defining railroad services as joint products may seem to justify different prices for these services, but it provides no answer to the question of whether the sum of the prices of the joint products should equal average or marginal costs.

Nearly all critics of price discrimination have concluded that rates should be uniform at the average-cost level. Since the social advantage of price discrimination has often been demonstrated, this conclusion also has been unsatisfying. A satisfactory theory must recognize both, (1) that railroad services are not joint products and should be uniform in price when they have the same cost, and (2) that reducing prices below average costs benefits the community. Only the theory of marginal-cost price-output control meets both tests.

Public hostility to price discrimination, or charging what the traffic will bear, was never based upon any awareness of the defects of the joint-cost theory of railroad rates. It was due directly to the well justified suspicion that rate discrimination was being used to secure monopoly profits, a suspicion which played a key role in bringing about the creation of our present complex system of federal and state regulation of railroads. This system greatly reduced monopoly profits, but it did so by lowering the level of discriminatory rates, not by eliminating price discrimination. Hence, we have today, a system of railroad and utility rates which is thoroughly discriminatory and therefore uneconomic, which contradicts the basic principles both of traditional descriptive value theory and of modern prescriptive (welfare) price theory, and is yet accepted without question by railroad and utility managers, by public regulatory officials, and by consumers. However, a few economists have recently applied the new theory of marginal-cost control to railroad and public utility rates. We have noted the first foreshadowing of this effort by Launhardt. We turn now to a review of recent efforts of this sort.[2]

HOTELLING

While the discussion of marginal-cost price-output theory started by Meade and Lerner in England was still in an early stage, two American

[2] This literature has also been reviewed by I. M. D. Little in Chap. XI of his *A Critique of Welfare Economics* (Oxford, 1950). He commented on the contributions of Hotelling,

economists, Harold Hotelling and R. M. Montgomery, restated the theory, in its price-control form, and applied it for the first time to railroad and utility rates. In this section we shall review Hotelling's contribution.

Although Hotelling's article was published in *Econometrica* in July, 1938, about two years after the publication of the first statements of the theory of marginal-cost output control by Meade and Lerner, there is no reference to these statements in it. He may have developed his theory independently.

The title of Hotelling's article, "The General Welfare in Relation to Problems of Taxation and of Railway and Utility Rates," is misleading, for it implies that the price theory in the article applies only or chiefly to taxation and to railway and utility rates. Actually, he opened his article with the arresting statement that:

In this paper we shall bring down to date an argument due essentially to the engineer Jules Dupuit, to the effect that the optimum of general welfare corresponds to the sale of everything at marginal cost. (p. 242)

The attribution of this theory to Dupuit has little basis. Dupuit was a pioneer in the use of marginal analysis and consumers' surplus, but no one except Hotelling has ever attributed the theory of marginal-cost control to him, and in a June, 1949, letter to the author he qualified his attribution as follows:

Dupuit mentions . . . the idea of a zero toll for which I argued in my 1938 paper. However, he fails to endorse it explicitly as he carried along at this point the common idea that maintenance costs and interest should be paid out of tolls. Thus, the writers to whom you allude are correct in so far as they imply that Dupuit did not explicitly endorse the idea of sales at marginal cost; at least I cannot point to any place in which Dupuit does this.

After mentioning Dupuit, Hotelling went on in his article to explain the opening sentence thus:

This means that toll bridges . . . are inefficient reversions; that all taxes on commodities, including sales taxes, are more objectionable than taxes on incomes, inheritance, and the site value of land; and that the latter taxes might well be applied to cover the fixed costs of electric power plants, waterworks, railroads, and other industries in which the fixed costs are large, so as to reduce to the level of marginal cost the prices charged for the services and products of these industries. (p. 242)

Coase, Wilson, Norris, Meade, Fleming, Lewis, and Henderson, giving most of his space to the last two.

One of Hotelling's chief contributions was his idea that "the considerations applicable to taxation are very nearly identical with those involved in proper rate making" (pp. 242–43). This is a very fruitful idea. He thought it justified the application of prescriptive tax theory to price determination, and developed this point with skill and profit. To us, it also implies that the theory of marginal-cost pricing can be directly applied to *price taxes,* namely those used to cover marginal costs (see p. 193 below). In either case, a single body of theory applicable to both taxes and prices results.

Hotelling attempted a mathematical proof of the major conclusions stated in his initial summary. He began by reviewing Dupuit's pioneer discussion of consumers' and producers' surpluses. Using a chart showing "a rising [long-run] supply curve, . . . sometimes regarded as coinciding with the marginal-cost curve," which intersects a falling long-run demand curve, he defined consumers' and producers' surplus, and concluded that "the total net benefit, representing the value to society of the commodity, and therefore the maximum worth spending from the public funds to obtain it, is the sum of consumers' and producers' surpluses" (p. 245). He illustrated the way a tax causes a net loss of total net benefit, and attributed the first description and measurement of this loss to Dupuit, who had pointed out that this loss is proportional to the square of the tax rate.

Hotelling thought that this "remarkable" analysis had often been ignored when it was relevant. It had also been subject to open attacks "based on an excessive emphasis on the shortcomings of consumers' and producers' surpluses as measures of benefits" (p. 246). The chief alleged shortcomings are that pleasure is non-measurable, that consumers' surpluses from different goods are not independent and cannot be added together, and that surpluses of different persons cannot be added. Hotelling offered a mathematical refutation to the last two objections. We shall not repeat it here because we do not understand calculus. He did not specifically refute the first objection, that pleasure is non-measurable. Although he was apparently skeptical of all three objections, he was sufficiently impressed by them, or by the emphasis placed upon them, to avoid using these surpluses to demonstrate his price theory. He did not see that the use of such surpluses is incompatible with marginal analysis as there can be no surplus at the margin. It is only in total analysis that surpluses should be measured and compared.

To avoid the unsound objections to the use of the surpluses in question discussed by him, Hotelling tried to establish "a generalized form of Dupuit's conclusions on the basis of a ranking only, without measurement of satisfactions, in the way represented graphically by indifference curves" (p. 246). To do this, he assumed the existence of an economy in which all prices equal marginal costs, and demonstrated algebraically a "fundamental theorem."

The fundamental theorem thus established is that *if a person must pay a certain sum of money in taxes, his satisfaction will be greater if the levy is made directly on him as a fixed amount than if it is made through a system of excise taxes which he can to some extent avoid by rearranging his production and consumption.* In the latter case, the excise taxes must be at rates sufficiently high to yield the required revenue after the person's rearrangement of his budget. The redistribution of his production and consumption then represent a loss to him without any corresponding gain to the treasury. This conclusion is not new. What we have done is to establish it in a rigorous manner free from the fallacious methods of reasoning about one commodity at a time which have led to false conclusions in other associated discussions. (p. 252)

This theorem assumes, without explanation, that all desirable excise taxes have been adopted and raised to the optimum level. Some government costs, such as the cost of repairing highways, vary with private use and should be partly financed by excise taxes on such use. Moreover, other excise taxes should be levied to reduce air and water pollution and other real costs not represented by money costs. If a certain sum of money must be raised by taxes, it is better to raise as much as possible of this sum by such excise taxes. Hence, Hotelling's theorem is invalid. It can be made valid, however, by assuming that all desirable excise taxes are already in use and that therefore additional excise taxes would be undesirable. All valid mathematical reasoning begs the question in this way because the conclusions are implicit in the definitions and axioms.

For Hotelling, that part of a price which covers overhead costs is like a tax, and therefore the above theorem proved to him that overhead costs should be covered by taxes which do not affect consumption rather than by prices which do. If this theorem applies to each individual, it applies to the community as a whole. Hence,

If government revenue is produced by any system of excise taxes, there exists a possible distribution of personal levies . . . such that the abolition of the excise taxes and their replacement by these levies will yield the same revenue while leaving each person in a state more satisfactory to himself than before. (p. 252)

Since that part of a price which covers fixed costs is like a tax, this implies that it is possible to change from so-called average-cost pricing or some other pricing system to marginal-cost price control without harming any individual and therefore without any compensation payments. Hotelling did not state and discuss the "principle of compensation," and there is no evidence in his article that he contemplated compensation payments to individual persons, other than subsidies to cover deficits. He believed in "a possible distribution of personal levies" which would yield net benefits to all consumers, but in our opinion no such distribution is possible. If marginal-cost control were adopted and financed by any possible (i.e., feasible) distribution of personal levies, net losses would be suffered not only by some consumers (those who consume chiefly goods whose prices would be raised), but also by some landowners (whose rents would be reduced), by some monopolists (whose monopoly profits would be reduced or eliminated), and by many other businessmen (through inventory losses, increased competition from substitute products, etc.). And even if such losses were recognized, it would be impractical to determine and make the innumerable compensation payments required to prevent any person from suffering a net loss. If Hotelling meant "conceivable" when he said "possible," his statement is irrelevant. Marginal-cost control must be proven beneficial in practice.

In other words Hotelling's effort to demonstrate the merit of marginal-cost price control by means of indifference curve analysis, without making interpersonal comparisons of utility, was unsuccessful. It is impossible to justify any economic act or policy without making interpersonal comparisons of utility because each individual economic act has repercussions throughout the economic system and affects the welfare of every person.[3]

Hotelling next discussed the problem of financing deficits due to ideal price control. He recommended the use of land taxes, taxes on quasi-rents, taxes on advertising, income and inheritance taxes, and "similar taxes which do not entail a dead loss" (p. 257). The last category includes poll taxes, but he did not mention them specifically.

He noted that the burden of these taxes might be greater for some persons than their benefit from marginal-cost price control, but offered

[3] See pp. 139–40, 161–62, 175–77 below.

reasons for believing that such cases would be few and minor if such control were generally adopted. Benefits which arise from such control in one area naturally spread throughout the nation. Moreover, the general adoption of such control would affect so many enterprises that direct as well as indirect benefits would accrue to nearly all persons. He thought that there are only two important groups of people who might not receive net benefits, namely, those possessed of great wealth and landowners.

One of the most significant new ideas in Hotelling's article is that marginal-cost control would reduce the severity of the business cycle. In his opening paragraph he announced that:

It will appear also that the inefficient plan of requiring that all costs, including fixed overhead cost, of an industry shall be paid out of the price of its products is responsible for an important part of the instability which leads to cyclical fluctuations. (p. 242)

Later he devoted a two-page section to this original thesis. He reviewed the causes of the 1930–40 depression and explained that:

If, as the general price level fell, railroad, utility and manufacturing concerns had reduced their selling prices proportionately, the prosperity of the years, 1922 to 1928, might have continued. But such reductions in selling prices were not possible when an increasing volume of overhead charges had to be paid out of earnings. (p. 266)

Hotelling did not add that when a depression first reduces output, it sharply lowers marginal costs in most firms, so that marginal-cost control would lower prices considerably at such times, but he vigorously condemned the absurdity of raising prices to cover higher average overhead costs due to a fall in sales.

To illustrate the application and benefits of marginal-cost control Hotelling preferred the case of a toll bridge because in this case marginal costs are neligible and the social gain from maximum use is obvious (p. 260). He thought, however, that the most important industries to which marginal-cost theory is applicable are railroads and utilities. These industries are large ones, and they have marginal costs well below their average costs. He was the first to apply the new theory to these industries, and he stated some very significant new ideas in so doing. For instance, he noted the perverse seasonal fluctuations in passenger fares, which are low in the summer when marginal costs are high and high in the winter when marginal costs are low (p. 263). He stressed "the extreme and uneconomic complexity of railway freight and passenger rates" and the "great simplification of the rate structure" which would result from application of the rule that all rates should equal marginal costs. He said that excursion rates, which must be above marginal costs to be profitable, were sometimes less than 20 percent of regular fares for the same trips (p. 263). He pointed out that some wholesale lumber prices in New York City were more than 100 percent above the level in Oregon, and implied that the freight rates were well above marginal costs. He explained that under marginal-cost control there should be no charge for the use of railroad facilities except in the most congested regions, but that, when facilities are congested, rates should be high enough to balance supply and demand (pp. 263–65). If Hotelling is right, orthodox railroad rate theory is almost entirely wrong.

One of the major faults of Hotelling's article is that he never defined marginal cost. In particular, he never explained whether he meant long-run or short-run marginal cost. Most of his analysis suggests that he used marginal cost to mean short-run cost at the margin, but there are passages which suggest that he meant long-run marginal cost. For instance, his restatement of Dupuit's theories has this effect. The graph (p. 243) used to illustrate Dupuit's work shows a *long-run* supply curve "sometimes regarded as coinciding with the marginal-cost curve."

Marginal short-run adjustments in output do not result in significant changes in total surplus; such changes result only from lumpy adjustments in fixed capital or land use. Hotelling failed to distinguish clearly between the problem of ideal price and output in the short run and ideal investment in fixed capital in the long run.

On the other hand, when he did discuss the problem of optimum investment at the end of his article, he did not make the error of saying it could be solved by the theory of marginal-cost pricing. Instead, he noted that it is the relationship of *total* investment revenue to *total* investment costs which guides private investment. He thought this criterion too conservative because it does not allow for the consumers' surplus on the additional output, and he vaguely suggested a better criterion of new fixed investment. "If some distribution of the burden is possible such that everyone concerned is better off than without the new investment, then there is a prima facie case for making the investment" (p. 267).

To summarize Hotelling's notable contributions to the theory of marginal-cost control, we repeat the following major points. He explained the close relationship of the theory of taxation to this theory. He made clear the way in which marginal-cost control would smooth out business fluctuations. He applied the theory to toll bridges, railroads, and public utilities. He answered in advance some of the major arguments against this theory. Unfortunately, he failed to define marginal cost, resorted to mathematical analysis to prove his theory, assumed that interpersonal comparability of utility is unnecessary, and did not distinguish clearly between optimum pricing and optimum investment in fixed capital. Nevertheless, his article made Hotelling the first and the outstanding American proponent of the marginal-cost price-output theory. Later writers have often called it the "Lerner-Hotelling" theory.

In a brief comment on Hotelling's article, Ragner Frisch asserted that excise taxes are as good as income taxes as a means of covering fixed costs, if they are proportional to prices which equal marginal cost (p. 145). In his reply Hotelling accepted this point, and rephrased it thus: "It is enough that all prices be *proportional* to marginal costs" (p. 151). We disagree. On their way to the consumer most goods are sold for a price several times, and the number of times this happens differs widely. If a turnover tax were levied on each sale, the tax would pyramid unequally and the proportion between the retail prices of different goods, and their marginal costs excluding turnover taxes would be variously affected.

It is possible that when Hotelling said "all prices" he meant only those prices paid by the final consumer, but even this qualification would not make his statement correct. Prices proportional to, but 100 percent above, marginal costs would create unbearable inflation and/or profits. And, as many goods are sold to both consumers and producers, they would have to have two prices if pyramiding were to be avoided.

MONTGOMERY

Hotelling's application of the new theory of marginal-cost price-output control to railroad and utility rates was followed within a year by another able discussion of this application of the theory by

R. H. Montgomery of the University of Texas, who was probably unfamiliar both with Hotelling's article and with the work of Meade, Lerner, Lange, *et al.* In January, 1939, two short articles [4] by Montgomery appeared in the *Annals* of the American Academy, and the new theory was stated in both of them. These articles have not received the notice they merit.

Montgomery used the new theory, which he called the theory of "incremental-cost pricing," [5] chiefly to support government ownership. He did this in both articles, but his detailed statement and demonstration of the theory are given in the article on railroads and merely summarized and applied to electric utilities in the first article. In the railroad article, nearly all of which is devoted to his new rate theory, Montgomery began with a brief critical history of doctrine on railway rates. He quoted statements by F. W. Taussig and Emory R. Johnson of the common but unsound theory that "a railway should pay its own way" and noted that they had ignored the contrary arguments by Marshall and Pigou. He quoted both the latter in support of subsidies to decreasing-cost industries. Since he referred to no other precursors, he probably developed his own ideas directly from their tax-subsidy proposal. He asserted that none of the proponents of this proposal "has specified the extent to which production should be expanded, or the point beyond which it should not go," and anticipated the conclusion of his later analysis at this point by stating that "production should be expanded to the point where incremental cost and demand price coincide" (p. 139).

To demonstrate the new theory, Montgomery used consumers' surplus and relied on partial rather than general analysis. He pointed out that as long as price is above incremental cost, additional output yields a net surplus to the community. This surplus can be measured in money. To illustrate, he assumed a total cost schedule, an incremental-cost schedule, and a demand schedule (unit elasticity) for a railroad.

Government regulation of the traditional kind would result in production being frozen at or near the 50-million unit point (where price equals average cost).

[4] "Government Ownership and Operation of the Electric Industry," pp. 43–49, and "Governmental Ownership and Operation of Railroads," pp. 137–45.
[5] He used "incremental cost" as synonymous with "marginal-cost" ("Governmental Ownership and Operation of Railroads," in American Academy, *Annals*, CCI, 139n) but did not define either.

On the other hand, large aggregate community gains would be derived from pushing production to the point of contact between incremental cost and demand price. . . . These community gains can be expressed in monetary values . . . the railroad would lose $417,000; the consumers would gain $645,627; the net community gain would be $228,627.

It is to be noted that the net community advantage would be greater at this point than at any other. (p. 141)

This demonstration is unsatisfactory because it uses *total* analysis to show the effect of *marginal* changes. A sound demonstration must use marginal analysis to prove that each marginal adjustment required by marginal-cost control is beneficial.

Montgomery also argued that marginal-cost control would restore price flexibility where prices are now most rigid or sticky, and thus help to smooth out so-called business cycles. He noted that during the thirties there was a small decline in output in industries whose prices were flexible and a large one in those with inflexible prices. The latter were, of course, chiefly responsible for unemployment. Hence, he thought they should be taken over by the state, which could practice marginal-cost pricing and thus increase employment (pp. 144–45).

In his article supporting state ownership of utilities, Montgomery merely summarized his railroad rate theory and applied it to electric utilities.

The writer submits two premises: (1) that railroad charges should cover only incremental costs; (2) that incremental costs should be kept well below average costs by continual expansion of facilities beyond the point of possible profit to private owners.

It is theoretically possible that this pricing theory could be effected under private ownership and operation, or under government ownership and private operation. Either would require huge government subsidies, and would not provide a reasonable probability that we would secure the possible benefit. Government ownership and operation offers the only practicable solution.

These arguments are equally valid for the electric industries. Power plants usually operate under more rapidly decreasing average costs than do railroads. Demand for electricity, within the range of rates possible under the proposed pricing policy, is far more elastic than is demand for railroad services. Consequently, gains to the community would be even greater. (p. 43)

Montgomery was the first to point out that, by using service charges, utilities could achieve nearly all the benefits of marginal-cost price control without incurring a deficit.

A ready-to-serve charge can be made to cover approximately the individual user's part of inflexible costs. This would undoubtedly prevent a few potential users from installing electric implements or machines; but the experiences of those communities which have employed the device indicate that the effect is negligible. Since current would be purchased at incremental-cost price, patently each user would extend his consumption without reference to the ready-to-serve charge. (p. 48)

Montgomery implied that service charges could be used to cover fixed costs only when utilities are state owned. In fact, such charges can be used as effectively by private as by state-owned electric utilities. Moreover, they are suitable for use by gas, water, telephone, and steam utilities, as well as by electric utilities.

In sum, Montgomery was a pioneer proponent, perhaps even an original codiscoverer of the new theory of marginal-cost price-output control, he understood its meaning and importance, he defended it forcefully and logically, and his discussion of the theory supplements earlier discussions in significant ways.

DICKINSON

At this point we must comment again on the work of the English Socialist, H. D. Dickinson. In his *Economics of Socialism* (1939), he was the first English economist to discuss the application of marginal-cost price theory to railroads and utilities. His discussion was, however, not equal to that of Hotelling and Montgomery, with whose work he seemed unfamiliar.

Dickinson discussed the application of marginal-cost theory to utility rates in Chapter V, "Price Policy of Public Utilities." He began with some comments on rate discrimination, and was probably the first economist to note that the orthodox defense of rate discrimination tends to justify marginal-cost price control (pp. 152–53). It is remarkable that economists had used the orthodox argument for price discrimination for a hundred years without seeing its obvious implication. But it is even more remarkable that Dickinson himself, after clearly stating this implication, after reading Lerner, Meade, Lange, *et al.,* and after stating the theory of marginal-cost control as a possible general theory, implicitly rejected the application of marginal-cost price control to railroads and public utilities, precisely the industries in which it would be most beneficial. In his words:

A sound system of social costing should render possible a threefold equilibrium: (1) within the enterprise, *a balance of receipts and costs* in each line of production where separate costs are ascertainable. . . . A system of transport, electricity, gas and water charges based on *mean cost* of service would afford a reliable indication to the planners of socialist industry of the most economic size and location for the manufacturing unit in different industries. (p. 153; italics added)

On the other hand, Dickinson specifically recommended the use of service charges under Socialism to cover capital costs, both for utilities (p. 155) and for transport (p. 156). Such charges would permit utilities to achieve most of the beneficial effects of marginal-cost price control, but Dickinson did not try to justify his proposal in this way. He noted that the use of such charges in transport industries "would be difficult under capitalism." We think it would be impractical under any economic system.

BONBRIGHT

The first economist to refer favorably to Hotelling's suggestion that public utility rates should equal marginal costs was James C. Bonbright, a colleague of Hotelling's at Columbia University. He did not attempt to contribute anything to the development of the new theory but his two-page discussion of it before the American Economic Association in December, 1940, is significant because he showed sympathy for the new theory and because he commented on the reason for the usual rejection of the new theory.

The more orthodox choice . . . is to retain the cost principle as a basis of general rate levels but to abandon it, or at least to modify it, in favor of the so-called "value of the service" principle in the fixation of specific rates. The more heterodox choice is to set all rates at marginal cost, relying on a system of subsidies and of excess-profits taxes to equate total costs.

The extreme social conservatism of most public utility and railroad specialists has prevented this latter point of view from gaining wide acceptance, or even from receiving any considerable notice, in the literature of rate theory. There is a fair chance, however, that it may become a live issue in the next few years, partly as a result of the recent mathematical defense of the principle by . . . Hotelling. Hotelling's defense . . . is, in my opinion, one of the most distinguished contributions to rate-making theory in the entire literature of economics.

Here, . . . there is time only for a few brief comments . . . First, I note that *Prof. Hotelling belongs to the amazingly small minority of ab-*

stract theorists who are bold enough to draw from their scientifically ortho-dox technique of static-equilibrium economics the socially radical conclu-sions which this type of analysis might seem to justify if it has any signifi-cance at all. Unlike Hotelling, most of these theorists have an almost magical ability suddenly to transform themselves into institutional econ-omists at the very moment when one would expect them to begin throwing bombs.[6] (Italics added)

Although Bonbright supported the new rate theory, he did not accept it as *"the* great cardinal principle of rate control"* (p. 388). He thought that utility rates should serve several useful functions and that marginal-cost rate control would not result in rates which would serve all these functions. One of these functions is to minimize public pro-tests, and, presumably, marginal-cost control would not do this because consumers do not understand it. This implies that economic theory is sound when it is popular and unsound when it is unpopular. It is much better, we think, to distinguish clearly between economic and educational problems.

THOMPSON AND SMITH

The first economists to discuss marginal-cost price control in a text-book on public utility economics were C. W. Thompson and W. R. Smith. Their *Public Utility Economics* (1941) contains a lucid two-page statement and discussion of the theory, including its implica-tions, a graphic demonstration showing the gain in consumers' surplus and net utility, and several arguments against the theory.

After pointing out that orthodox utility rate theory holds that net income should just cover average costs, the authors called attention to the new theory that rates should equal marginal cost.

Strangely enough, the literature on public utilities is quite silent on this point, but that silence is not surprising. There is, nevertheless, sound so-cial basis for the advocacy of marginal cost as a rule of reasonableness, be-cause at that price there would be a maximum of satisfaction of wants and at no increase in fixed costs. This appears in Chart 18, . . . No one doubts the wisdom of regulation's forcing prices from P^1 [monopoly price] to P [competitive price], thereby doubling output and eliminating monopoly profits. Why not push it to P^2, the marginal cost, thereby gaining a maxi-mum of want satisfaction at no increase in fixed costs? Such a proposal is entirely valid as a rule of reasonableness. (p. 272)

[6] "Major Controversies as to the Criteria of Reasonable Public Utility Rates," *American Economic Review*, XXX, Supplement (Feb., 1940), 385.

The authors noted, as the chief disadvantage of marginal-cost control, that taxpayers would have to meet the fixed costs. They ignored the fact that service charges of various kinds might be used to cover most if not all of these fixed costs, and that price discrimination also makes possible a much closer approach to optimum output without any government subsidies than does uniform average-cost pricing. Partly for these reasons, they concluded that "so long as private ownership continues in the United States, we shall not have utility prices set by marginal costs" (p. 273).

LEWIS

The next economist to discuss the application of marginal-cost theory to public utilities was W. A. Lewis of Birmingham University, England. He was primarily interested in what he called "two-part" pricing, and gave his twenty-two-page article, in the August, 1941, issue of *Economica,* the title, "The Two-Part Tariff," [7] but he discussed briefly the relationship of such tariffs to the theory of marginal-cost price control. He seems to have been unaware that Montgomery and Dickinson had explained the relationship of monthly service charges to such pricing.

Lewis defined two-part pricing as follows:

The essence of two-part charging is that the consumer is called on to pay two charges, one which varies directly with the amount of the commodity that he consumes, and another which does not. Thus the Post Office charges for the use of the telephone (1) a quarterly rental, payable whether any calls are made or not, plus (2) a charge for each call. Similarly for electricity one may be asked to pay a fixed charge depending on e.g. the size or rateable value of one's house, plus a charge per unit of actual consumption. (p. 249)

The chief defect in this definition is that it covers two entirely distinct pricing principles: (1) the use of fixed charges to cover continuing overhead costs and (2) the use of separate charges to cover one-time special marginal costs necessary to the provision of some service—for instance, phone installation costs. Moreover, since there may be more than one of these special marginal costs—for instance, phone directory costs, phone directory listing costs, and phone installation costs—

[7] This article was revised and reprinted as Chapter II in Lewis's *Overhead Costs* (London, 1949).

which should be covered by special charges, two-part pricing type (2) may require three or more charges, which makes the term "two-part" inaccurate. The illustrations given in the above quotation suggest that Lewis intended his definition to cover only two-part pricing type (1), but he made it clear later (pp. 264–67) that it also covers type (2).

The greater part of Lewis's article is devoted to the reasons why two-part pricing has been used. He noted five motives for such use and devoted eighteen pages to individual discussions of them. The following list of these motives is thus also an outline of the major part of this article.

1. To allocate "standing charges" to individual consumers. (pp. 250–56)

2. "To escape the risks of unforeseen changes" by allocating overhead costs to consumers by contract before they occur. (pp. 256–59)

3. To "extract some of the consumers' surplus" without reducing consumption. The fixed charge may be raised high enough to yield a considerable profit from such an expropriation of consumers' surplus. (p. 260)

4. To achieve price discrimination, and thus increase profits. (pp. 262–64)

5. To allocate "customer costs" to those responsible for them. (pp. 264–67)

There are several errors in the statement and discussion of these motives. Motives (1) and (5) are *social* rather than *private* motives. Why should a private entrepreneur seek to allocate costs in a socially desirable manner when this does not increase his profits? Moreover, it is impossible to allocate overhead costs to customers, a fact which Lewis himself later admitted in his reply to critics (p. 407). It is only possible to charge prices which cover total costs, and there are many price structures that would achieve this end. It is possible, on the other hand, to allocate special customer costs, such as the cost of telephone directories, to those customers who are responsible for them, but few if any telephone companies charge for directories, which indicates that the use of such charges is often not considered profitable. In other words, motive (5), like motive (1), does not influence businessmen because it is not a profit motive. As social motives both should have been treated only in Lewis's separate discussion of optimum price.

In the last three pages of his article, the only pages ostensibly devoted to the effect of two-part pricing on the "public interest," Lewis offered a demonstration of the social utility of two-part tariffs which is really a proof of the benefits of marginal-cost pricing.

It is now generally agreed that the "ideal" output of a concern is such that every consumer is getting every unit for which he is prepared to pay marginal cost. . . . But if marginal cost is less than average cost, ... It is easily shown that it is better to recoup the difference between average and marginal cost by a fixed charge than to add it to the variable. Consider the following diagram where AD is the demand curve . . . and ON the marginal cost. (p. 269)

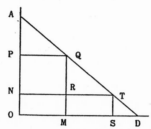

The proof is that lowering the variable charge from Q (average cost) to T (marginal cost) increases net welfare by QRT. Lewis thought that the loss caused by this price cut may be covered by fixed charges, which may be adjusted to each consumer so that they do not decrease output below the ideal amount OS. In fact, however, such ideal adjustments are not practical.

In a footnote he briefly noted that:

some writers have favoured an alternative solution, viz.: to charge only a price equal to marginal cost, and to meet the difference by a subsidy out of general taxation. The points of issue between this solution and two-part charging involve questions of social justice rather than economics. (p. 269n)

This implies that the two pricing policies have the same economic effects, which is not true. Fixed charges prevent some consumers from buying any service and thus reduce output below the ideal level. Moreover, "social justice" is a meaningless religious or philosophic concept and has no place in a scientific article.

CLEMENS

The first economist to discuss and reject the Hotelling-Montgomery proposal to apply marginal-cost price control to railroads and utilities was E. W. Clemens,[8] now at the University of Maryland. In a nine-page article called "Price Discrimination in Decreasing Cost Indus-tries," in the *American Economic Review* for December, 1941, he argued that there is no need for such a price reform because "in the railway and utility industries . . . the desired objective [optimum output] is actually obtained in practice by the much deprecated dis-criminatory pricing system" (p. 794).

Clemens used the term "discriminatory pricing" in a very broad sense. "In the railroad and utility industries," he explained, "dis-crimination is usually effected by differentiating between customer classes, geographical areas, or between different units of output taken by the same customer" (p. 801). Later he stated that the pricing of joint products so as to cover joint costs is also a form of price discrimi-nation (p. 802), and he probably meant to include other forms of non-uniform pricing under this term. Apparently, he wished to defend all rate variations now used by railroads and utilities.

Such a broad use of the term price discrimination is confusing. Each type of pricing included by Clemens under price discrimination de-serves a separate name and a separate theoretical analysis. Some of them are completely consistent with marginal-cost pricing, some help to achieve similar results, and some are inconsistent with such pricing and/or with each other.

The claim that railroads and utilities achieve optimum output with their existing rates is, of course, unjustified. Every class of consumers required to pay a rate above marginal cost would increase its con-sumption if this rate were reduced. Clemens also assumed that block or class rates can achieve full expropriation of all consumers' surpluses, which is impossible.

On the other hand, it is true that price discrimination, fixed serv-ice charges, block rates, incentive rates, and other similar pricing methods have increased the output of railroad and utility services beyond the average-cost level and towards the marginal-cost level. Clemens was therefore justified in claiming that "price discrimina-tion thus liberally interpreted would seem to deserve a more ex-tended place within the framework of analytical economic theory" (p. 802).

8 Clemens was also the first writer on marginal-cost theory to cite the earlier litera-ture in some detail. He noted the work of Lerner, Durbin, Hotelling, Montgomery, and Thompson and Smith. His discussion is based primarily on Montgomery's article.

BARNES

The second public utility economist to discuss marginal-cost price control in a book on public utilities was Irston R. Barnes. In the *Economics of Public Utility Regulation* (1942), he gave a clear summary of the theory, as then known, and its advantages and disadvantages. We quote below the key sentences in his three-page section on "The Increment-Cost School":

The Plan. One of the most sweeping proposals for the reform of utility rate regulation is that advanced by the increment-cost school. This program would provide for the establishment of utility rates at the marginal cost of providing the service. The marginal cost is the additional or increment cost that could be avoided if that unit of service were not supplied. . . .

The Merits of the Plan. The chief advantage claimed for the plan is that this price policy would encourage increased consumption. . . . [It] would . . . maximise the general welfare by creating the largest possible aggregate of consumers' surpluses.

The other advantages [are] . . . (1) . . . full utilization of . . . plant capacity. . . . (2) . . . increased investment [in utilities which] . . . would help to eliminate . . . the idle capacity of the capital-goods industries. . . . (3) . . . overhead cost . . . would be taken care of through . . . taxes which would not . . . lessen production or investment. . . . (4) . . . economic stability and fuller employment. . . . (5) . . . great simplification in rate structures. (pp. 586–87)

Advantage Number 3 is really a restatement or explanation of the first two advantages. Advantage Number 2 is a new one not mentioned in earlier literature, but it is an illusion. When properly stated, the theory of marginal-cost price control has nothing to say about investment in fixed capital.

In his "Critical Appraisal of the Plan," Barnes wrote:

the plan rests rather heavily upon the assumption that the general welfare which is to be balanced against . . . total economic cost . . . is to be measured by the amount which consumers are willing and able to pay. . . . [This] depends upon the amount and distribution of income and . . . it is doubtful whether the existing distribution of income may be assumed to maximise the general welfare. (p. 588)

This is a criticism which affects equally all prescriptive theories of utility rate determination.

"A more practical objection to the plan," Barnes continued, "has to do with the difficulty of assuring efficiency where . . . all overhead costs will be covered through a government subsidy" (p. 588). This objection assumes private management of utilities. It is not valid when utilities are publicly managed, as they are in most countries today. The same argument has been used against government regulation of utility profits. If the state restricts profits to 6 percent, why should a utility management strive to be efficient? And since nearly all utilities not state managed are state regulated, the argument that marginal-cost control would reduce the efficiency of management is not very persuasive.

Barnes also noted that under marginal-cost control "the earnings on utility properties would cease to guide the investment of capital," and asked, "What would prevent the uneconomic expansion of the utility industries?" This argument implies, without justification, that existing utility rates result in "economic investment" in utilities whereas marginal-cost price control would result in overinvestment. We believe that the truth is just the opposite. While the theory of marginal-cost control is not a theory of optimum investment, such control is a prerequisite for optimum investment.

On the whole, however, Barnes's early textbook treatment of the application of marginal-cost price theory to public utilities was a much-needed step towards the popularization of the new theory.

TROXEL

The most prolific writer on the application of marginal-cost theory to utility rates is Emery Troxel, of Wayne University, who published three journal articles on this subject in 1942–44 and who devoted some thirty pages of his *Economics of Public Utilities* (1947) to it. In general, he approved of the theory, at least as a social ideal, but stressed the technical and political difficulties of applying it. He seems to have been unaware of the work of most previous writers on the new theory. We shall comment now only on the three articles.

Troxel's first article [9] consisted largely of a summary and criticism of the earlier statements of the theory of marginal-cost control by

[9] "I. Incremental Cost Determination of Utility Prices," *Journal of Land and Public Utility Economics*, XVIII (Nov., 1942), 458–67.

Hotelling and Donald Wallace. He defined marginal cost as the increment in total cost (p. 459), not cost at the margin, and implied that there is a difference between short-run and long-run marginal costs.

Both of these writers propose to make all public utility prices equal to incremental costs. They advocate complete use of the incremental cost rule. Moreover, it is conceived as a short-run rule of pricing, i.e. incremental cost is measured principally in terms of an existing plant. (p. 460)

A few pages later (p. 465), Troxel explained that Wallace really thought all prices should be above marginal costs. The idea that there are two kinds of incremental costs, short-run and long-run, is a common error. Hotelling did not use short-run cost curves and did not state a "short-run rule of pricing."

Troxel went on to explain some of the advantages claimed for marginal-cost price control by Hotelling, among them fuller use of existing capital facilities and greater price flexibility. He summarized Wallace's views at some length, including his reason for advocating prices above marginal costs, namely, to guarantee a fair return to private investors.[10]

In his second article,[11] Troxel described the practical difficulties of applying marginal-cost price theory to privately owned utilities. He began by discussing the problem of determining incremental costs, and asserted that it is more difficult to determine incremental costs than to determine average costs. Since the latter usually requires the determination of incremental costs as a basis for the allocation of overhead costs, his claim is questionable. He also noted that marginal-cost price control without subsidies would not assure a fair return for investors in private utilities, and concluded that such control is inappropriate in these cases. Apparently he was unaware of the earlier suggestions that service charges might be used to assure a fair return to investors.

In his third article [12] he explained that marginal-cost price control is particularly suitable for publicly owned utilities because they can afford to place social welfare above profit. However, he stressed the fact that voters, politicians, and administrators of publicly owned

[10] We have not discussed Wallace because his comments on marginal-cost pricing (1940–41) were extremely brief and confusing.

[11] "II. Limitations of the Incremental Cost Patterns of Pricing," *Journal of Land and Public Utility Economics,* XIX (Aug., 1943), 28–39.

[12] "III. Incremental Cost Control under Public Ownership," *Journal of Land and Public Utility Economics,* XIX (Aug., 1943), 292–99.

utilities do not accept the theory of marginal-cost control and implied that they would not be likely to accept it in the future. He overlooks the fact that they had scarcely heard of the theory, which suggests real modesty, for Troxel's chief merit is that he was one of the first to bring the theory of marginal-cost control to the attention of public utility economists and administrators. Hence, it was surely too early to despair of their acceptance of the new theory.

PEGRUM

After Troxel had written his three articles, but before he had published his *Economics of Public Utilities* (1947), D. F. Pegrum criticized and rejected Troxel's major thesis concerning marginal-cost price control in a three-page reply, "Incremental Cost Pricing: A Comment," in February, 1944, in the *Journal of Land and Public Utility Economics.* He gave no evidence of being aware of earlier discussions of the theory not mentioned by Troxel. He summarized Troxel's conclusions as follows:

In his recent articles on "Incremental Cost Determination of Utility Prices," Prof. Troxel comes to the conclusion that it "is unworkable as a means of price control of privately owned utility companies." He regards this, however, as a "social misfortune" which in many respects "becomes another argument for public ownership of public utility plants." In the section dealing with the application of incremental cost to public ownership, he concludes that it "affords a better social concept of pricing than the objective of liquidating public investments." He feels, nonetheless, that "it is not yet an accepted pricing policy" and that it is a difficult administrative task to equate prices to incremental cost.

Pegrum pointed out that Troxel had not discussed "the issues which arise in connection with the making of the investment decision" in publicly owned utilities under marginal-cost pricing, and then suggested three methods of making this decision:

There are three possibilities. The decision may be made on political or on social grounds which are not readily amenable to economic tests. It may be made on the same basis as a private investor would use, that is, on the prospect of self liquidation. Or thirdly, it may be made on estimates of general economic welfare, in which case the funds to be invested would be determined by estimating the size of the plant the operation of which would equate incremental cost and price.

Pegrum thought the third method of making investment decisions is the most consistent with marginal-cost pricing. We disagree. Short-run marginal cost can be equated to price regardless of the size of the investment, so this solution is completely indeterminate. Long-run marginal cost is an illogical concept.

Pegrum next attacked the belief that, when prices equal marginal costs, the benefits from fuller use of existing capacity offset the loss to taxpayers who meet the resulting deficits. He questioned both the belief that the utility gains of one group are comparable with the utility loses of another group and the idea that "taxes can be imposed in such a way as to avoid offsetting the very gains that incremental cost-pricing is designed to secure." These points contradict each other. The argument that utility to different persons cannot be compared is nihilistic. The argument that taxes imposed to cover deficits will offset the gains achieved by marginal-cost pricing assumes that utility gains and losses to different persons can be measured and compared.

"Presumably, tariff policies based on the same theoretical principles as incremental-cost pricing would have to be adopted," Pegrum continued, and "this does not fit well in a world looking towards freer trade." It is impossible for this critic to understand how such tariff policies would limit free trade. All tariffs violate the theory of marginal-cost price-output control because they raise prices still further above marginal costs. For this reason, therefore, they would be eliminated by the full adoption of marginal-cost control.

The chief reason for Pegrum's rejection of the new price theory may have been his recognition that "the implication of incremental-cost pricing is that a Socialist economy is more capable of maximizing welfare than is a private one."

Troxel's reply to Pegrum's comment does not take issue with his critic on any of the above points. It repeats his previous ideas and also comments on the difficulty of persuading public authorities to "accept dispassionate reasoning when they want to stay alive politically."

LEWIS

W. A. Lewis resumed the discussion of the application of marginal-cost price control to public utilities in a twenty-eight-page article,

"Fixed Costs," in the November, 1946, issue of *Economica*.[13] His primary purpose was to prescribe the proper method of price control in

the case where similar services are supplied by two different industries, one or both of which has a high ratio of fixed to variable expenses. Gas and electricity and road and rail transport are the outstanding examples, and special reference will be made to them.

This implies that a different prescriptive theory of price is needed for industries which produce close substitutes than for those which compete less directly, at least when one or both competitors have large fixed costs. This is contrary to the theory of marginal-cost control, and Lewis therefore tried to refute this theory before offering what he called "the principles of coordination" of such industries. To introduce this refutation, he devoted four pages to a discussion of fixed costs. Hence, the title of the article.

Lewis defined "fixed" costs as those which cannot be escaped by a reduction in output. Other costs are "the economists' costs." He classified fixed costs as follows:

Fixed or inescapable costs fall into four categories:

(a) Some are inescapable in the short run but not in the long run;
(b) Some are joint costs, and inescapable only in that sense;
(c) Some are inescapable for small but not for large changes in output; and
(d) Some are inescapable in all senses. (p. 231)

This classification seems unsatisfactory because the classes overlap and because it is of little help in determining whether individual costs—research, advertising, etc.—are marginal costs. In fact, it was not designed for this purpose, but rather to serve as a basis for an attack on the theory of marginal-cost control. We shall therefore refrain from criticizing Lewis's brief effort to justify this classification, even though it includes such unsound claims as that depreciation is a joint cost (p. 233), and shall proceed to his use of it to refute marginal-cost theory.

1. It has now become an axiom that if the price mechanism is accurately to allocate resources, price must equal marginal cost, and recent writers have said even that this rule simplifies the administration of state undertakings since it is virtually the only instruction that need be given to man-

13 Reprinted as Chapter I in *Overhead Costs*.

agers to determine output. We are now in a position to grapple with some of its hidden difficulties.

They are four, corresponding to the categories of fixed cost:

(a) the fact that there is a whole range of marginal costs, depending on how far ahead one looks;

(b) the fact that marginal cost may fluctuate from one moment to the next;

(c) the fact that indivisible escapable costs must be covered; and

(d) the fact that the accounting and the economic cost are different. (p. 236)

The mere statement of the first two difficulties implies that so-called average cost would not depend upon how far one looks ahead and would not fluctuate, which is untrue. Moreover, the claim that marginal cost may be based upon a long look ahead is inconsistent with the statement that it "fluctuates from one moment to the next." Actually, marginal cost is the cost at a given moment. Hence, the first difficulty is an illusion. It is so-called average-cost pricing which raises the problem of how many future costs should be averaged.

The second difficulty describes what is really a great merit of marginal-cost pricing, for the price fluctuations in question would reduce or eliminate many harmful output cycles. Lewis conceded that price fluctuations are needed to offset regular demand or cost cycles for all goods and irregular cycles for goods sold in an organized market, but he objected to "irregular and unforeseeable" price fluctuations on the grounds that they are a nuisance. Orthodox economists have long taught that the function of prices is to adjust demand and supply when any change in cost or demand occurs, and it is scarcely necessary for us to support traditional value theory on this point. There are practical limits to the number of times a price should change in any given period, but this has nothing to do with whether the change in demand or cost on which it is based is a regular or irregular change.

"The third difficulty in equating price to marginal cost," according to Lewis, "is that it leaves uncovered escapable indivisible expenses which ought to be covered if the retention of these resources by consumers of this commodity is to be justified" (p. 234). This is a vague statement, which may mean only that marginal-cost control is bad because it results in deficits, the same point made in his fourth difficulty.

"The fourth consequence of equating price with escapable cost is that . . . receipts may be greater or less than . . . expenses" (pp.

244–45). This is a familiar point. Lewis apparently believed that every enterprise should cover its costs.

Lewis summarized his conclusions as follows:

The net conclusion is that, at least in public utility undertakings and state industries, price should not fluctuate irregularly; should cover not only short-run but also long-run marginal cost; not only long-run marginal cost but also, preferably by way of price discrimination, escapable indivisible cost as well; and not only these, but as much of the cost of non-renewable assets as can be extracted from consumers' surplus by price discrimination. (p. 246)

All of these conclusions seem wrong. They result chiefly from a failure to distinguish between the problem of ideal price and the problem of ideal investment in fixed capital.

The last twelve pages of this article are devoted to an effort to apply these dubious principles to the problem specifically stated at the beginning of the article, and contain nothing new on the theory of marginal-cost control.

TROXEL

In his *Economics of Public Utilities* (1947), C. Emery Troxel devoted a twenty-three-page chapter (Number 20) to "A Proposal: Marginal-Cost Pricing," and also gave other pages (439–40, 755–61) to this theory. His attitude towards it in the book remained essentially the same as that in his journal articles.

Troxel opened this textbook discussion of the theory of marginal-cost price control with a statement that it resembles the theory of pricing under perfect competition because both theories make price equal to marginal cost. He then described the great difference between marginal-cost pricing of utility services and the traditional theory of utility regulation—fair return on a fair value—and noted the reluctance of regulatory commissions to make such a radical change.

He defined marginal cost as increment in total cost, not cost at the margin; pointed out that it is a concept familiar only to economists; and discussed some of the practical problems of using the concept. First, there is the problem of whether short-period or long-period marginal costs should be used. The latter includes plant expansion and management costs, "because these costs, like raw material and labor costs, vary with output changes in long-period operations" (p. 445). Several graphs are used to explain the relationship between short-period and long-period cost curves. Since he thought that long-period marginal costs are higher than short-period marginal costs, Troxel suggested that long-period marginal costs would be "possible measures of reasonable costs for the commission that wants to encourage new investments and reinvestments" (p. 448). However, due to the difficulty of measuring long-period marginal costs, he used short-period marginal costs in his main exposition of marginal-cost price control.

The chief merit of Troxel's discussion of long-run marginal cost is that it helps to show the confusion of those who use this term. He defined long-run marginal cost by deriving it from a smooth long-run average-cost curve. This is the method approved by Chamberlin and Robinson. It assumes that marginal analysis can be applied to large indivisible investments in fixed capital, and puts marginal cost below average cost as long as the latter is declining.

Most firms have continually decreasing costs (see pp. 213–16 below). In such cases every short-run average-cost curve is above the long-run average-cost curve except where tangent to it, and the latter is well above the so-called long-run marginal-cost curve derived from it. Hence, what Troxel, Chamberlin, and Robinson call the long-run marginal-cost is below their short-run marginal cost (increment in total cost) most if not all of the time in most firms. Yet Troxel and others have argued that price should equal long-run rather than short-run marginal cost because they think the latter policy would result in deficits.

Troxel next raised the question of which costs are short-run marginal costs when a company has several plants supplying the same market and each plant has different marginal costs. "To solve this practical problem, a commission can equate the 'average' marginal costs to the demand prices of consumers" (p. 449). Both the statement of this problem and the solution offered are incorrect. A public utility with one high-cost and one low-cost plant supplying the same market should expand its use of the low-cost plant to the point where its marginal costs become equal to those of the high-cost plant. It is always wrong to average different marginal costs in different plants. There can only be one marginal cost at any given time because marginal cost is the cost of additional output produced in the most economical way.

There are always many uneconomical ways to increase output, but their costs are not marginal costs.

After these comments on the definition of marginal costs, Troxel undertook a general statement of "the way in which marginal costs of production can be used to control public utility prices." He proposed that price should, (1) equal marginal cost when excess capacity exists, and (2) balance supply and demand when demand at a price equal to marginal cost exceeds capacity (p. 454). This distinction between two pricing rules is sound, but the second method is important only if marginal costs cannot be raised gradually by efforts to increase output beyond capacity, an unusual situation (see p. 174 below).

Perhaps the chief merit of Troxel's entire discussion of marginal-cost price control is his recognition of the fact that such pricing ought to be adopted by publicly owned utilities. He had devoted the last of his three journal articles to this thesis, and he restated it in *Economics of Public Utilities* (pp. 760–61).

There are other points in Troxel's long discussion of marginal-cost control which might be commented upon, but we can not give him more space. To summarize, Troxel's greatest service was to bring the new rate theory to the attention of a larger number of public utility experts. He also deserves credit for recognizing the merit of marginal-cost price control as an economic ideal, but he was hesitant in supporting its practical application. He did not grasp the possibility of using service charges to cover fixed costs in privately owned utilities, and he despaired prematurely of public acceptance of the theory.

HENDERSON

We come now to the work of A. M. Henderson of Manchester University, the third English economist to discuss the application of marginal-cost price theory to public utilities. A twenty-seven-page article by him, "The Pricing of Public Utility Undertakings," appeared in *The Manchester School* for September, 1947. Like Dickinson and Lewis, he rejected the new rate theory. It is notable that while seven American economists (Hotelling, Montgomery, Bonbright, Thompson and Smith, Barnes, and Troxel), supported the application of the new price theory to utility rates between 1939 and 1950, only three English economists discussed this proposal and all rejected it.

This is surprising since English economists had been primarily responsible for the development of the general theory.

Henderson began his criticism by considering "the simplest possible case," that of a toll bridge, where "the marginal cost is nothing" (p. 225). He restated Hotelling's argument for abolishing tolls on toll bridges, and then criticized the methods suggested by Hotelling and Lerner for covering the costs of free bridges. He remarked, quite properly, that the land tax proposed by Hotelling should be used whether or not toll bridges are made free, if it has the merits ascribed to it, but he ignored, at this point, Hotelling's alternative suggestion of higher income, excise, and other taxes (p. 229). He noted that Lerner's suggestion of a lower social dividend really implied higher taxes, for the social dividend could also be reduced in order to lower taxes. He accepted Lerner's suggestion of a negative social dividend, a poll tax, as the ideal source of revenue, but argued that it is a very regressive tax in most societies. On the same page (p. 229), however, he implied that a non-regressive income tax is bad because it falls on marginal income.

The chief error in Henderson's discussion of taxes to finance free bridges is his neglect of the fact that bridge tolls have similar disadvantages. He implied that poll taxes are regressive while bridge tolls are not, that income taxes stimulate tax evasion while bridge tolls do not stimulate evasion of bridge tolls, that the collection of taxes is expensive while the collection of bridge tolls is costless. These unjustified implications were achieved by mentioning only the disadvantages of taxes.

We turn now to a new line of reasoning. After stating that "it is simplest to judge various pricing policies by considering the ideal as charging a price equal to marginal cost," he added that "this will cause a loss which must be met by a tax, which may take various forms —income tax, local rates, a toll on users, or the sale of season tickets" (p. 233). Since some tax (or price) must be imposed, the problem is to determine which is the best. This sound approach closely resembles that used by Hotelling. Henderson suggested four criteria to be used in solving this problem.

1. Ideal output from a given investment. A tax is good if it insures that once investment has taken place it is used by all who are willing to pay the marginal cost.

2. Ideal investment. A tax is good if it insures that a bridge which can-

not be made to pay with any rate of toll can still be built. It is also good
to the extent that it insures that bridges are not built where the cost exceeds
the consumers' surplus.

. . . .

3. Distribution of the burden. A good tax is one which places the burden
where political preferences wish it to be put. If the distribution of incomes
was ideal before the bridge was built, this involves putting it on the users of
the bridge.
    4. Autonomous financing. (p. 233)

This is notable as the first attempt after Hotelling's to formulate
the radically new principles of taxation implicit in the theory of marginal-cost control. When properly stated, the first two principles should
form the basis of all tax theory, and they directly contradict orthodox
tax theory.

However, they are not properly stated. The ultimate ideal is a price
which equals a marginal money cost which measures marginal real
cost. Hence, the first principle should be restated to say that a tax is
good if it insures that, once investment has taken place, it is used by
all who are willing to pay a marginal money cost (including taxes)
which measures marginal real costs. His version justifies all excise
taxes if they are included in his definition of marginal cost. If they
are not included, excise taxes that measure real marginal costs not
measured by other marginal money costs (such as the costs of air and
water pollution) are ineffective because they do not raise price and
restrict output. The second principle is also imperfect. It is the total
monetary loss, not "the cost," which should not exceed the consumers'
surplus.

By autonomous financing, Henderson meant a system under which
the firm covers its costs. He explained that firms with deficits require
state subsidies and, hence, state control. "This means nationalization,
but nationalization with political control of detailed operations" (p.
234). State subsidies imply state control, but they do not always require nationalization, let alone "nationalization with political control of detailed operations." In the very next paragraph, he noted that
state regulation of utilities has already largely eliminated "the automatic incentive to efficiency which is supplied by the profit motive."
Thus, state subsidies to utilities would not seriously reduce existing
incentives to efficiency.

Even under Socialism, there would be no need for "political control of detailed operations" of utilities if marginal-cost price control were adopted. The central authorities would have to prescribe a uniform system of accounting and check accounting statements periodically; but both of these measures are desirable for many other reasons and have already been widely adopted, and neither requires "political control of detailed operations."

With his four criteria in mind, Henderson proceeded to describe and evaluate five methods of financing fixed costs. The first method is:

(a) Subsidy from national funds; this is equivalent to an increase of national taxation, of which we need only consider an increase of income tax or of indirect taxes on consumption.

Here we have another indication of bias. Other and more suitable taxes, notably poll taxes, are available and had been recommended by proponents of marginal-cost control. Henderson was aware of the prejudicial character of the above assumption, and tried to excuse it in a footnote by claiming that the taxes he mentioned are widely used and "can be taken as those which will be raised to meet additional outgoings" (p. 235n). But it is illogical to condemn a proposed reform on the ground that politicians will not adopt it.

At this point Henderson repeated his doubtful claim that income taxes fall on marginal income and therefore lead to maldistribution of resources, without adding that they may also make taxation less regressive, and asserted that there is no reason why this maldistribution should not be as important as the gain from marginal-cost price control. In reply, one can claim with equal logic that there is no reason why the gain from less regression in taxation may not fully compensate for any bad effects of additional income taxes upon the distribution of resources, leaving the full benefits from marginal-cost control as a net gain. Any statement about unknown quantities is irrefutable.

Henderson criticized the use of indirect taxes as a means of covering fixed costs on the ground that "it means that marginal-cost pricing is obtained in one industry at the cost of a departure from marginal-cost pricing in some other direction" (p. 236). But later (p. 242), he said that a uniform degree of departure from marginal-cost pricing in all industries is preferable to a nonuniform degree.

On the basis of these arguments he concluded, "To argue, therefore, that the use of general (national) taxation must be the right answer in all cases of public utilities is wrong" (p. 237). The rejected conclusion is a sort of straw man; it is stated in such terms that it is not very likely to be true, especially under Capitalism, but Henderson's denial of it is not justified by his arguments.

After denying that general taxation is the right method in all cases, he added that it is equally wrong to maintain that general taxation should never be used to support utilities, noting with approval the use of such taxes to finance roads, bridges, and "the general services of the state." He even thought that state subsidies for railways "may well be justified."

The rest of his list of methods of financing fixed costs follows:

(b) The two-part tariff; this is a tax on real property as a condition of supply by the public utility.

(c) Subsidy from local funds; in the United Kingdom this is equivalent to a tax on real property.

(d) Average cost pricing; this is equivalent to marginal cost pricing plus a tax on the consumption of the service of the public utility (levied directly by the public utility).

(e) Discriminating pricing; this is equivalent to marginal cost pricing plus a tax on consumption at different rates for different classes of consumers. (p. 235)

Henderson thought that the use of "two-part tariffs" has four advantages. (1) It limits investment by allocating capital costs to consumers. (2) It preserves autonomous financing. (3) It allocates overhead costs to beneficiaries. (4) It enables consumers willing to pay the fixed charges to consume the ideal quantity of service. The chief defect is that it excludes consumers unwilling to pay the fixed charge. The system is most suitable, and indeed the best available, for electrical utilities, but Henderson apparently considered it unsuitable for gas, water, and telephone companies (pp. 235–39).

Turning to the use of local property taxes, Henderson asserted that "except for the fact that it involves a loss of financial autonomy, it is exactly equivalent to the use of a two-part tariff in the case of any service which all ratepayers will consume" (p. 239). Water supply is such a case. He also hinted that local taxes should be used to finance refuse collection, local roads, and local busses.

In discussing average-cost pricing, Henderson claimed for it the same advantages he had claimed for two-part pricing and the same single disadvantage. He emphasized that it restricts investment more than previously discussed methods of financing deficits, but treated this as an advantage in spite of the fact that he conceded that average-cost pricing "reduces the amount of investment undertaken below the ideal." *He failed to explain that it reduces output from existing plant much farther below the ideal level than does a two-part tariff.* He concluded that when the four advantages of two-part tariffs noted above are particularly great and "where no suitable basis is available for a two-part tariff," average-cost pricing may be desirable (p. 240). This seems a perfect *non sequitur*. Here as elsewhere, moreover, he confused the problem of optimum investment with the problem of optimum price.

Price discrimination, the fifth and final method of covering fixed costs, is preferable to average-cost pricing, according to Henderson, because "differential rates can always be found which will increase output and investment above the level reached by single-pricing." (p. 240). He claimed that discriminatory railway rates "were not unsatisfactory" before the rise of road transport because financing fixed costs through general taxation would have required nationalization of the railways, which he deemed incompatible with the "climate of opinion of the nineteenth century."

Since the English government had finally nationalized railways, whose average costs were above highway transport costs, Henderson thought that "some modification involving finance of the railway losses either through general taxation or taxation on all forms of transport is necessary" (p. 241). Presumably, however, he desired to retain the highly complex and discriminatory rate structure condemned by Hotelling.

One of Henderson's principal purposes in this discussion of methods of financing deficits was to show that there is no one right method. Thus he recommended two-part tariffs for electrical utilities, local taxes for water and urban bus service, average-cost pricing for other but unspecified utilities, price discrimination for railways, and national taxes for roads, bridges, and the "general services of the state." The role of marginal-cost price control would be a relatively small one under his plan.

At this point, Henderson turned from the problem of the ideal method of financing fixed costs to discuss four "complications" which he thought would arise in any effort to bring prices closer to marginal costs. He argued first that it is an error to reduce price to marginal cost in one industry if prices remain above marginal costs in some other industries, and suggested that in such cases prices should be re-duced only part of the way towards marginal cost. He thought that, "the ideal distribution of resources . . . will be obtained if the ratio of prices to marginal costs is the same in all industries" (p. 242). This is an error we have already explained (see p. 89 above). He did note that "if prices are above marginal cost the supply of factors . . . will not be ideal," but he failed to add that equal ratios of price to mar-ginal costs pyramid unequally and affect retail prices very unequally.

The second complication "concerns the control of investment policy," but it is not clear what problem Henderson meant. He used the unsound distinction between short- and long-period marginal costs without explaining it (p. 243), and tried to apply marginal analysis to the problem of lumpy investment. All of his numerous references to investment in fixed capital are confusing because he failed to see that the problem of optimum price is distinct from the problem of optimum investment in fixed capital.

The third and "major" complication is also stated vaguely, but ap-parently means that marginal costs change as time passes, that they differ from place to place, and that they depend upon the size of each sale. After barely mentioning these three quite unrelated difficulties, Henderson defined "multi-part pricing" as the practice of charging a special price to cover each additional special marginal cost and noted that this is quite different from two-part pricing, an important point ignored by earlier writers. He did not, however, explain the relation-ship of multi-part pricing to the three unrelated difficulties previously hinted at in the same paragraph, and the disconnected statement of all four ideas in a single paragraph as one "major complication" is confusing.

The fourth and final complication is "due to the fact that marginal costs may fluctuate widely over short periods" (p. 244). He solved this problem by asserting that:

The only solution is to average the marginal cost over the range for which uniform prices are decided. This solution is a compromise between exact equality of marginal cost and price and the gains of convenience both to consumers and the enterprises from some degree of stability. (p. 245)

The problem of how often prices should be changed is an important problem under any system of pricing. The theory of marginal-cost price-output control suggests the disadvantages of price stability, but it does not create the problem. And the "only solution" given by

Henderson is no solution at all since it fails to tell us how often prices should be changed.

In his final section the author tried to analyze an imperfect market, one in which "price exceeds marginal cost for each firm" (p. 245). If all firms were required to equate price and marginal cost, he claimed, they would all try to increase output. "But all firms cannot do so simultaneously," he asserted, without offering any reason. Presumably he had tacitly assumed full employment, an assumption which begs the point at issue. "If all firms are affected equally," he continued, "they will all be producing the same output as before, and thus marginal costs will have risen to equal price" (p. 245). Here the explicit assumption, "if all firms are affected equally" is completely unrealistic and again begs the question at issue. Moreover, the conclusion that marginal costs would rise to equal price ignores the serious inflation of consumer incomes which would accompany such a bidding up of factor prices, and its effect upon prices.

He went on to claim that "the profits of each firm will be reduced" and some will go out of business. The elimination of some firms by marginal-cost pricing would, he argued, reduce total consumers' surplus because it would eliminate the consumers' surplus from the goods produced by the eliminated firms. But individual marginal adjustments do not affect consumers' surplus appreciably. Surpluses must be measured in total analysis, but not in marginal analysis.

Our general conclusion must be that, although his article contains some new insights, especially concerning the financing of fixed costs, it is biased against marginal-cost price control, and arrives at conclusions which are largely unsound.

SUMMARY

The chief facts revealed in this chapter may be summarized as follows. The theory of marginal-cost price control has never been explicitly stated and distinguished from the theory of marginal-cost output control. It was first applied to railroad and public utility rates by two American economists, Harold Hotelling and R. M. Montgomery, who apparently developed their theories independently of each other and of the earlier English proponents of marginal-cost output control. The level of analysis in these pioneer articles was of an extremely high order, in sharp contrast to most of the subsequent discussions of the same subject. Hotelling and Montgomery had a notable early influence upon American public utility economists. Two American textbooks on public utility economics containing a sympathetic statement of their proposals were published within five years of the publications of the original proposals, and another followed in 1947. On the other hand, no such textbook statements have appeared in England, and, more important, no textbook on railroad or transportation economics has stated the theory in either England or America. The new proposals have been vigorously attacked by several writers on public utility economics in both countries. Most of these critics seem unfamiliar with the scant but significant earlier literature, especially the contributions of Meade, Lerner, and Montgomery. For instance, they have repeatedly ignored Montgomery's suggestion that service charges may be used to approximate the desirable results of marginal-cost price control without incurring a deficit.

The general conclusion must be that the theory of marginal-cost price control has to date (1951) been accepted by only a handful of public utility economists and by scarcely any transportation economists. The vast majority of contemporary writers on railroad and utility rates have not only failed to endorse marginal-cost theory, but have even failed to mention it. This generalization applies both to specialists in transportation and public utility economics and to the authors of treatises or textbooks including one or two chapters on these fields. Either these writers are simply not familiar with the journal literature on the new theory or they dislike its implications and have decided that silence is the most effective weapon to use against it.

VI

THE DEVELOPMENT OF
MARGINAL-COST PRICE-OUTPUT THEORY
AS A GENERAL PRICE-OUTPUT THEORY
1942 TO 1950

INTRODUCTION

THE FIRST ECONOMISTS to state and discuss the theory of marginal-cost price-output control were Socialists who wrote from 1933 to 1939. The first Capitalist economists to discuss the theory were interested solely or chiefly in the application of the new theory to railroad and public utility rate theory. In this chapter, we turn to a third group of writers on this theory, namely, those who debated its merits as a general prescriptive price-output theory during the years 1942 to 1950. This group includes both Socialists and Capitalists.

No hard and fast classification of economists into these three groups is possible. For instance, Hotelling considered the new theory a general prescriptive theory applicable to all prices, but most of his discussion dealt with railroad and utility rates. Hence, we reviewed him in the previous chapter. However, some of the writers discussed below limited themselves to the pricing problems of state enterprises, a class which now consists largely of public utilities.

SCHUMPETER

In a chapter on "The Socialist Blueprint" in his admirable book, *Capitalism, Socialism, and Democracy* (1942), Joseph A. Schumpeter devoted two pages to the principle of marginal-cost output control in a Socialist economy. We quote first his statement of the general theory.

Third, the managements [of Socialist trusts] are required to call for and to use such quantities as (and not less than), producing in the most economical manner, they can use without having to "sell" any part of their products for less "dollars" than they have to transfer to the central board for the corresponding amounts of means of production. . . . this condition means that production in all lines should be such as to make "prices" equal (not merely proportional) to marginal costs. (pp. 175–76)

This is a theory of marginal-cost output control, not a theory of marginal-cost price control. Prices, he added, should be directly fixed so as to "clear the market" (p. 177).

Unfortunately, Schumpeter did not really accept marginal-cost output control in any but a nominal sense. In a long footnote to the above statement, he made clear that when he said marginal costs he really meant so-called average costs. He attempted to draw a sharp distinction between short-run marginal costs, which usually do not include depreciation, interest, taxes, etc., and long-run marginal costs, which, he believed, do include these costs. And he argued that the theory of marginal-cost control does not mean that prices should equal short-run marginal costs, but rather that it implies "equating prices to total cost per unit of product as long as things develop according to plans." Hence, he not only claimed that "it is never part of that [marginal-cost control] logic to operate an industry at a deficit" but even went so far as to imply that the fixed costs of a bridge should be met by tolls rather than by taxes. This interpretation of marginal-cost control amounts to a repudiation of the theory.

PUTNAM

If marginal-cost output control is desirable and is easier to adopt and apply under Socialism than under Capitalism, this is a new argu-

ment in favor of Socialism. The first Socialist to use this argument was
John Putnam. In his *Modern Case for Socialism* (*1943*), he wrote: [1]

It has long been recognized by bourgeois economists that in industries
of increasing costs, for instance agriculture, market prices ought to be
equal to the marginal costs of production. They are slowly becoming aware
of the fact that the same principle is valid in industries of decreasing costs.
This latter application of the principle is practical only under Socialism,
however.

When the products of agriculture are sold at the marginal cost of
production, intra-marginal producers receive a large surplus called rent.
However, if automobiles were sold at the marginal cost of production
(the additional costs of producing one more car), all automobile manufacturers would incur a constant heavy loss which we may name negative
rent. This is impossible under Capitalism. Hence, automobile manufacturers charge a price high enough to cover their average costs. As a
result, the output of automobiles is far below the optimum level, for the
production of additional cars would bring in a revenue more than
sufficient to cover the additional costs of producing them. Under Socialism the output of automobiles, and all other products of industries of
decreasing costs, will be increased to the optimum level where market price
equals marginal cost. The negative rent created in this way will be offset
by ordinary or positive rent derived from other industries plus, if necessary,
income taxes. This will bring about a different and more desirable distribution of invested capital among individual industries, and a considerable
increase in the size of the national income. (p. 152)

This was meant to be a popular statement of the new theory and
its relationship to Socialism for nonprofessional readers. Written in
1936, it contains nearly all the errors found in the pioneer statements
of marginal-cost price-output theory by Meade and Lerner. There is
no distinction between the theory of ideal price or output and the
theory of investment in fixed capital. Hence, the misuse of concepts
like increasing and decreasing costs, positive and negative rent, etc.
The relationship of marginal-cost price control to marginal-cost output control is not explained. The methods of approximating the desirable results of marginal-cost price-output control under Capitalism
(service charges, special charges for optional services, etc.) are ignored,
and the need for adopting Socialism to achieve these results is thus
exaggerated.

[1] John Putnam is a pseudonym for B. P. Beckwith. This book was actually written
in 1936.

LERNER

In 1944, A. P. Lerner restated the theory of marginal-cost output control and made it the foundation of most of his analysis in *The Economics of Control*. This was an epoch-making general treatise because it was the first to be based upon marginal-cost price-output theory. The index includes almost a hundred references to "the *Rule*," i.e., to this theory.

While writing this book, Lerner retreated from Fabian Socialism to radical interventionism. He started out to state the economic theory of a Socialist economy and ended up with a general theory of economic control under Capitalism. However, his new Rule is so stated that it could be applied only under Socialism; in other words, it is stated as a rule of output control.

Lerner led up to his first statement of the Rule by explaining why factors should be allocated to producers so as to make their marginal value productivity the same in all uses. He then asserted that it would not be possible either for central or local managers to allocate factors in this way because they would be lost "in the hopeless intricacy of the problem" (p. 62). Under Socialism, however, this problem of the ideal allocation of the factors "can be solved with the help of the price mechanism and a simple Rule that must be followed by the managers of every production unit." There are two prerequisites: there must be a free market in the sale of both consumption goods and factors in production (p. 63). By free market he meant that prices must balance supply and demand, not that there must be many buyers and sellers. Under these conditions

the optimum division of each factor . . . can . . . be fixed by issuing a simple *Rule* which every manager must obey. The *Rule* is:
If the value of the marginal (physical) product of any factor is greater than the price of the factor, increase output. If it is less, decrease output. If it is equal to the price of the factor, continue producing at the same rate. (p. 64)

This first statement of the Rule professes to apply to "each factor" and to "the marginal (physical) product of any factor." However, it occurs in a chapter explicitly devoted "only" to the analysis of "simple production," which is the use of one factor to produce one good (p. 57).

Lerner claimed that his Rule could be applied to "three different kinds of transformation. . . . First, the transformation of factors . . . into products. . . . Second, the transformation of one product into another. . . . Third, the transformation of one factor into another or the technical substitution between factors" (p. 125).

He recognized that this threefold application of the Rule might seem complicated, and explained that:

It is sufficient if the Rule is applied only in the literal sense.

The managers who keep the Rule in the literal sense will increase or decrease the amount of each factor applied to the production of each product . . . until the value of each marginal product is equal to the price of the factor. (p. 126)

In his 1936 article Lerner had proposed two separate rules of economic control under Socialism: (1) that price should be proportional to marginal cost, and (2) that production should be carried on economically, which means that total and average cost should be minimized. In *The Economics of Control* he substituted for these two rules a single Rule which covers both factor combination and output control. He thought this an important step forward. To us it seems a step backward.

There are two serious faults in the idea that a single rule should be used to determine both factor or agent combination and the volume of output. In the first place, a rule requiring direct control of factor combination and output cannot be applied to any firms producing services, since this would mean direct regulation of people receiving services, and cannot be applied to privately owned firms producing other goods, since this would end private control (see pp. 197–98 below). As Lerner wrote his book primarily to guide state control of private industry, rather than the management of state trusts under Socialism, his Rule was inappropriate to his purpose. He ought to have stated and stressed the theory of marginal-cost *price* control, not the theory of marginal-cost *output* control.

In the second place, the new single Rule ignores the practical advantages of treating factor combination and output control as two separate problems. Plant managers now treat these as separate problems because this helps clear thinking and quick action on each problem. When demand suddenly rises or falls, it is necessary to change output quickly without stopping to discover a new and better method of combining the factors. And if better methods of combining the factors can be discovered, these improved methods should be introduced regardless of whether a change in total output is needed. Of course, improved methods should result in lower prices and higher output, but the introduction of such methods is not usually the best method of securing a desired increase in output.

To support his case for a single rule, Lerner criticized his old second rule, that goods should be produced in the cheapest possible manner. Total cost is often affected by changes in intramarginal factor costs, due to increased use, as well as by the additional cost of additional factors. Hence, an effort to minimize total costs will not necessarily minimize real costs. In expanding output, a producer may prefer to use more of factor A instead of factor B because increased use of factor A will not raise its unit cost. Therefore, rule two must be qualified by explaining that the manager should assume that his actions will not affect factor costs. This involves certain complications which are avoided by the use of his new single Rule. However, as we have noted, there are much more serious defects in his Rule. Hence, we prefer his earlier use of two separate rules.

Lerner also objected to the use of the term *marginal cost* because he identified it with the increase in total cost, which may be affected by changes in factor prices due to increased use of them as well as by the use at the margin of additional factors (pp. 99–100). We prefer to avoid this difficulty by defining marginal cost as the cost of the additional factors required to produce the marginal unit of output, as Lerner himself once defined it (p. 70 above).

Lerner noted that his Rule can be expressed in terms of marginal cost—defined as the value of the marginal factors (vmf)—and treated the rule that output should be increased or decreased until price equals vmf as an alternative but inferior statement of the Rule (pp. 96–100). It is inferior because the original formulation "shows up more clearly the fundamental nature of a scarce factor of production" (p. 100). Moreover, this version of the rule is often stated in terms of marginal cost without explaining that marginal cost must be defined as vmf to make the rule valid. As we have noted, we prefer this version and consider this criticism of it unconvincing.

One defect in Lerner's discussion of the Rule is that he assumed that price equals the marginal social benefit (msb) and that the money cost of the marginal factors equals the real marginal social cost (msc). He treated the equation, $msb = msc$, as equivalent to the equation,

$p = mc$ (pp. 75–76, 96–97). The rule that output should be controlled so as to make p equal mc is under certain conditions a corollary, but never an alternative version, of the rule that msb should equal msc. There are many reforms which should be adopted, such as the levying of taxes on those who pollute the air, to make mc a better measure of msc, and there are many other reforms, such as better consumer education and laws increasing the honesty of advertising, which would make price a better measure of msb. The rule of marginal-cost output control is only one of the corollaries of the more basic principle that msb should equal msc. In order to solve the problem of ideal output, it is wise to ignore the other problems involved in making msb equal msc. Only when isolated in this way, can this problem be clearly discussed or easily solved. Lerner did not explicitly isolate the problem of ideal output from these other problems. However, he did isolate it practically, for he did not discuss any of the other problems of making msb equal msc—one of the chief defects of his book—but he did not explain why he failed to discuss the other problems.

In his 1936 article Lerner, unlike Meade, had claimed that prices need only be *proportional,* not *equal,* to marginal cost. In *The Economics of Control* he reversed himself on the grounds that (1) it is impossible for prices to be proportional to marginal cost unless they equal it, and (2) prices should equal marginal cost in order to achieve an ideal balance between work and leisure (pp. 100–5). He did not make clear why he thought proportionality is impossible without equality but he explained why it is not ideal. If prices are proportional to but above or below marginal cost, workers will be under- or overpaid, and they will work more or less than they should. This is a good point. However, we can think of no reason why money prices cannot be proportional but unequal to marginal money cost.

According to Lerner the basic argument for the use of his Rule is that, assuming freedom of choice for consumers and a free market in the sale of factors, the value of the marginal factors will measure marginal social opportunity costs and the value of the marginal unit of output will measure the marginal social gain from production. Hence, output should be increased until the value of the marginal product equals the value of the factors used to produce it (pp. 66–67). Apparently he considered it obvious that the transfer of a marginal unit of any factor from a less to a more productive use promotes welfare. But this has been repeatedly questioned, notably by "new welfare" economists. The transfer of factors from one use to another has different effects upon different persons. Some workers get higher wages and some lower as a result of each transfer. Some consumers enjoy lower prices and some higher. It is impossible to conclude that there is a net increase in welfare from any transfer of factors from one use to another unless gains and losses to different men can be measured and compared (see pp. 161–62, 176–77 below).

Lerner seems to have been strongly influenced by the new welfare school of economists, who reject interpersonal comparisons of utility. However, there is no mention of interpersonal comparability of utility in the eleven-page analytical table of contents or in the thirty-five page index of *The Economics of Control,* nor is there any reference to compensation payments made possible by the existence of consumers' surplus. These are curious omissions to be noted in a book on welfare economics.

Lerner tried to distinguish between short and long-run marginal cost. He raised and offered a solution for the problem of whether price should equal short or long-run marginal cost.

The *mc* of producing another unit of any product depends on the *period* allowed. There may be a different *mc* for every different period. If very little time is allowed, the increased output can be obtained only by increasing the few factors that can be adjusted at very little notice. If more time is allowed, a different kind of adjustment may be more appropriate. . . . The Rule is ambiguous. Which of the different *mc's* should be equated to the price? (p. 213)

· · · ·

Fortunately, this is not a real ambiguity. . . . The appropriate *vmf's* for producing an additional unit of output *at a certain point of time* are definitely known. Many different factors can be applied at the margin . . . at different points of time. . . . The Rule says that all those whose value *vmf* is less than the price of the product *p* should be applied. . . . The matter becomes clearer still if we use the first formulation of the Rule . . . which tells us to apply factors where *vmp* is greater than *pf*. . . . If the *vmp* of a factor accruing at any future time is expected to be greater than its price, the factor should be applied. That is all there is to it. (pp. 214–15)

This analysis is obscure and misleading because Lerner failed to distinguish between the problem of optimum output with no change in fixed capital and the problem of when to invest in additional fixed capital.

On the basis of this analysis Lerner concluded, "The appropriate *mc* to equate to the price . . . at a particular date . . . is that which would be incurred in . . . producing an increment of output at that date" (p. 215). This sounds plausible but is ambiguous. It does not answer the main question, which is whether marginal cost at any given time is a long-run marginal cost or a short-run marginal cost, whether it includes the costs of investment in fixed capital or not. Our guess is, however, that if he had faced this problem squarely, he would have said that marginal cost includes the costs of investment in fixed capital when such costs are incurred to expand output, and this is a serious error.

There are numerous other references to marginal-cost output control in this book, but we cannot devote more space to it. *The Economics of Control* is a notable book precisely because it is based upon the new output theory and makes use of it very frequently. Its chief faults are: (1) the neglect of the theory of marginal-cost *price* control, (2) the failure to use interpersonal comparisons of utility to prove the advantages of marginal-cost control, and (3) the failure to distinguish between the problem of optimum price and output with existing fixed capital and the problem of investment in fixed capital.

MEADE, FLEMING, WILSON

In a symposium on "Price and Output Policy of State Enterprise," in the *Economic Journal* for December, 1944, J. E. Meade restated and elaborated his pioneer (1936) formulation of the theory of marginal-cost control. He led up to it by stating a theory of ideal factor allocation:

In order to achieve that use of . . . resources which is . . . the most efficient . . . they should be distributed among the various uses in such a way that the value of the marginal product of a given factor is the same in every occupation. In so far as the reward paid to any factor is the same in every occupation, this rule means that the value of the marginal product of a factor should, in every occupation, bear a constant ratio to the price of that factor. (p. 321)

This restates the erroneous doctrine of Lerner and Hotelling that prices only need to bear a "constant ratio" to marginal costs. Meade proceeded to correct this error as follows:

If labour is paid everywhere a reward which is not merely in a constant ratio to, but actually equal to, the value of its marginal product, two additional advantages may be achieved: (i) A larger proportion of the total national income will accrue to labour than if labour is paid everywhere a wage lower . . . than the value of its marginal product. . . . (ii) Labour has the choice between earning more income or enjoying more leisure. The more nearly the reward for an additional unit of work approaches the value of the marginal product of labour, the greater . . . will be the welfare achieved by means of a proper balance between work and leisure.

Meade next applied his general theory to the management of a socialized plant. He explained that "output should be increased so long as the price of the product exceeds the marginal (not the average) cost of production" (p. 322). Here we have again the theory of marginal-cost output control stated as if it applies to services as well as commodities.

Although Meade never distinguished clearly between the problem of ideal output in the short run and the problem of ideal investment in fixed capital, and presumably continued to include capital costs in marginal cost and to blame deficits on decreasing costs, he did state an independent theory of ideal investment in fixed capital.

A greater amount of fixed capital should be invested so long as the annual interest on the capital plus the annual cost of repair, depreciation, etc., is less than the price of any additional output expected from the investment plus the price of any existing prime factors which it is expected to save, minus the price of any additional prime factor which it is expected to take on as a result of the investment. (pp. 322–23)

This is a step towards total analysis, but it does not go far enough. A year's cost or gain is much too small to use in determining the wisdom of a new investment in fixed capital. One must compare the additional costs with the additional gains over the *entire life of the fixed capital,* which may be over a hundred years. Moreover, one must allow for the effect of new investment on consumers' surplus. Meade called attention to this latter defect when the rule is applied to a "large new investment," noting that "in the exceptional cases, however, one cannot afford to neglect the consumers' surplus involved," (p. 325) both in the industry where output is increased and in alternative investment fields. This errs in the opposite way, for the effect on consumers' surplus in other industries should be ignored (see pp. 210–11 below).

Because of the size of the expected deficits, Meade favored both socialization of decreasing-cost industries and a capital levy and noted two "incidental advantages" which would result:

First it would open up a large new range for capital investment . . . in an economy otherwise threatened with large-scale unemployment. . . .

Secondly, these principles of pricing . . . involve a shift of income from profits to wages. . . . Such a shift will be brought about by bringing down to the marginal cost . . . prices without reducing money wages. (pp. 327–28)

Only the second of these should be credited to marginal-cost control, and it is badly stated. The fall in the price level which would result from marginal-cost output control would affect all shares in income equally.

J. M. Fleming, the other participant in this symposium, began with a statement of general agreement with Meade (p. 329).

However, he differed from Meade in "attaching greater importance to the administrative and less to the financial difficulties involved in applying these principles," and he devoted most of his comment to this difference.

Before discussing these administrative difficulties, Fleming criticized Meade because "he neglects the producers' surpluses (which may often be more important than the consumers' surpluses)." This suggests a confusion of the theory of optimum output with the theory of optimum investment. Marginal analysis, which solves the problem of ideal price and output, ignores all surpluses because they are not marginal factors.

To support his argument that the difficulties would be more administrative than financial, Fleming questioned Meade's stress on the size of the deficits. Fleming explained that when demand exceeds capacity in a decreasing-cost industry, the industry operates temporarily under conditions of increasing costs, and large profits may be earned before new capacity is or should be added (pp. 330–31). Meade conceded the justice of this criticism and applied it to Lerner in his review of Lerner's *The Economics of Control* three months later.[2] However, Fleming pressed this argument to an unsound extreme, asserting, "In any event, there is, as we have seen, no particular reason to expect the average cost curve in socialised undertakings to be falling rather than rising" (p. 332). Since only those industries most subject to decreasing

[2] *Economic Journal,* LV (April, 1945), 58.

costs were to be socialized, this claim is unreasonable, and Meade rejected it (pp. 337–38).

Fleming next argued that marginal-cost control "will make it more difficult to weed out the inefficient managers" (p. 336), because it would abolish the profit-loss criterion. He did not deny the possibility, suggested by Meade, of using comparative unit cost data as a basis for judgment, but claimed that this method is also useful as a supplement to the profit-loss criterion and is not an alternative only. However, marginal profits and losses could also be used to judge state managers practicing marginal-cost control. The manager whose total marginal profits and losses (added as if of the same sign) were the smallest would, other factors being equal, be the best manager. And such profits and losses would reflect real errors in judgment of social welfare, whereas average profits and losses do not.

Fleming concluded: (1) that "trust-busting" and other antimonopoly measures are preferable to socialization and marginal-cost pricing "at the cost of *some* reduction in the unit of management below the optimum size," and (2) that, when monopoly makes socialization necessary, marginal-cost control should be used only if expansion of output is "more important than the preservation of the maximum incentive to maintain technical efficiency and progress" (p. 337). He did not attempt to name the industries suitable for marginal-cost control under these rules.

Perhaps the greatest mistake Fleming made, from his point of view, was to ignore the use of utility service charges as a means of covering fixed costs. This would have given him a much better basis for questioning socialization than any he actually used. Moreover, there seems to be a contradiction between his initial acceptance of Meade's theory of marginal-cost output control and his final rejection of most applications of it.

R. H. Coase contributed a two-page comment on the Meade-Fleming symposium to the next (April, 1945) issue of the *Economic Journal.* "It is my opinion," he wrote, "that they have stated the proposition [of marginal-cost control] in such a way as to confuse rather than clarify an important issue in public utility pricing." He endorsed the old but often disproven theory that "a consumer should pay the [full average] cost of any product which he buys," and also called attention to the serious failure of Meade and Fleming to discuss service charges.

A seven-page comment on this symposium by T. Wilson appeared in the *Economic Journal* for December, 1945. In this highly critical article, the author charged that the theory of marginal-cost control "is familiar enough, but, in spite of the weight of authority behind it, it is . . . inadequately supported in logic and likely to be highly dangerous in practice—if, indeed, one can conceive of an attempt being made to apply it" (p. 455).

As his first objection to the theory, he noted that it implies a need for socialization of decreasing-cost industries since "it is rightly regarded as inconceivable that the State should subsidise a private monopoly." But since state subsidies have actually been granted to numerous private firms for many years, this statement is false, and the degree of exaggeration in it is typical of Wilson's entire comment. This objection also overlooks the important point, stressed by Coase, that service charges would make it possible to achieve most of the benefits of marginal-cost utility rates without socialization of utilities.

Wilson repeated the traditional Capitalist arguments against socialization, and claimed that marginal-cost control would encourage excessive overhead costs because such costs would not affect prices. He argued that "the sanction of dismissal for inefficiency is a poor one as compared with a profit motive" (p. 457). This claim was repeated by Durbin and refuted by Fleming a few years later (see pp. 151–52, 158 below).

Like Fleming, Wilson argued that Capitalism is superior to Socialism in spite of the fact that rational economic pricing is possible only under Socialism. *This just reverses the argument of Mises, Hayek, and others that Socialism is impossible because it is incompatible with rational economic calculation.*

COASE AND NORDIN

The first detailed attack by a Capitalist economist upon the new theory of marginal-cost price-output control as a general price theory was published by R. H. Coase in the August, 1946, issue of *Economica* under the title, "The Marginal Cost Controversy." The application of the new theory to a Socialist economy had been briefly criticized by Hayek, Dobb, and Durbin, and its application to public utilities had been criticized in more detail by Clemens, Pegrum, and Lewis, but Coase was the first to attack the theory directly and in detail as a general theory of price. The lateness of this first general attack is probably due to the facts that, (1) the theory of marginal-cost price-output control was first stated by Socialists and applied by them only to a Socialist economy, and (2) the theory was then extended only to railroads and public utilities under Capitalism. In other words, about ten years passed after the original statement of the new theory before its critics began to realize that the new theory may be presented as the only valid prescriptive theory of price under both Capitalism and Socialism. Coase therefore introduced his attack on this theory by noting correctly that "despite the importance of its practical implications, its paradoxical character, and the fact that there are many economists who consider it fallacious, it has so far received little written criticism."

Coase stated the theory of marginal-cost control as a theory of *price* control. "The amount paid for each unit of the product (the price) should be made equal to marginal cost" (p. 169). To refute this theory, he assumed a case in which the producer paid delivery charges and in which the total delivery charges are the same regardless of the number of units delivered, pointed out the obvious need for different prices on the first and subsequent units because of the difference in marginal costs, and asserted that the theory of marginal-cost control denies this need.

The Hotelling-Lerner solution, if adopted in the case of my example, would mean that the cost of the goods at the central market would be paid for by consumers but that the cost of carriage would be borne out of taxation. (p. 174)

Coase argued that consumers should pay the delivery costs separately and called this "multi-part pricing." He also used this phrase to describe price discrimination, the use of service charges, and cases in which a consumer pays more than one price for a single unit of a good, for instance, when consumers of utility services pay connection fees or monthly service charges. He did not define multi-part pricing, and the specific cases to which he applied it have little in common.

The second argument against marginal-cost control stressed by Coase is that we need a "subsequent market test of whether consumers are willing to pay the total cost of the product." He noted Hotelling's denial of this need and asserted:

Nowhere in Prof. Hotelling's article does one find recognition of the fact that it will be more difficult to discover whether to build new railroads or new industries if one does not know whether the creation of past rail-roads or industries was wise social policy. (pp. 175–76)

This begs the whole question by assuming that profits and losses are a good test of the wisdom of past investments. Moreover, it assumes that the theory of marginal-cost control can be applied to the problem of controlling investment in fixed capital.

Coase's third major argument against marginal-cost control is that it will cause a redistribution of income "in favor of consumers of goods produced under conditions of decreasing average costs." He noted Hotelling's claim that the benefits of marginal-cost control would be so widespread that few if any would suffer a loss and replied:

But this argument stands or falls by the assumption that there will be no significant redistribution as between consumers of different kinds of prod-ucts. There is no reason to assume that this will be so. (p. 177)

On this ground, Coase proceeded to assume conditions which would justify the opposite conclusion. He explicitly assumed that utility in-dustries are the only ones in which costs decrease and he implicitly assumed that no interconnections exist between utilities in different cities. He then reasoned that under such conditions marginal-cost price control would benefit certain utility consumers—those whose demand is the most elastic and who are served by plants with the most unused capacity—at the expense of other taxpayers.

Coase's fourth objection to marginal-cost control is that it requires taxes to cover deficits and that these taxes will have harmful effects. He ignored Hotelling's demonstration and italicized conclusion that *"if a person must pay a certain sum of money in taxes, his satisfaction will be greater if the levy is made directly on him as a fixed amount,"* and devoted his criticism largely to income taxes, also mentioned by Hotelling as a possibility. He claimed that "an income tax will have the same unfortunate effect on consumers' choice as a tax on goods and will produce results similar in character to those which follow from charging "prices above marginal costs" (pp. 178–79). We disagree. An excise tax, or a price above marginal costs, deflects demand from one good to another, and also reduces total demand (which further changes the consumption pattern) while an income tax merely reduces total demand. This is orthodox tax theory, yet Coase charged that "Prof. Hotelling does not give any reasons why he thinks income taxes will tend to be less harmful than excise taxes" (p. 179).

In the May, 1947, issue of *Economica,* there appeared a sixteen-page reply to Coase's article by J. A. Nordin. He interpreted "multi-part" pricing to mean price discrimination (p. 134) and devoted his reply to proving that marginal-cost price control is superior to price discrimination. He began by pointing out that Coase's illustrative case was badly chosen.

The carrier example is not closely analogous to the situation in an electric light plant. It amounts to artificially putting together two successive stages of production. There should indeed be separate prices for the good at the central market, and for the services of the carrier. But this fact will not clarify the problems of a light plant, where fixed and variable agents are combined in one production process. (p. 135)

To Coase's argument that marginal-cost control redistributes income for the worse, both by changing prices and by requiring higher taxes, Nordin answered that this assumes without ground that the previous distribution of income was ideal (p. 143).

Much of Nordin's comment on Coase takes the form of mathematical demonstrations which this critic is not competent to criticize. We must rely on his verbal translation of them. This claims that the first three pages of mathematical reasoning demonstrates that "making prices proportionate to marginal costs will bring about the optimum allocation of resources" (p. 138). It is not necessary to use mathematical reasoning to refute this theory. We have already done this with verbal reasoning (pp. 89, 123).

The following summary tells briefly how Nordin approached the problem of optimum pricing and what positive conclusions he arrived at:

Summary—In connection with the allocation of resources, marginal-cost pricing has been examined in a case in which there are two agents (one of them being fixed), two finished goods and one consumer. At the beginning of the first period an allocation is made. At the beginning of the second period there is a reallocation of the variable agent.

The marginal-cost pricing policy discussed makes prices proportionate to marginal costs, and equates the value of the marginal product for both goods. The following conclusions have emerged:

1. If the authority knows the consumers' indifference map and both the fixed and variable agents can be allocated, the authority can maximise the consumers utility by using the marginal-cost pricing system.

2. If the authority knows the consumers' indifference map and only the variable agent can be allocated, the authority can make the optimum allocation by using the marginal-cost pricing policy.

3. If the authority does not know the indifference map, it can make successive approximations to the optimum allocation by using the marginal-cost pricing policy.

4. The marginal-cost pricing policy provides a method for determining whether a given product ought to be produced. (pp. 148–49)

In our opinion, these conclusions are not justified by Nordin's analysis because he failed to assume interpersonal comparability of utility. His analysis is also defective because he failed to distinguish between optimum price-output control (the allocation of variable capital) and optimum investment (the allocation of capital funds to fixed investments). Both his first and his fourth conclusion illustrate this.

In spite of these defects, Nordin's article is much superior to Coase's. But it illustrates again how easily rigorous mathematical reasoning can lead to error. And when such reasoning yields correct results, it always begs the question by using assumptions which imply the desired conclusion.

Coase's article also provoked a five-page comment, "The Marginal Cost Controversy: A Note on Mr. Coase's Model," by G. F. Thirlby in the February, 1947, issue of *Economica*. Thirlby argued that the cost of "administration, credit and the time-dimension" cannot be allocated to output and that therefore "cost" is indeterminable. This argument is valid against average-cost pricing, but not against marginal-cost pricing (see pp. 196–97 below).

In reply, Coase published, "The Marginal Cost Controversy: Some Further Comments," in the May, 1947, issue of *Economica*. He devoted most of his four-page reply to a restatement of his main points, but in so doing he generalized his argument that marginal-cost control results in "maldistribution of resources."

My position can be simply stated. If certain factors of production can be obtained free in one use (because they do not enter into marginal cost) but have to be paid for in another use (because they enter into marginal cost), consumers may choose to employ these factors in the use in which they are free even though they would in fact prefer to employ them in some other way. (p. 150)

But, if the cost of "certain factors" does not enter into marginal costs, consumers do not increase their use of these factors by increasing their consumption. Hence, this argument is invalid.

BERGSON

In 1947 there was published under the auspices of the American Economic Association a review of the developments in economic theory during the previous ten to fifteen years. This book, *A Survey of Contemporary Economics*, has chapters on "Value and Distribution," "Price and Production Policies," and "Socialist Economics." Only the last mentions marginal-cost control, a significant fact which suggests that the theory of marginal-cost price-output control has as yet achieved very little acceptance by Capitalist economists.

The chapter on "Socialist Economics," by Abram Bergson of Columbia University, is not a review of the development of Socialist economic theory in general. Rather, it is a review of the development of non-Marxian Socialist price and output theory from Pareto to 1946, with special emphasis upon the contributions of "welfare" economists. It contains a sympathetic statement and discussion of the new theory of marginal-cost price-output control.

The first three sections of this chapter are devoted to "I. The Ends" of economic policy, "II. Optimum Conditions" of economic activity, and "III. 'Marginal Costs' vs. 'Average Costs.' " It is certainly proper to discuss the purpose of economic policy before discussing the policies themselves, but Bergson's review of this subject is unsatisfying. He noted Pareto's rejection of the interpersonal comparisons of utility long used by neo-classical economists, but he did not make clear how far this rejection was accepted by other writers on Socialist price theory or by himself. He seems to have followed Pareto in thinking that "utilities are incommensurable" (p. 418), but he accepted the theory of marginal-cost control, which we have argued is inconsistent with Pareto's doctrine (pp. 86, 123, 176).

Bergson's discussion of ends suggests that he considered them to be absolute philosophical or religious goals which no scientist can determine or question (pp. 413–20). He seems to have believed that economic policies, including that of marginal-cost control, are sound only if the results which they produce are approved by priests and philosophers. In fact, however, these non-scientific thinkers disagree violently among themselves, so it is impossible to use their dogmas to determine the validity of economic policies.

When he turned to discuss optimum conditions and optimum price, however, Bergson avoided this difficulty by ignoring such dogmas and assuming that optimum conditions and optimum price are those which maximize welfare or want satisfaction. He also ignored both the "new welfare" definition of welfare-increasing policies and the case for interpersonal comparison of utilities.

Bergson presented the theory of marginal-cost control as a corollary of the optimum conditions.

It is an easy matter to restate the foregoing optimum conditions in terms of "costs." The total cost incurred in the production of the optimum output must be at a minimum and, in the optimum, price must equal marginal cost (since we say nothing about rent, costs may be understood here to comprise material costs, interest, and wages). (p. 424)

Here we have a return to Lerner's original argument that two separate rules, one prescribing minimum cost and the other prescribing prices equal to marginal cost, are needed.

On the next page Bergson restated the theory of marginal-cost control as follows:

To repeat, . . . the rule for the attainment of the optimum is that price must equal *marginal* cost. The principle is perfectly general: it holds regardless of the relation of marginal and average cost, regardless of whether price is above average cost and there are "profits" (as might be in the case of "fixed factors") or below average costs and there are losses (as might be also in the case of "fixed factors," and very likely would be so in the case of large indivisibilities). (p. 425)

Actually, the theory is not "perfectly general." It applies only to the prices of *reproducible* goods in adequate supply whose production the state does not desire to restrict by means of special excise or other taxes because it deems them harmful.

A much more serious fault is that Bergson tried to distinguish between "long-run" and "short-run" marginal costs. His explanation of the difference is vague, but he seems to have identified long-run marginal costs with the marginal costs of additional output which would require an expansion of fixed capital (p. 427). However, he claimed that "long-run marginal cost will generally be less than short-run marginal cost," which is contrary to the usual view and shows how nebulous the concept of long-run marginal cost is. He never explained whether price should equal short-run or should equal long-run marginal money cost.

Bergson devoted only one paragraph to the history of the marginal-cost rule.

For this very fundamental proposition, we are indebted chiefly to Marshall and Pigou, who long ago advanced it boldly even for cases of decreasing costs. In recent years, however, the rule has had to be defended and re-affirmed on a number of occasions in the face of recurrent confusion. In this connection, mention should be made of the contributions of Lerner and Hotelling. Both writers, Lerner with special vigor, have championed the Marshall-Pigou position against doctrinal deviations. (p. 425)

Our analysis of the tax-subsidy scheme supported by Marshall and Pigou does not support these conclusions.

NORRIS

The second criticism of the theory of marginal-cost price-output control as a general theory by a Capitalist theorist was offered by Harry Norris, an English accountant, in the February, 1947, issue of *Economica*.[3] He began with a just evaluation of Coase's comments:

I cannot feel that Mr. Coase has added a great deal to the development of the analysis in his article, though his support of the proposition that multi-part pricing is a possible solution in some cases is valuable. In choosing for an example the incidence of delivery costs, he considerably restricts the scope of his analysis. I cannot imagine that the Lerner Rule would be applied so literally that a manager would charge each customer with the central market cost only. (p. 55)

Norris began his own criticism of the Lerner Rule by arguing that it would require too frequent price changes:

The impact of indivisibilities . . . may therefore vary quite spectacularly in a short period, and the only course to be followed in the vast majority of cases is to treat the cost of the indivisible factors as apportionable to customers. A railway company cannot adjust its fares to maximise revenue from each train—it cannot even cancel a train if there is insufficient revenue to meet the total marginal cost of running it. And in no type of business that I can think of would one be able to make the constant changes in price necessary to satisfy the Rule. (p. 56)

But the fact that a rule cannot be applied perfectly and without cost does not prove it is unsound. It is impossible to keep prices equal to

3 "State Enterprise and Output Policy . . . ," *Economica*, XIV (Feb., 1947), 54–62.

so-called average costs at all times, but this alone is a trivial argument against average-cost pricing. Railroad rates should not be different for each train because marginal or average costs are different for each train, but it is feasible to reduce fares until on an average day they do equal either marginal or average costs. The Rule is not impractical because it uses marginal instead of average costs as its criterion.

Norris's second objection to the Rule was that "in nearly every case, as a matter of practical administration, one would not dream of fixing prices by reference to supply considerations" (p. 56). In other words, prices should reflect demand as well as supply or cost considerations. He immediately vitiated this criticism by conceding that Lerner had made the same point and had merely proposed that output should be so altered as to make prices equal to marginal costs, but he tried to maintain his criticism by claiming that such output control is difficult if not impossible because it is hard to predict demand, especially in the absence of economic planning. This argument applies to all efforts at rational pricing.

The third argument, "that it is extremely valuable to have more or less uniform prices for similar goods in different shops," is equally dubious. It implies that large cost variations between different stores should be ignored.

Norris noted that Lerner and other proponents of marginal-cost control had neglected retail pricing, thus implying that this had been treated in detail by neo-classical economists. Actually, they offered no solution of the retail pricing problem, and there is none compatible with orthodox value theory. One of the many virtues of marginal-cost theory is that it does suggest specific measures to solve this problem, notably quantity-pricing; charging admission to retail stores; special prices for special services; seasonal, weekly and daily price changes; etc. (see pp. 184–90 below).

Retailing also provided Norris with a fourth criticism of marginal-cost control, "the impossibility of measuring marginal cost" (p. 57). In fact it is the so-called average cost of retail sales which it is impossible to measure because this requires the allocation of overhead costs (see pp. 196–97 below). Measuring marginal costs is relatively easy.

As his fifth criticism, Norris repeated Coase's argument that taxes to cover deficits would fall on some nonusers of the subsidized good. We have discussed this point (see pp. 110, 131).

Norris supported both price discrimination and multi-part pricing as means of approximating the results of marginal-cost control, which suggests that he recognized these results as beneficial, yet he concluded that "the golden rule of administration under public enterprise is to fix prices so as to equate demand with current output, and to expand or contract according as there is a profit or loss until price equals average cost."

REDER

We come now to the first discussion of the theory of marginal-cost control by a "new welfare economist." In his lucid *Studies in the Theory of Welfare Economics* (1947), Melvin W. Reder, now at Stanford, attempted to state this theory without using interpersonal utility comparisons. In this effort, he was following Lerner and Hotelling, but his rejection of traditional analysis was more explicit and more complete, and he was the first to discuss compensation payments in connection with marginal-cost control.

Reder explained the concept of welfare accepted by new welfare economists, namely that welfare is increased only when some persons are benefited and none are harmed. Since every economic policy harms some persons, new welfare economists have developed the "compensation principle," which asserts that welfare will be increased if due compensation is or can be paid to all persons who suffer from an economic policy, out of taxes on those who benefit from it, without eliminating such benefits.

Some new welfare economists have argued that the mere possibility of full compensation is enough to justify a proposed economic measure. This is illogical if inter-personal comparisons of utility are invalid. Other new welfare economists have argued that compensation must be paid before any economic measure can be said to promote welfare. This point of view is nihilistic because it is never possible to make all the required compensation payments. Reder did not explain clearly which view he held. His final statements on this point (pp. 98–100) suggest that a reform increases welfare if *full* compensation is possible and *partial* compensation is paid. If this interpretation is correct, he was really making interpersonal comparisons of utility at this point, for he assumed that the gains of certain persons offset the uncompensated losses of others.

Reder did not attempt to improve upon earlier statements of the theory of marginal-cost control. Indeed, he did not even choose the best previous statement of the theory, for he never noted that cost at the margin, not increment in total cost, is the correct price criterion. He was interested primarily in explaining how the compensation principle can be used to justify the new theory. The following quotation shows how he did this:

> In such cases [when average costs exceed marginal costs], welfare economists [Hotelling and Lerner are mentioned in a footnote] have recommended either, that the government purchase the firm . . . and run it on a welfare-maximizing basis, or that it regulate the firm so that it produces an output such as to make marginal cost equal to price, paying the firm a subsidy sufficient to cover its overhead costs. In either case . . . the government's action is justified on welfare grounds, as can be seen from the following: assume that the government charges a price equal to the marginal cost of the equilibrium output, but restricts actual output to that which would have been produced by the monopolist and supplies each customer only the amount that he previously purchased. The government can then pay the monopolist the same total revenue he would have received from the unhampered use of his monopoly, the revenue being derived from the sale of the products plus the proceeds of a tax levied upon each of the customers equal to the difference between what he pays to the government . . . and what he would have paid to the monopolist. . . . Thus without harming any *other* individual (taxpayer) the government can . . . compensate the monopolist . . . *providing output is restricted to the level that would have maximized the monopolist's profit.* But allowing output to expand freely to the equilibrium level (where marginal cost = price) cannot reduce either welfare or profits and will almost certainly increase both. For . . . purchasers of the units in excess of the amount that the monopolist would produce can pay a positive compensating tax. . . . Thus the government can increase welfare, by renting a monopoly from its owner and operating it so as to make marginal cost equal price. That this is a welfare-maximizing policy . . . follows directly from the previous argument. (pp. 51–52)

This reasoning is questionable because it assumes that it is feasible to impose on the intra-marginal consumers of a good taxes high enough to cover the loss from marginal-cost control without harming any such consumers and without reducing output below the ideal level. We have already criticized this assumption (see pp. 98–99, 131–32 above). Moreover, all changes in output harm some workers and some producers and consumers of competing products by undeterminable amounts (see pp. 85–86 above), and therefore require compensation payments, which cannot be paid. For instance, an increase in the output of rubber heels injures most workers and firms producing leather heels. Since new welfare economists reject interpersonal comparisons of utility and since compensation of all injured persons is impossible, these economists cannot justify any changes in output.

Reder noted that his attempted demonstration of the theory of marginal-cost control was based upon partial rather than general equilibrium analysis, and implied that this is a serious defect.

> The welfare arguments that we have developed . . . are partial equilibrium arguments. . . . But, in order to determine (say) the optimum output of a particular product, we must know (inter alia) the actual outputs of other products, the quantities of the factors used in producing them, etc. (p. 57)

He should have used the term *partial optimum* instead of *partial equilibrium* here and elsewhere, for welfare economics deals with optima, not with equilibria, but this is a minor point. The serious fault is that he implies that all economic theory is useless. If action requires full knowledge of all economic variables, no action is ever possible. Even partial knowledge of the numerous variables mentioned is difficult to obtain and largely useless when obtained because no feasible method of using such data is known. Reder and other new welfare economists have made no effort to explain a practical method of using it. The effect of stressing the need for such data is to discredit the only available practical method of approaching optimum price, namely partial adjustment based on partial optimum analysis. Here again new welfare economics is nihilistic.

The chief merit of Reder's discussion of marginal-cost control is that he made more explicit the relationship of new welfare theory to this theory and that he was the first to raise the question of compensation payments.

BOWEN

The first economist after Meade and Lerner to state and support the theory of marginal-cost control in a book on general economic theory was Howard R. Bowen of the University of Illinois. In his stimulating and readable book, *Toward Social Economy* (1947), he stated and explained the new theory in a form well suited to the needs of students (pp. 164–69).

Bowen began his explanation by assuming the case of a highway whose use involves no marginal costs.

Under these assumptions, . . . the price of the use of the road ought . . . to be zero. . . . The charging of a price . . . will . . . prevent the achievement of a part of the satisfactions which the road is capable of yielding, . . . the necessary "finance" must be raised through some form of payment that will not, like a price, be made a condition of using the highway. This . . . means taxation . . . but . . . over and against any social gain from finance through taxation must be set the possible redistribution of income which would be undesirable, assuming a "correct" distribution of income to begin with. (pp. 165–66)

The last qualification is unnecessary. The present distribution of income is far from "correct." Moreover, the problem of the ideal distribution of income is quite distinct from the problem of ideal price-output control and should be separately treated.

Bowen next assumed that some costs of highway use are marginal, and explained that prices above marginal costs would restrict highway use unduly. "It would pay to increase the use of the highway," he reasoned, "so long as the *additional* satisfactions (as measured by the price paid for them) were sufficient to warrant the *extra* cost" (p. 168).

Bowen used marginal cost to mean the increment in total cost, not cost at the margin. More serious is the fact that he explicitly stated that he meant "long-run marginal cost" (p. 171). He thus repeated the common error of trying to apply marginal analysis to the problem of lumpy investment in fixed capital. He did explain, however, that the problem of whether to start a new decreasing-cost industry should be solved by total analysis (pp. 169–71).

VICKREY

In answer to the criticisms of marginal-cost control by Coase, Norris, and others, there appeared in *The Journal of Political Economy* for June, 1948, an able reply by William Vickrey.[4] He classified the objections to such control into four groups: (1) difficulties in the selec-

---

[4] "Some Objections to Marginal-Cost Pricing," *Journal of Political Economy*, LVI (June, 1948), 218–38.

tion of projects, (2) difficulties in the computation of marginal cost, (3) fluctuations in marginal costs, and (4) sociopolitical considerations.

Under the first heading he noted, "One of the leading objections to the marginal-cost pricing policy for decreasing-cost industries is that the admitted necessity for a subsidy leaves no simple and obvious test of whether or not the project is worth while as a whole" (p. 218). On the other hand, the simple test of profitability now used is not a sound test because it rules out worth-while projects. Price discrimination and multi-part pricing improve the accuracy of profitability as a test but do not make it a sound test. Hence:

Either we accept marginal-cost pricing, with attendant subsidies and the necessity for making the over-all decision as to whether to undertake a given service, without any positive check (even retrospectively) on whether the decision was right or wrong; or we accept a more or less substantial misallocation of resources. (p. 225)

Earlier, Vickrey had discussed Coase's article in some detail. Coase had not made clear what he meant by "multi-part pricing" but Vickrey gave a definition and attributed it to Coase.

R. H. Coase . . . has suggested that this result [a closer approach to optimum output] may be achieved by "multi-part pricing," in which the total amount charged each customer is the sum of a flat "customer charge" for each consumer regardless of the quantity of the service taken (provided it be greater than zero), and a charge per unit of service taken, set at the marginal-cost level. (p. 219)

This is a good definition, but it is not to be found in Coase's article, and much of Coase's discussion, notably his assumed case, is inconsistent with it. However, Vickrey's discussion of various methods of price discrimination and multi-part pricing and of their relationship to marginal-cost price-output control was more detailed and more stimulating than any previous one.

He stated the second objection to marginal-cost control as follows:

Another objection . . . is based on the fact that reality does not conform to the regular and perfectly defined curves of the theorist, so that, in practice, marginal cost may not be only quite difficult to determine with any approach to accuracy but also subject to extreme and erratic fluctuation, depending on the precise circumstances of the moment. (230–31)

Vickrey answered this argument by claiming that, (1) in the case of perishable goods prices should balance supply and demand because marginal cost is opportunity cost in the short run, and (2) it is easier to determine marginal costs than average costs. He used the case of TVA to illustrate the difficulty of allocating overhead costs. And he stressed that "even when only one uniform product is being produced, there is always the question of how much of the cost of the capital employed should be charged to past production and how much to future" (p. 231). He concluded that

marginal cost is a definite concept, though it may be difficult to measure, while average cost for a specific date or type of output may be completely arbitrary, though accountants may be able to compute it with great accuracy in accordance with their more or less arbitrary rules.

The third objection to marginal-cost control is that "marginal cost is subject to extreme and erratic fluctuations." After doubting that anyone "has ever seriously proposed that prices should slavishly follow marginal costs" regardless of cost and convenience, Vickrey analyzed in some detail a rare case in which a close approach to such a slavish observance of marginal costs might be proper, namely, the case of transatlantic plane service. He recommended daily and hourly changes in fares in order to fill all planes and satisfy all demands at the market price. More important, he noted that price fluctuations based on changes in marginal costs are socially desirable and that price stability may reflect "sluggish competition combined with a not inconsiderable remnant of the medieval idea of the *justum pretium*" (p. 234). He also shrewdly observed that, by means of more price cycles based on cycles in demand, "a much closer approach to marginal-cost pricing than now generally prevails should be possible even without a subsidy" (p. 234).

In the fourth section of his article, "Sociopolitical Considerations," Vickrey asserted that marginal-cost pricing: (1) would remove utility rates from politics and provide an objective basis for their determination; (2) would end the need for legally prohibiting private competition with public monopolies; but (3), on the other hand, is unsuitable for application to firms "purveying . . . literature, information, news, entertainment, opinions, and the like" (p. 236), because it would require state determination of subsidies, which would amount to state censorship. We shall comment only on his third point. Vickrey was the first economist to suggest marginal-cost control of these industries, and he devoted only one paragraph to this idea. To conclude that it is impractical without a detailed study of the many possible ways of subsidizing these industries is surely hasty.

The above review of Vickrey's article, like most reviews in this monograph, is incomplete because we wish to keep our history of marginal-cost price-output theory within certain space limits. In Vickrey's case this treatment is especially questionable. He deserves to be ranked with Meade, Lerner, Hotelling, and Montgomery as one of the most able proponents of the theory of marginal-cost control.

HENDERSON

The attack on marginal-cost control was continued by A. M. Henderson in two journal articles, "The Pricing of Public Utility Undertakings," in the *Manchester School* for September, 1947, and "Prices and Profits in State Enterprises," in the *Review of Economic Studies* for 1948–49. Since the former article was discussed in Chapter V, we shall comment here primarily on the latter.

Henderson began this article with some timely remarks on the need for a price theory for state enterprises, but failed to note that such a theory is implicit, if not explicit, in Capitalist books on the regulation of utility and railroad rates. The traditional theory that such rates should be based upon ability to pay and should yield a net income equal to a fair return on the investment is so like the price theory which he himself finally proposed that his neglect of it is odd.

Instead of stating this orthodox theory, Henderson criticized "the standard economist's solution; the solution of Pareto and Baronne" that prices should equal marginal costs (p. 16). (We have already noted the error of such references to Pareto and Baronne [pp. 30–31].) "The principle [of marginal-cost pricing]" he continued, "has been discussed *ad nauseam* in recent literature." If this means that the theory had been adequately discussed, generally accepted, or included in many textbooks, it is very misleading.

Aside from such indirectly revealing remarks, his attitude towards marginal-cost control was equivocal. For instance, he asserted that "the marginal-cost pricing principle must always remain of fundamental importance in a pricing system," but on the same page (17) he stated that "the . . . principle is disqualified from being the sole or even the main principle of pricing on the score of administrative difficulty."

Actually, the later statement represents Henderson's real belief. To justify it, he stated and briefly discussed nine difficulties involved in the application of marginal-cost control.

The first difficulty is that "marginal cost is not nearly as simple a concept as it appears in the text-book" (p. 17). It depends upon changes in the output of other goods, the marginal-cost function is not continuous, marginal costs change with the passage of time, current marginal costs include an estimate of unknowable future replacement costs, and they are difficult to determine. These sound like serious difficulties unless one stops to realize that they all apply equally to so-called average costs. Henderson failed to see that the relevant question is not whether these difficulties exist but whether they are greater for marginal costs than for average costs. Moreover, much of his criticism of marginal costs seem to result from his erroneous belief that marginal costs include some fixed costs.

His second criticism is that under marginal-cost control there is no practicable criterion for determining which investments are justified. We have criticized his earlier statement of this point (p. 114).

His third point is that such control creates deficits which require additional, perhaps intolerable, taxation. We have discussed this argument repeatedly.

His fourth argument, that state enterprise should yield a profit which will lower the need for taxes, is merely a variation of the third.

His fifth point is that in a mixed economy marginal-cost control for state enterprises only would result in their overexpansion (p. 18). This implies that such overexpansion is more harmful than the gross underexpansion due to so-called average-cost pricing. But in a mixed economy, state enterprises are usually found in those industries—railroads, canals, public utilities, bridges, dams, etc.—where the greatest difference between average and marginal costs exists and where average-cost pricing therefore results in the greatest degree of underexpansion and idle capacity. Hence, a small overexpansion due to the application of marginal-cost control would be much less of an evil.

His sixth criticism is that marginal-cost control by state enterprises would not eliminate local unemployment due to the immobility of labor. But in such cases the solution is to reduce the wages or increase the mobility of the surplus labor, not to distort the prices of finished goods enough to compensate for wage distortions. In any case, so-called average-cost pricing also fails to eliminate local unemployment.

The seventh alleged difficulty is that marginal costs do not reflect external economies and diseconomies (p. 19). However, most external economies and diseconomies are internal to supplying firms, and would affect the prices charged by these firms to the ideal extent under marginal-cost control. The taxes and subsidies proposed by Henderson would result in 100 percent over-reaction to such economies.

The eighth alleged defect of marginal-cost control is that it does not subsidize the output of goods whose output ought to be subsidized. The mere statement of the argument in this form suggests the answer, which is to adopt the desired subsidies openly, so that they can be measured and independently debated, instead of distorting prices to achieve the same end.

The ninth and final criticism is that marginal-cost control theory is an "economic formula" and that prices charged by state enterprises should reflect noneconomic needs, such as needs for a better social structure, for immunity from the trade cycle (surely an economic need), for military preparedness, for health, and for rural beauty. Here again, Henderson wished to distort prices in order to solve problems which should be separately handled. Special appropriations can and should be made for all of these purposes. Only when special appropriations are made can voters have any idea of the sums being devoted to each of these ends.

This nine-point criticism of marginal-cost control is followed by a curious paragraph in which Henderson stated that such control and arbitrary planning of output "for the whole economy" are both ideally perfect but are not administratively feasible, and that a compromise between them is desirable. In our opinion, marginal-cost control is absolutely inconsistent with planning of production and the latter is a bad ideal.

As an alternative to marginal-cost control, Henderson suggested that the state should determine in advance an "Annual Payment" to the state to be made by each state enterprise and that each such enterprise should fix prices so as to cover total costs including this payment. The payment should, in most cases, equal a fair return on the capital invested, but in some cases the state should raise or lower this payment to help to achieve numerous special purposes such as national defense, greater equality of income, promotion of certain industries, full employment, etc., etc.

The determination of the Annual Payment by politicians would relieve the individual enterprise of the difficult problem of determining capital and land costs (interest and rent), but it would still have to allocate these costs, i.e., the Annual Payment, to individual products. Henderson proposed that this allocation should, in nearly all cases, be proportional to marginal costs, which would require the prior determination of marginal costs. Thus, his proposal does not avoid any of the difficulties of determining marginal costs.

BECKWITH

It is hard for any author to evaluate objectively his own contributions to a new theory, and perhaps he should not attempt this. However, this author has participated in the development of the theory of marginal-cost price-output control since 1932, and a factual account of his work and what he feels its contribution to be should at least help others to judge it.

The author's *Economic Theory of a Socialist Economy* was not published until 1949, but it was written, essentially in its present form, in the years 1932-34. It contains a detailed statement of the theory of marginal-cost output control and a larger number of specific applications of the theory than any other article or book to date (1952).

The manuscript on Socialist economics was read by at least a dozen economists in the years 1934 to 1937, but the author could not find a publisher at that time. In the meantime, he had written in 1936 and published in 1943 his book, *The Modern Case for Socialism,* which contains a brief statement of the theory of marginal-cost control, discussed above (pp. 118-19).

The Introduction to *The Economic Theory of a Socialist Economy* ends with the following paragraph:

The fourth major contribution [of this book] is the application of the old but largely neglected theory that prices should equal marginal costs to all the pricing problems of a Socialist Economy. The few economists who accept this theory have failed to realize its significance because they are unaware that virtually all non-extractive industries have decreasing costs. (p. 22)

There are two errors in this paragraph. First, the theory was not old and neglected, but essentially new at the time this book was written (1932-34). Secondly, the last part of the last sentence implies that the author then believed that, (1) the theory of marginal-cost control solves the problem of optimum investment in fixed capital, and (2) the general application of such control would result in a large deficit. In fact, the theory of optimum investment is quite distinct from the theory of optimum price, and it is the application of the former, not the latter, which would result in deficits in decreasing-cost industries.

The first general statement of the new theory of price-output control in this treatise occurs in Chapter VII, "The Theory of Production Control Over Price Goods," but this is preceded by three chapters on the measurement of utility, in which the role of prices in measuring marginal utility and marginal disutility is discussed in detail. It is argued that utility to different persons is comparable (pp. 38–41) and that the function of prices is to make possible comparisons of marginal utility and marginal disutility in order to permit rational economic decisions which will maximize the net surplus of total *utilitum* (experienced pleasure) over total *disutilitum* (pp. 25–28, 70–75). It is also asserted that prices should always equalize supply and demand (pp. 80–82).

The following quotation contains the heart of the general statement of the theory of marginal-cost output control.

> In the first place, *a Socialist economy ought to produce every good whose production yields net utilitum at any volume of production. In the second place, the production of such a good should be increased whenever the production of an additional unit . . . would yield additional net utilitum, and should be curtailed whenever the production of the marginal unit yields net disutilitum.* (p. 152)

> . . . .

> To permit their practical application in a Socialist economy, it is necessary to translate the two basic principles of production control . . . into principles which prescribe the proper reaction to properly determined prices. (p. 153)

> . . . .

> The second basic principle of production control can be easily translated into one simple and universal principle of response to marginal profits and losses: *the output of any good . . . should be increased or decreased until its marginal cost (cost at the margin) of production becomes equal to its sales price.* Control over the production of price goods in a Socialist economy will therefore not be more difficult, but far less difficult

than under Capitalism. All that is necessary is to strive to eliminate both marginal profits and marginal losses, to regard the former as evidence of underproduction, the latter as evidence of overproduction. (p. 154)

In the discussion of this general principle, it is argued that past losses should never be balanced by later profits because a price above marginal costs is as uneconomic as a price below marginal costs, and a new wrong never rights an old one (p. 155). It is also asserted that marginal-cost output control is incompatible with arbitrary planning of the type practiced in the USSR and favored by many democratic Socialists (pp. 168–71).

Negative rent is defined (p. 159) and the methods of covering it are discussed (p. 288). Poll taxes are highly recommended because they do not distort marginal money costs (pp. 217–19). Marshall's tax subsidy proposal is criticized (p. 159). A graphic demonstration of the way marginal-cost control maximizes consumers' surplus in decreasing-cost industries is attempted (p. 160). The deflationary effect of the introduction of marginal-cost control, the stability of money-wages during this deflation, the resulting increase in real wages, and the expansion of decreasing-cost industries at the expense of increasing-cost industries are all noted (p. 161).

The Economic Theory of a Socialist Economy also includes a twenty-page chapter (VIII), "The Determination of Marginal Profits and Losses," in which the problem of what costs should enter into marginal costs and affect ideal prices is discussed in detail, for the first time so far as we are aware. It is argued that certain costs, once incurred, are never affected by later changes in the volume of output, and these costs, nine of which are individually discussed, are called "pure intramarginal costs." In the discussion of pure marginal costs it is noted that the basing-point system of pricing is inconsistent with marginal-cost control because freight charges are always a marginal cost (p. 187).

Finally there are six chapters on the application of pure Socialist economic theory to specific industries (agriculture, transportation, marketing, foreign trade, public utilities, and building). In each of these, the effect of marginal-cost control upon specific prices is explained and illustrated. Hotelling and Montgomery described in general terms the effect of such control upon railroad and utility rates, but this application is treated in much greater detail in this book (pp. 355–62, 406–10). For instance, the role of service charges is discussed, and the need for varying rates hourly and seasonally is noted. Perhaps the most novel applications of marginal-cost control are those in the chapter on marketing, where it is proposed that, (1) retail stores charge admission, (2) retail prices be lower in off-peak hours than during peak hours, (3) separate charges be made for all optional services (since service costs are pure marginal costs), and that (4) the second and latter units of identical merchandise in the same sale be sold at cost price since the marginal cost of selling two units instead of one is negligible (pp. 373–76).

One of the defects in the general statement of the theory of marginal-cost output control is the failure to explain that it can be applied only to tangible goods. Since services cannot be stored, their output should be controlled directly by the consumer responding to price changes. In this case, therefore, marginal-cost price control is applicable but marginal-cost output control is not. This point is made in discussing utility rates (p. 407), but there is no mention of it in Chapter VII, "The Theory of Production Control Over Price Goods."

Another defect of this treatise is that there is no discussion of the way in which marginal money costs should be corrected by the use of special taxes and bonuses so that they will measure marginal real costs more accurately. The correction of marginal money costs is not a part of the theory of marginal-cost price-output control, but it should have been discussed and clearly related to this theory.

The chief error in the treatment of marginal-cost output control is the failure to distinguish between the problem of controlling output from existing plant and the problem of controlling investment in fixed plant. This serious error is responsible for such false conclusions as that, (1) fixed capital costs are often marginal costs (pp. 183–86), (2) all decreasing-cost industries should operate at a loss (p. 159), (3) this loss should be called negative rent, (4) losses should result only from marginal-cost control (pp. 159–61), and (5) the benefits of marginal-cost output control can be proven graphically by using *long-run* demand and marginal-cost-curves, unfortunately not labeled as long-run curves (p. 160).

To summarize, *The Economic Theory of a Socialist Economy* is a general treatise on economics built around the central theory that output is ideal when prices equal marginal costs. With the exception of Lerner's *Economics of Control*, it is the first treatise of this type. It suggests many applications of marginal-cost price-output theory, not noted by him, but it repeats nearly all of the serious errors common to most contemporary statements of this theory.

DURBIN

Ten years after his first discussion of marginal-cost control, Durbin restated his views in greater detail and with some changes in his reasoning, but reached the same conclusion, namely, that the prices charged by state enterprises should equal average rather than marginal costs.[5] Before beginning to criticize it, he stated the theory of marginal-cost output control in these words:

> The strictly logical directive that should be given to all managements [of state enterprises] runs as follows: "Produce at the level of output where the price of the commodity you are producing is equal to the *marginal* cost of production."
> This is the correct instruction since the real cost to society of the last increment of the output of any commodity is the additional in-puts of labour, material, capital and management required to make it. (p. 84)

This statement was followed by a confusing argument that marginal-cost control works in industries in which there are many production units but not in industries where there is only one plant. By this he apparently meant that it does not result in losses in increasing-cost industries and does result in losses in other industries. He asserted that it should not be applied to one-firm industries for two reasons:

> In the first place it would reduce the status of accountancy and the principle of accountability to empty formularies. . . . If managers and workers can make large surpluses, or appear responsible for large deficits, without any change in their application or efficiency, the set of accounts by which they are supposed to be guided will become meaningless and irritating to them. (p. 86)

This argument ignores the fact that profits have often turned into deficits without any change in the efficiency of management or labor. The deficits of 1931 to 1935 were not due to a decrease in efficiency, and the unusual profits of 1941 to 1951 were not due to an increase in efficiency. It is odd that a Socialist economist should assume there is a close relationship between profits and efficiency under Capitalism

---

[5] "The Problems of the Socialized Sector," in *Problems of Economic Planning* (London, 1949), pp. 84–89. This article was first written in 1946.

or assert that accounting would be discredited if Socialists learned that private profits do not measure efficiency!

Durbin ignored the possibility that better methods of measuring efficiency could be developed under Socialism. For instance, efficiency might be measured by intraplant unit costs, especially if all plants were required to use uniform cost-accounting methods. In making comparisons between plants, it would be necessary to allow for differences in equipment and other factors, but these differences affect profits also, and unit costs are not affected by many factors unrelated to efficiency which do affect profits.

If the "principle of accountability" merely means that a firm must cover its total costs, it is inconsistent with marginal-cost control. But this is not evidence as to whether such control is sound. If such control is sound, the "principle of accountability" should not merely be reduced to an "empty formulary"; it should be repudiated as unsound.

We turn now to Durbin's second objection:

> In the second place, the consistent application of the marginal directive would reduce price policy to confusion. . . . Pure logic requires that only current costs—or today's inputs—should be considered in fixing today's prices. . . . Unfortunately, any attempt to apply it . . . would produce fantastic results. Consider a socialised railway system. On any given day the cost, in the above sense, of carrying an additional passenger would be zero. . . . Hence . . . transport would be free. As an immediate consequence the railways would become congested and extra trains would have to be organised. The cost of the extra trains would be true marginal costs . . . and prices have to be raised at once to cover them. Empty places would then appear once more and fares would again disappear. (p. 87)
>
> . . .
>
> It is in order to avoid this absurd and disastrous instability of prices that cost calculations should include an estimate of all the future payments that can be foreseen. (p. 88)

The essence of this argument is that if the only sound theory of pricing cannot be perfectly applied to certain difficult cases, no effort to apply it imperfectly to such cases or to easy cases is worth while.

In this railway case some compromise with perfection is both practical and wise. For instance the fare might equal the average marginal cost per passenger seat of operating the marginal passenger car or train. The result of such a compromise would not be fares equal to so-called average costs but fares normally far below this level, for the costs of operating one more existing car or train include none of the costs of building cars or the railway.

The operation of extra trains changes average as well as marginal costs. If one kind of cost change is unpredictable or difficult to measure, the other is equally so. If raising prices to cover additional marginal costs results in empty seats, raising prices to cover additional average costs has the same effect. In both cases, however, it is possible to raise prices just enough to balance supply and demand at the higher prices.

KRISHNAMURTI

We turn next to a stimulating little (139-page) monograph, *Pricing in Planned Economy* (1949), by B. V. Krishnamurti. In it, the author ably restated the Lerner-Hotelling case for marginal-cost control. In addition, he stressed the fact that orthodox value theory assumes small-scale production and increasing marginal costs, characteristics of Adam Smith's world but not of our own, and argued briefly that the application of marginal welfare analysis to the modern world of large-scale production and decreasing marginal costs results in an entirely new theory of price. We shall not repeat his restatement of the ideas of Lerner and Hotelling (he largely ignored Meade), but shall stress the two notable contributions of this study.

In the first place, *Krishnamurti was the first to make the vital distinction between the problem of ideal price or output, assuming no new investment in fixed capital, and the problem of determining whether a proposed investment in fixed capital is desirable.* He explained, repeatedly, that the first problem can be solved by marginal analysis while the latter cannot.

It has been clearly demonstrated in the last chapter that the *ideal* output that the firm should produce with a given stock of fixed equipment is given by the position at which the price of the product is equal to the marginal cost of production. It has been further shown that this marginal-cost price equality also implies the *ideal* adjustment of inputs of variable factors. Fixed equipment was intentionally kept out of account as an irrelevant consideration. . . . The problem now is to examine the considerations that enter into the determination of the correct size of the fixed equipment. (pp. 62–63)

He went on to explain that in planning fixed investment the area under the demand curve and above the marginal-cost curve should be maximized (p. 73). In other words, proposals for investment in fixed capital should be evaluated by means of a comparison of *total* gain with *total* cost, which is obviously not an application of marginal analysis.

Krishnamurti did not fully realize the meaning and significance of his brilliant distinction between the problems of optimum price and optimum investment in fixed capital. At one point he claimed that by his analysis "the short-run and the long-run problems are brought under one standard criterion" (p. 68) which, though vague, may contradict his main thesis. He failed, moreover, to state and properly develop the chief implications of his pioneer distinction. *Nevertheless, his imperfect statement of one of these implications, the fallacy of using the concept of long-run marginal cost, is his second major contribution.* He introduced his discussion of this concept as follows:

It is often asked whether it is the short-period marginal cost or the long-period marginal cost that should be equated with price. That the question framed in this form itself is wrong becomes obvious by a careful examination of the definition of marginal cost. For, marginal cost which is the cost of producing an additional unit implies the production of the particular unit at a certain point of time. And this is all that matters. (p. 82)

Unfortunately, this is not what matters. In determining the cost of a particular marginal unit at a certain point of time, one may include the cost of new fixed capital built to produce that unit, or one may exclude such costs. The correct criterion to be used in determining which costs enter into marginal costs is not whether they occur "at a certain point of time," but whether they are divisible and can be allocated to marginal units of output. The costs of fixed capital are not divisible and cannot be so allocated. Hence, they cannot be subjected to marginal analysis and never enter marginal cost. Krishnamurti was vaguely aware of this, though he failed to see that it contradicts the above quotation. His awareness is suggested by the next paragraph which contains his main criticism of the concept of long-run marginal cost.

The distinction between short-period and long-period costs persists because of the fallacious belief that the long-run marginal cost inclusive of changes in the long-run variable factors (short-term fixed factors) is greater than the short-period marginal cost. This is used to prove the short-coming of the price short-period marginal cost rule. A. P. Lerner has neatly demonstrated that this is not necessarily so. But the point is that the long-run marginal cost is not a very helpful concept. The reason is that the application of the marginal concept to long-run variable factors is a matter of estimating marginal costs or marginal returns of significantly indivisible units which involves considerable numerical imprecision.

This passage is of great significance because it is a part of the first open attack upon the concept of long-run marginal cost, but the attack is not properly developed and pressed home. The quotation contains evidence that the author had not freed his own analysis from the fallacies implicit in the concept of long-run marginal cost. For instance, the first sentence suggests that he believes that short-run fixed costs turn into variable costs which enter marginal cost at a later date. Actually, short-run fixed costs are the costs of fixed capital and never enter marginal cost. Moreover, the last sentence implies that long-run marginal cost is a concept of little utility only because there is "considerable numerical imprecision" in allocating the costs of indivisible fixed capital to marginal units of output. In fact, no degree of precision whatever is possible. Rational allocation of fixed costs is impossible. The concept of long-run marginal cost is not only "not a very helpful concept"; it is a contradictory concept which has caused a vast amount of confusion in welfare price theory, in orthodox neo-classical value theory, and in the theory of imperfect competition. Recognition of its faults should lead in time to the abandonment of all theories that price is or should be determined by the intersection of the long-run marginal-cost curve and some other curve.

There are other errors in this monograph. In restating older arguments for marginal-cost control, Krishnamurti repeated many of the mistakes we have noted in earlier writers. He rejected the measurement and comparison of personal utility (p. 5), described Hotelling's faulty proof of the marginal-cost rule as "impeccable" (p. 36), implied that higher mathematics is needed to show that price should equal marginal cost, recommended that rent (a surplus) should be controlled in order to control price (pp. 85–86), assumed that economic planning is consistent with marginal-cost control (p. 2), and argued that marginal money costs are perfect measures of marginal real costs when income is equal and, hence, that all inequality of income weakens the case for marginal-cost control (p. 114). In spite of such errors, Krishnamurti made very important contributions to the new price-output theory.

It is noteworthy that these contributions were not mentioned in Lerner's sympathetic review of *Pricing in Planned Economy* in the

American Economic Review for December, 1950. Lerner not only failed to call attention to the novelty of the vital distinction between marginal analysis and total analysis, but criticized Krishnamurti for calling a certain curve a long-term average-cost curve instead of a long-term marginal-cost curve. If he had grasped the meaning of Krishnamurti's contributions, he would have seen that the concept of long-run marginal cost is meaningless.

FLEMING

In February, 1950, J. M. Fleming resumed his discussion of marginal-cost control in a twenty-two-page article on "Production and Price Policy in Public Enterprise" in *Economica*. In this article he replied to some of the numerous criticisms of such control, particularly those which claim the theory is impractical, and proved himself to be both a greater friend and a shrewder analyst of the theory than he was in his 1945 article.

He began by stating the theory as a "rule of optimal output" and tried to present it "in the most general and least ambiguous way."

> *Assuming that the prices of factors and of products are such as to bring demand and supply into equilibrium, an optimal position will result from each enterprise undertaking any changes of input and/or output such that the value of additional outputs less the value of subtractional outputs exceeds the value of additional inputs less the value of subtractional inputs.*

. . . .

From the above formulation the following points emerge:

(a) The Rule in its pure form relates *not to pricing but to production.* This is of great importance and is constantly being overlooked. Prices should be determined by demand and supply. It is only where circumstances forbid the integral application of the Rule, and even then only in certain cases, that the question of costs (marginal or other) enters directly into the determination of price. (pp. 1–2)

Fleming did well to stress that the theory of marginal-cost control may be stated as a theory of ideal output, but he exaggerated the importance and misinterpreted the meaning of this fact. Since price and output ought to be dependent upon each other, any theory of ideal price is also a theory of ideal output, and vice versa. Moreover, under capitalism direct control over price is usually preferable to direct control over output. Finally, as he himself was one of the first to point out (pp. 7–8), the marginal-cost output control rule cannot be applied to firms producing services under any economic system.

The second point which emerges from the above formulation of the rule "of optimal output in the most general . . . way" is that:

(b) The various marginal rules about which controversy has centered, e.g., that the value of marginal product should equal the factor price, or that the marginal substitutability of factor for factor should equal their regular prices, are but special applications of a general rule which is equally applicable to large input/output variations, such as that involved in setting up an entire new plant. (p. 2)

Fleming went on to explain that when the change in output is "significantly large," the effect upon both consumers' and producers' surplus must be allowed for. Since the gains from and costs of new investment may continue over many years, he pointed out that they must be discounted "by the aid of an appropriate rate of interest" to permit their consideration at the time the investment is being weighed. "With this interpretive gloss," he concluded, "it is clear that the rule governing investment is precisely the same as that governing current production."

This is a serious error. Marginal analysis is not suitable for the evaluation of non-marginal quantities like the total costs and gains from a large investment in fixed capital. Discounting future gains and costs and adding in consumers' and producers' surpluses does not solve the basic problem, which is how these total gains and costs can be allocated to individual marginal units of output. Fleming did not try to solve this problem.

He next argued that the effect of a large output change in one industry upon the price and output of complementary or substitute products must be considered in evaluating the initial change. This assumes again that marginal analysis can deal with large non-marginal quantities. It is also in error because it implies, (1) that general analysis is practical, and (2) that all changes in consumers' and producers' surplus are significant (see pp. 210–11 below).

Fleming restated the argument that prices should not be reduced all the way to marginal costs in state enterprises because, due to imperfect competition, prices are above marginal costs in private firms, and lowering prices to the marginal-cost level in state enterprises would cause "an excessive diversion of resources" to the latter (p. 4). We have already answered this criticism (see p. 145).

He also suggested that the marginal-cost rule should be modified to compensate for the distortion of wages due to collective bargaining (pp. 4–5). To us it seems more logical to modify wage determination methods so as to prevent the distortion of wages by wage contracts. Moreover, it would certainly not be practical to estimate the margin between actual and ideal wages in each occupation in each plant and then raise or lower prices enough to compensate for this margin.

Fleming's discussion of the effect of marginal-cost control upon income distribution is more satisfying. He not only noted that any bad effects should be compensated for by fiscal means rather than by modifying the method of pricing, but that those who, like Coase, have argued that marginal-cost control would worsen the distribution of income have begged the question by assuming that the distribution of income resulting from so-called average-cost pricing is ideal (p. 10).

Thus far, we have been discussing Fleming's suggested "modifications" or qualifications of the basic rule of ideal output and price. We turn now to his reply to various attempts to refute the rule itself. He began by remarking that few opponents of marginal-cost control have stated clearly the alternative theory which they prefer, and proceeded to do this for them, describing two alternatives, (1) average-cost control, and (2) multi-part pricing. He then pointed out that a profitable monopoly may alter its average costs in many ways (for instance, by advertising more) and can make prices equal any one of many alternative average costs (p. 11). Hence, neither average-cost price-output control nor multi-part pricing designed to cover average costs can solve the pricing problem. This is a sound and vital point.

Turning to multi-part pricing, he noted that this term has been used to cover several different ideas, one of which—making a separate charge for a necessary incidental service if its cost is independent of the amount of the serviced good consumed—is not only compatible with but required by the marginal-cost rule (p. 12). Hence, it is not, like average-cost control, an alternative rule.

Fleming next replied to the objection of Wilson and Durbin that marginal-cost control would make it impossible to use profits as a measure of managerial efficiency. He asserted that, where the output of individual plants is small relative to the size of the market, managers may be told to maximize their profits, so that this objection "clearly would not apply" (p. 15). The assumption of many small firms however, implies that marginal costs are above average costs. Otherwise, output would be concentrated in one firm. Hence, the assumed case is one in which marginal-cost control would not change prices or profits and could not affect incentives. Fleming went on, however, to offer a better reply. He explained that profits are a poor measure of efficiency because they reflect physical differences between plants, unpredictable price changes, and other factors beyond the control of the manager (p. 16).

In answer to the common argument that it is too difficult to measure marginal cost, he pointed out that if managers are to be efficient, they must increase the use of each agent in production until its marginal productivity equals its cost. This involves all of the difficulties of measuring marginal cost. If marginal-cost control is impossible, so is efficiency. Average-cost pricing does not reduce these difficulties, but rather adds others to them. So great are these added difficulties that multi-product firms fix their prices in an arbitrary manner without regard for indeterminable average costs. By avoiding the insoluble problem of allocating common overhead costs to individual products, marginal-cost theory greatly simplifies the problem of pricing, in addition to offering a more rational criterion of ideal price (pp. 19–20).

"Quite the strongest argument against the rule," he concluded, "is simply that it is unfamiliar to the man in the street and fails to command his assent" (p. 21). He considered this more than a transitional difficulty because he thought it very difficult to educate the public to a new price-output theory. He also suggested that in socialized industries the unsound idea that prices should equal average costs might be a useful defense against the wage demands of organized labor. At the last, however, he denied his previous implication that sound theory should be taught only to those who will accept it.

I myself believe that it never pays in the end to propitiate an economic fallacy, and that the mental confusion engendered by following a false principle will have worse practical consequences than the difficulties encountered in understanding and applying the true one. (p. 22)

This is a vital point which few critics of marginal-cost control have grasped. On the whole, this article is a valuable contribution to the literature on ideal price and output.

RUGGLES

In the spring and summer of 1950 the *Review of Economic Studies* published two lucid articles containing a critical history and evaluation of the theory of marginal-cost price-output control by Nancy Ruggles, based upon her Ph.D. thesis at Harvard. Their principal purpose was to show that this theory is invalid because it violates the basic assumption of new welfare economics—namely, that interpersonal comparisons of utility are impossible—and she made little effort to improve the theory she was criticizing.

As implied by its title, "The Welfare Basis of the Marginal Cost Pricing Principle," the first article is devoted chiefly to a critical history of new welfare economics. However, the last pages of this article and the bulk of the second, "Recent Developments in the Theory of Marginal Cost Pricing," offer the first critical history of the new price-output theory. We shall not comment on the history of new welfare economics. We shall also largely refrain from comment on her history of the new price theory because we have already criticized parts of it (see pp. 58, 63, 78 above) and because a detailed criticism would require too much space and would duplicate many of our previous points. But we do wish to note her treatment of the relationship between these doctrines.

Mrs. Ruggles prefaced her discussion of marginal-cost control with a discussion of new welfare economics because she thought that "present-day proponents of marginal-cost pricing almost universally couch their arguments in terms of the 'new' welfare economics" (p. 29). She did not cite any explicit statements of the basic premise of new welfare economics by proponents of marginal-cost control. Actually, we can recall only one in the English language literature on marginal-cost pricing, namely, that by Reder. Lerner, Lange, and Hotelling were influenced by new welfare theory, but they never explicitly rested their entire case for the new price theory upon new welfare economics, and they repeatedly contradicted implicitly the basic premise of this school. Finally, proponents like Meade, Montgomery, Thompson and Smith, Barnes, Troxel, Fleming, Vickrey, Bowen, and the present author have never based their case for the new theory on the assumption that interpersonal comparisons of utility are impossible. Mrs. Ruggles assumed too often that when proponents ignore or contradict this premise they are inconsistent. She ought to have concluded that most of them are not new welfare economists by her definition.

Mrs. Ruggles thought that it is impossible to achieve both an optimum distribution of income and optimum prices. She asserted that Lerner "advocated equality of income" (p. 114), whereas he merely proved that equal distribution of a *given* stock would maximize utility,[6] and she claimed that equality of income is incompatible with marginal-cost control. She also asserted that it is very difficult, if not impossible, to finance deficits due to such control without using taxes inconsistent with an optimum distribution of income. This argument implies that the existing distribution of income is ideal, or if it is not that the taxes needed to correct it are inconsistent with those required to finance deficits. Both implications are questionable, and she did not try to justify them.

In her final "Summary and Evaluation," Mrs. Ruggles repeated her two chief points against marginal-cost theory, namely, (1) that it is based on interpersonal comparisons of utility, and (2) that the resulting deficits must be financed, in part at least, by taxes which affect marginal costs. The claim that some of the taxes used to finance deficits must fall on marginal costs is unjustified. A variety of taxes which do not fall on marginal costs have been suggested. The best of these suggestions, the use of poll taxes under Capitalism and interest and rent under Socialism, were ignored by her. She noted the possible use of taxes on inheritance and land rent, but rested her case upon the argument that these taxes would not yield enough to cover the deficits. Since Hotelling had suggested income taxes, she assumed unjustifiably that such taxes *must* be used, and argued that they would change the distribution of income and reduce the supply of labor. But if a redistribution of income from the rich to the poor is desirable, as most economists believe, the change in income distribution created by an income tax would be beneficial, and Mrs. Ruggles's only counterargument is based on the invalid assumption that interpersonal comparisons of utility are impossible. Moreover, she asserted that both Meade and Lerner "failed to consider the question" of how to finance deficits (p. 119), and then, paradoxically, cited Meade as one of those who recognized that income taxes are unsuitable because "they will prevent

[6] Lerner, *The Economics of Control* (New York, 1944), p. 39.

the marginal conditions of production from being met" (pp. 116, 119).

Like other new welfare economists, Mrs. Ruggles seems unaware that in the real world one must choose among price-output policies and that a critique which equally invalidates all of them is useless. There is no evidence in her articles to suggest that she is aware that one must assume the interpersonal comparability of utility in order to demonstrate that any price-output policy is desirable. Nor, on the other hand, is there any rejection of all such policies. She used new welfare economic theory against marginal-cost control, and conveniently forgot it when discussing the alternatives to it.

In spite of these defects, Mrs. Ruggles made one contribution. She made it clear that the theory of marginal-cost price-output control is incompatible with new welfare economics because the former assumes, while the latter denies, the interpersonal comparability of utility. This means that the few new welfare economists who have supported such control have been inconsistent. It does not mean that the new price-output theory is invalid, as she argued.

LITTLE

The long series of attacks upon the new theory of marginal-cost control by Capitalist economists was continued in *A Critique of Welfare Economics* (1950) by I. M. D. Little of Oxford. He revised and/or restated in more lucid form most of the unsound arguments against the new theory developed by his predecessors. He explained better than any previous writer the way in which welfare economics could be used to attack Capitalism and support Socialism, and he offered a more plausible defense against this new threat to the present order.

He opened this defense with a long discussion of what he called ethical value judgments. His book contains over a hundred references to "ethical values," "value judgements," "ethics," "values," and other synonyms, as well as a chapter (V) on "Value Judgements and Welfare Economics." In this chapter, he tried to explain what he meant by values, but his explanation (pp. 69–71) is extremely obscure. His use of the term in the remainder of the book is only slightly more revealing. He seems to have used ethical value, and its synonyms, to describe personal prejudices (see pp. 67–68, 108, 268–69). In other words, if A prefers equality or inequality of income but cannot justify his prefer-

ence by scientific reasoning, his prejudice is a value judgment. Similarly, prejudices for or against slavery, free trade, and private ownership of property are ethical values. Little thought that "there is no
alternative to the view that welfare conclusions must be deduced from
value premises" (p. 84). As we shall see, he based his own theory of
welfare economics upon two explicit value judgments or personal
prejudices.

For some unexplained reason Little ignored the modern positivist
view that ethical propositions are meaningless if no method of verifi-
cation can be conceived and that if they are meaningful they are a part
of some science. Meaningful ethical doctrines that solve economic
problems fall within the science of economics. Hence, in our positivist
opinion there is no basis for Little's claim that welfare conclusions
must be derived from ethical propositions outside the science of economics. This point of view has been brilliantly presented in *Language,
Truth and Logic* (1936), by A. J. Ayer.

As its title implies, Little's book is a review and restatement of welfare theory as a whole. His criticism of the theory of marginal-cost control is incidental to his critique of welfare economics. However, he
laid the basis for one of his major arguments against such control, the
perfectionist argument for doing nothing, by restating the new welfare
theory that an economic measure is desirable only if, "(a) it does not
result in a bad redistribution of welfare, and (b) the potential losers
could not bribe the potential gainers to vote against the change" (p.
116).

The idea that this criterion could be applied to practical problems
in the real world is, we believe, completely visionary. It is never possible to determine the effect of a price change on the distribution of
welfare. A price change affects all consumers, indirectly if not directly.
Hence, it is impractical to discover whether the potential losers could
bribe the potential gainers to vote against the change.

Little approached the pure theory of marginal-cost control as follows. He first stated two ethical value judgments, which he thought
widely held, namely, that, (1) the welfare of the community is an increasing function of the welfare of individuals, and (2) an individual is
better off if he is in a chosen position. These two "value judgements"
seem meaningless or tautological. In our opinion, there is no such
thing as a community with a welfare distinct from that of its members,
and if it is not distinct the first assumption is a tautology. In the second

value judgment, the term "better off" is meaningless if it is metaphysical, and the statement is a tautology if it merely means that more want satisfaction results when a person is in a "chosen position."

From these two dubious assumptions, Little thought he could derive nine optimum conditions of production and exchange (pp. 121–43), two of which follow:

II (b). The marginal rate at which one "good" can be transformed into another must be equal to the "individual's" common marginal rate of substitution of one for the other.

II (c). The rate at which "work" can be transformed into any given "good" must equal the marginal "individual" rate of substitution of "leisure" for consumption of that "good."

These two conditions "require that output should always be adjusted until, if possible, price is equal to marginal cost" (p. 148). This seems a poor method of demonstration. For instance, nothing has been said about the need for a price system, without which prices are obviously impossible, about the advantages of marginal analysis, or about the interpersonal comparability of utility. More important, there seems to be no gain from going through this incomplete and questionable line of deduction instead of directly stating the theory of marginal-cost control itself.

In Little's opinion, his reasoning proves only that prices should equal marginal costs when six of his nine conditions are perfectly achieved (p. 150). Here we have again the perfectionist argument for doing nothing. Sound pricing is invalid because other conditions necessary to complete achievement of Utopia have not been realized.

Little accepted the common but mistaken belief that marginal-cost control would result in continuing deficits which would make heavy taxes necessary. He claimed "that the 'optimum' conditions rule out both direct and indirect taxation" (p. 151), and then contradicted himself by conceding that "the only permissible tax is a poll tax." This last claim is dubious because there are many other taxes—on rent, inheritance, profits, etc.—which do not affect marginal costs. Little asserted that a poll tax cannot be assessed fairly and "would inevitably give rise to such grave injustices that it would be considered intolerable" but offered no evidence to support this view (p. 152).

His book has a thirty-page chapter (XI) on "Output and Price Policy in Public Enterprise," which "is an essay in applied welfare economics." Here the author proposed "to review and discuss some of the contributions to the marginal-cost controversy," namely, those which apply the price theory to public utilities. He devoted nearly all of his space to English critics of such an application, notably to Henderson and Lewis.

The prices charged by public enterprises should be above marginal cost, according to Little, because "price is not equal to marginal cost elsewhere, and . . . there is some marginal taxation" (p. 180). We have answered both of these objections (pp. 111, 145).

His chief contribution to the theory of marginal-cost price-output control was his clear statement that marginal analysis is not applicable to lumpy adjustments. He devoted a separate chapter (X) to "Indivisibilities and Consumers' Surplus," and opened it by asserting that:

The "optimum" conditions of exchange and production . . . apply only to marginal changes. That is sufficiently obvious. . . . Where . . . the amount of a thing bought or produced can only be varied in jumps, i.e. where there are "indivisibilities," there again by definition, the marginal analysis cannot apply. (p. 160)

Unfortunately, Little did not grasp the novelty, the significance, or the practical implications of this vital new point. He did not criticize proponents of marginal-cost control for claiming that their theory solves the problem of lumpy investment. He assumed that marginal adjustments in output must produce large continuing deficits (which in fact result only from lumpy investments in fixed capital). He asserted that marginal costs may be either short or long-run (pp. 154–55), and he failed to point out that decreasing costs are not responsible for deficits under marginal-cost control.

Moreover, Little restated and rejected the only sound theory of ideal investment in fixed capital, namely, "the traditional consumers' surplus criterion" that an investment should be made "if the sum of money represented by the area under the relevant section of the demand curve is greater than the change in total cost" (p. 167). He rejected this sound criterion for three reasons. "One of its chief demerits is that it is the result of a partial analysis only" (p. 168). Another is that "it still requires to be assumed that price is equal to marginal cost elsewhere," and these other prices are not equal to marginal cost and cannot be made so. This is another perfectionist argument for doing nothing. Both points have been discussed (see pp. 4, 59, 140). In developing the second point, Little offered a third criticism of the consumers' surplus criterion, namely, that it ignores loss of profits and/or producers' surplus due to contraction in other lines of production (p. 169). He did not attempt to prove that such losses are significant but merely asserted that they "might" be. Actually, such losses do not represent a real net cost to the economy (see pp. 210–11 below). The fall in prices which causes them is as beneficial to consumers as it is harmful to producers. Moreover, new investments increase the productivity of land and labor and raise rather than lower the total surplus accruing to landowners and workers. Little explained that when new investment increases the output of A and reduces the output of a substitute, B, the loss in consumers' surplus on B represents no real loss since voluntary changes in consumption benefit the consumer. (pp. 169–70). He did not add, however, that a similar argument proves that a loss of producers' surplus on B reflects no real loss.

Little concluded that "the general case against marginal-cost pricing is clearly over-whelming" (p. 189), but he did concede that, when marginal cost is zero or much below average cost, such pricing may be desirable.

A zero marginal cost means that the good in question could not be transformed into anything else. Therefore the complication engendered by the fact that price is not equal to marginal cost elsewhere does not arise. Moreover, when marginal cost is zero, all the other "optimum" conditions . . . do not require to be satisfied. If marginal cost can be zero, one can be fairly sure that some people could be made better off without making anyone worse off, simply by lowering the price. Admittedly there will be some small production changes elsewhere. . . . But, at least, the deduction is very much less shaky than when marginal cost is very small. (p. 189)

This is one of Little's best analyses, but it contains errors. A reduction in tolls on a toll bridge may make many people worse off, for instance the owners of competing ferries and restaurants on other roads, and the changes in their production might be large. Even if these changes were small, the deduction that no one would be worse off is not "less shaky" but wrong.

Although the above analysis applies only when marginal-cost is low or zero, Little apparently also believed that price should equal marginal costs when marginal cost is above average cost, especially when such pricing yields land rent. This position is, of course, inconsistent, for nearly all of his arguments against marginal-cost control apply to such pricing when it yields surpluses (rents). For instance, it changes the real distribution of income and is sound only if six optimum conditions have been met.

Little made other concessions to marginal-cost control theory. He stated that both two-part pricing and price discrimination may be desirable in order to reduce some prices nearer to marginal cost, but he insisted that "socialised undertakings should aim at covering *at least* total costs (with possibly rare exceptions)" (p. 195), and he probably included land rent in total costs. He did not see that there are several applications or corollaries of marginal-cost theory—such as quantity pricing and charging prices for optional services (see pp. 184–93 below) —which involve no deficit. If he had, he might have approved them, for in his discussion of practical pricing problems he wisely "set little weight" on his general arguments against marginal-cost theory (p. 195). What he did set great weight on is the fact that this theory justifies deficits in some industries and thus implies the need for public ownership (p. 154). He expressed no objection to marginal-cost control which results in profits or rents to private owners under Capitalism.

CONCLUSION

This chapter offers further evidence that the majority of non-Marxian, English-speaking Socialist economists have accepted the theory of marginal-cost price-output control as the basis of all prescriptive price-output theory. Durbin was the only such economist who explicitly rejected the new theory in these years, and he had already done this in the earlier period. On the other hand, the majority of Capitalist economists covered here rejected the new theory.

Perhaps the most conclusive evidence of the neglect or rejection of the theory of marginal-cost price-output control by orthodox Capitalist economists is the treatment of the new theory in the authoritative *Survey of Contemporary Economics* (1948). This official American Economic Association review of significant contributions to economic theory during the fifteen years ending in 1948, the very years in which the new theory was first stated, contains no mention of it in the two chapters on value and price.[7] The forty-eight page chapter, "Value and Distribution," was written by B. F. Haley and was criticized by Edward H. Chamberlin and J. M. Clark. The thirty-four page chapter, "Price and Production Policies," was written by Joe S. Bain

[7] We have already criticized the treatment of marginal-cost price-output theory in Bergson's chapter, "Socialist Economics," in this book.

and criticized by Joel P. Dean and Donald H. Wallace.[8] Both chapters
were also presumably criticized by the general editor, Howard S. Ellis,
President of the American Economic Association in 1949. These men
are representative of orthodox Capitalist economic thinking in America. Moreover, none of the reviewers of this book called attention to
the neglect of the new price-output theory in these chapters. In sharp
contrast to these men, we believe that writers on the history of economic doctrines will in time describe the rise of this theory as the
most significant development in economic doctrine during the years
1933 to 1948.

In 1950 there was, so far as we are aware, not a single elementary
textbook on the principles of economics in which the theory of marginal-cost control was stated or referred to in the chapters on value,
price, allocation of the factors, or output. Only one such textbook—
Samuelson's—referred to the theory in its discussion of utility rates,
and then only briefly and slightly in a footnote. There were but
three advanced general textbooks or treatises on Capitalist economics
which stated the new theory, namely, the books by Meade, Lerner,
and Bowen. In contrast again, we predict that within a generation or
two nearly all such textbooks will discuss the theory and that eventually most of them will be largely based upon it, like Lerner's *Economics of Control*.

Before ending our history of the theory of marginal-cost price-output
control, we wish to offer some criticism which applies to all the writers,
Socialist as well as Capitalist, on this new theory. First, few of these
writers have stated any of the nine vital corollaries of the basic principle of marginal-cost price-output control, most of which are readily
applicable under Capitalism without causing a financial loss. This
helps to explain the hostility of Capitalist economists to the theory.
They have mistakenly assumed that it is applicable only or chiefly
under Socialism.

Secondly, most of these writers failed to explain how the theory
could be applied to individual industries or goods, and those who
made stimulating incidental remarks on this subject never attempted
even a brief systematic survey of the practical application of marginal-
cost control theory to individual cases throughout the economy. Thus
the history of the new theory is almost entirely a history of the basic

8 Bain specifically stated that his subject included "the evaluation of [pricing] behavior
and results from the standpoint of total welfare" (p. 132), but he did not mention marginal-cost price-output theory.

general principle that price and/or output is ideal when price equals marginal cost. The corollaries and practical applications implicit in the basic principle have been largely ignored.

In the third place, the discussion of the theory of marginal-cost price-output control has been seriously handicapped by an almost universal failure to distinguish between the problem of ideal price and output with existing fixed capital and the problem of evaluating proposed investments in fixed capital. This failure is probably due to continued acceptance of the traditional illogical distinction between short-run and long-run price determination. The orthodox theory of long-run price determination assumes incorrectly that marginal analysis can be applied to output problems involving heavy investment in fixed capital, that fixed capital costs enter into marginal costs, that there is such a thing as a long-run price and a long-run marginal cost, etc. All of these errors have been carried over into the theory of marginal-cost control because it has usually been stated as a theory of *long-run* price-output control.

In the fourth place, few efforts have been made to define marginal cost, and these efforts have been abortive because of the belief that marginal cost is a long-run quantity. Morover, there are other obvious errors, due chiefly to a lack of care, in all previously given definitions of marginal cost.

Finally, the usual treatment of the effect of marginal-cost control on profits and losses is full of errors. It is argued, without reason, that marginal-cost control would result in large losses in decreasing-cost industries but none in increasing-cost industries and that these losses should be called negative rent. The fact that the application of most of the corollaries of the marginal-cost rule would not cause losses even when combined with ideal investment in fixed capital is ignored. No one has ever suggested that it is ideal investment, not ideal price-output control, which should result in continuing losses.

Certain writers on marginal-cost control have avoided some of these errors, but this usually seems to be accidental. In other words, they have not called attention to the errors they have avoided, and brevity rather than insight seems to be the most common reason for their success in avoiding them.

PART TWO

A RESTATEMENT OF

MARGINAL-COST PRICE-OUTPUT

THEORY

VII

THE PURE THEORY OF
MARGINAL-COST PRICE-OUTPUT CONTROL

As SHOWN in Part One, the theory of marginal-cost price-output control has been stated by a number of writers since 1936, but their statements all have serious defects. Our critical review of the literature should permit a more correct and more complete statement. Part Two will be devoted to an effort to achieve this.

The phrase, "marginal-cost price-output theory," is used in a broad sense in the title of Part Two. It includes not only the statement and demonstration of the basic principle that price or output should be controlled so as to make price equal marginal costs but also the facts about marginal costs that make the theory significant, its relationship to the theory of optimum investment, the application of marginal-cost price output control to certain industries, and the general economic effects of such application.

In this chapter, we shall state the pure theory of marginal-cost price-output control. We use pure to mean the opposite of applied.

THE BASIC PRINCIPLE OF MARGINAL-COST
PRICE-OUTPUT CONTROL

Summary Statement

Briefly stated, the basic principle of marginal-cost price-output control is that *in every plant either the price or the output of each reproducible price good should be directly raised or lowered until price becomes equal to the marginal money costs of production, defined as current costs at the intensive margin of production.*

This new version is superior to the most common earlier version, the rule that price should equal marginal cost, because it states that this result may be achieved either by direct price control or by direct output control. The earlier rule may be interpreted to mean this, but it has often been interpreted to mean that price should always be directly controlled to achieve prices which equal marginal costs. The new version is also superior to the rule that output should be controlled so as to make price equal marginal cost because it implies that it may be better to control price rather than output directly.

It is often assumed that in most plants there is an absolute limit beyond which output cannot be increased. When there are such limits, output cannot always be increased until marginal costs become equal to market price. Another principle is needed to solve the problem of optimum price when output is at the maximum level and a price equal to marginal costs at this output level will not limit sales to output. The correct rule to use in such cases is the same one which should be applied when supplies are inadequate to meet demand, namely, the rule that price should be raised or lowered until sales just equal supply.

It seems very unlikely, however, that such cases occur very often. It is nearly always possible to operate existing equipment at a higher rate by running extra shifts, by improving the fuel or supplies used, by hiring more workers, by employing operatives and repair men who are more capable, by reducing shutdown periods, or simply by taking greater risks as to breakdowns and rapid depreciation. Once equipment is being operated at normal capacity, twenty-four hours a day, all speed-up measures increase marginal costs. Hence, when capacity is inadequate to meet the demand, it is nearly always possible to increase the output of price goods until marginal costs equal the market price. Theaters and toll highways are among the few exceptions to this rule.

Production often results in real social costs and/or benefits which do not affect either the money costs or money income of the producer. In so far as marginal money costs fail to measure these real human costs accurately, they are imperfect. Many ways of increasing this accuracy, chiefly through the use of appropriate taxes and subsidies, are available. The marginal costs to which prices should be equal are subject to indefinite refinement by such means, as well as by improvements in accounting, but the fact that real social marginal costs could be better measured if such improvements were adopted is not an argument against marginal-cost control. It is merely an argument for further improvements of the price system, regardless of whether or not such control is adopted.

Assumptions

The principle of marginal-cost price-output control obviously assumes the use of money and prices. It assumes in addition that workers are free to choose their jobs, that consumers are free to buy what they can afford, and that both workers and consumers will use this freedom to maximize their want-satisfaction. As a result, money costs at the margin are the best available measures of real costs and market prices are the best available measure of real marginal benefit. All of this is implicit if not explicit in most modern non-Marxian welfare theory and therefore deserves no elaboration here. We shall also make other conventional assumptions. We do not accept the view that all assumptions of a theory can or should be stated and justified in a study such as ours. It suffices to state new assumptions and those as to whose meaning or validity there is serious doubt. We are making no new assumptions, and we shall comment on very few of the customary ones.

The principle of marginal-cost price-output control is valid only when output reacts properly to price changes, and vice versa. Properly does not mean perfectly here, but only a rough or reasonably satisfactory approach to perfection. A perfect reaction is impossible, but the closer the approximation on the average, the more beneficial is marginal-cost control.

The assumption that output will react properly to price changes means that if the prices charged by private firms are lowered by the state these firms will try to increase their output until demand is satisfied. This is reasonable, even when the prescribed price results in a deficit, if the additional output will reduce the deficit. Moreover, proper control of output could be made a prerequisite for payment of the subsidies needed to offset such deficits.

All prescriptive price and output theories assume the interpersonal comparability of utility and disutility. The denial of the validity of this assumption is nihilistic. It frustrates all efforts to justify existing price and output practices as well as all efforts to develop better practices. In this treatise we are primarily interested in proving that marginal-cost control is better than average-cost control, which also assumes the interpersonal comparability of utility. We shall, however, comment briefly upon the chief argument against this assumption, namely that individuals differ widely in tastes and strength of desire and that equal price and wage offers by different persons therefore cannot be assumed to represent equal utility or disutility, even if income is equal.

Consumers undoubtedly do differ in their desire for individual goods. It is possible that some consumers feel a stronger average intensity of desire for economic goods. If this were so and if we could measure this average intensity of desire, a division of income based upon it would maximize the utility of a *given stock* of goods. But in fact we have no means of demonstrating or measuring personal differences in average intensity of wants. To reason or act rationally in economics, we must make some assumption concerning such personal differences. If these differences exist and are indeterminable, the only reasonable assumption is that each person has the same average intensity of wants. This is a closer approximation to the truth than any other assumption. We know from numerous inductive studies of measurable personal traits that they usually follow the so-called normal distribution curve.[1] This means that most persons are near the average, and that the number of persons above and below the average is about the same. Hence, the assumption that they are actually at the average does not ordinarily result in large absolute errors and gives more accurate results than any alternative assumption.

It is sometimes stated that the fact that a 100 percent increase in real income does not increase welfare by 100 percent proves that welfare cannot be measured, and that if it cannot be measured the welfare experienced by two different persons cannot be compared. But in marginal analysis it is not necessary to compare the total welfare of one person with the total welfare of another. It is only necessary to compare small marginal gains or costs to some persons with similar gains or costs to others.

All prescriptive price and output theory assumes either, (1) that on the average the effect of the approved policies on income distribution does not reduce welfare more than the effect on output increases it, or (2) that if this is not true the undesirable effects on income distribu-

[1] R. S. Woodworth, *Psychology*, 4th ed. (New York, 1940), pp. 61–64.

tion can be avoided or offset by direct control of the distribution of income, for instance by personal subsidies or taxes. We believe that both
assumptions are valid.

The argument that marginal-cost price-output control would worsen
the distribution of income is used chiefly by economists who deny the
possibility of determining an ideal distribution of income and therefore have no way of detecting a worsening in this distribution. If it
is possible to determine an ideal distribution of income, it is always
possible to achieve and maintain it by suitable taxes and subsidies
without controlling or forbidding control of individual prices and
outputs (see Chapter IX below). And it is highly desirable to distinguish between and handle separately the problems of ideal price and
output and the problem of an ideal distribution of income.

An ideal system of income distribution would probably involve notable inequality of income under present conditions. The mere fact
that income is unequal does not prove that prices fail to measure
utility and therefore cannot be used as a basis for interpersonal comparison of utility. Desirable differences in income serve to weight the
wants of individuals in a socially beneficial way. They reward those
who make personal efforts to increase their output and also benefit all
consumers by increasing consumers' surplus. Too many economists
who see the need for differences in income to stimulate production refuse to concede that the effects of such income differentials upon price
offers are equally desirable. Social utility is personal utility weighted
by an optimum personal income. The fact that prices reflect this social
utility rather than personal utility is one of their great merits.

Finally, we assume that an ideal program of simplification and
standardization of goods has been carried out or will be carried out
independently of our program of ideal price-output control. If the
continued production of a good is condemned by a sound theory of
ideal simplification, it should not be produced, regardless of the relationship of its price to marginal cost. We have stated a theory of ideal
simplification elsewhere.[2]

Definitions of Terms

REPRODUCIBLE PRICE GOODS. Marginal-cost price-output control is
obviously inapplicable to goods like land and old paintings which

[2] Beckwith, *The Economic Theory of a Socialist Economy* (Palo Alto, Calif., 1949),
pp. 162–65.

cannot be reproduced and therefore have no marginal costs. Such goods should be sold at a price which balances supply and demand.

Price goods are those which are sold for a price, and include all articles and services produced by private firms under Capitalism. There is a trend towards increasing the free state provision of economic goods under Capitalism, however, and under Socialism the state might produce and distribute without charge over half of the total output of economic goods. Hence, the restriction of marginal-cost control to price goods is important, and will become steadily more so.

MARGINAL COST. It is a remarkable fact that there is no reference to a definition of marginal cost in the fifteen-page analytical table of contents or in the fourteen-page index of the last (1920) edition of Marshall's *Principles of Economics*. In fact, if he defined the term in this book, we have not found his definition. However, his usage of the term suggests that at times (in long-period analysis) he meant the increment in total money costs, including the costs of land and fixed capital, resulting from the production of the marginal unit on the extensive margin and that at other times (in very short-period analysis) he meant the increment in total variable costs due to marginal output at the intensive margin. Marshall's successors have also neglected the problem of defining marginal cost precisely, and have generally followed him in using it to mean the increment in total cost.

While the great majority of orthodox economists since Marshall have defined or used marginal cost as the increment in total cost due to the production of the marginal unit, which is consistent with Marshall's usage, a few of the more advanced have defined or used it to mean cost at the margin, the value of the additional factors used to produce the marginal unit. Members of both groups have distinguished between long-run and short-run marginal cost. As a result, writers on marginal-cost price-output control have used marginal cost in at least four senses: (1) the increment in variable costs and rents, (2) the increment in total costs and rents in the long run, (3) variable cost and rent at the intensive margin, and (4) total cost and rent at the extensive margin in the long run.

The first two definitions of marginal cost have been developed and used by those interested in business problems. The businessman must cover all of his costs, and he can maximize his profit by balancing increment in income (marginal revenue), against increment in variable costs, assuming no new investment. The use of the concept of the increment in total costs, including fixed costs, is based upon a failure to realize that marginal analysis is not suited to the control of fixed costs. But the definition of marginal cost as increment in variable cost is well suited to the needs of businessmen trying to maximize their profits and of economists who wish to explain how profits can be maximized. However, it is not suited to the problem of explaining how welfare should be maximized, which includes the problem of ideal price-output control.

To maximize welfare, it is necessary to balance money cost at the margin against market price because these are the best available measures of marginal social real cost and marginal social real gain. This point will be elaborated later (pp. 194–97). Hence, for marginal analysis of the problem of ideal price and output, marginal cost must be defined as money cost at the margin, the value of the additional factors required to produce a marginal unit of output.

But cost at the margin has ordinarily been defined so as to include fixed cost. Our next task therefore is to explain why this is a serious error. In our introduction we explained the difference between marginal and total analysis. The problem of determining ideal price or output is one which can be solved only by marginal analysis. This means that we must define marginal cost so as to make it suitable for marginal analysis. Such analysis can handle only variable quantities which are affected by every marginal change in output. Therefore, marginal cost should include only *continuously* variable costs. It should exclude all fixed costs. Since the latter are increased only by output at the extensive margin, we can exclude them by measuring marginal cost at the *intensive margin,* i.e., where output is increased without any expansion in fixed plant.

Those who believe that fixed costs should be included in marginal cost often claim that nearly all fixed costs eventually become variable costs. In reply, we must emphasize that fixed costs become only *temporarily,* i.e., discontinuously, variable and that marginal analysis can deal only with *continuously* variable costs. In accordance with common usage, we shall use *variable cost* hereafter to mean *continuously variable cost,* and fixed cost to mean both permanently and temporarily fixed cost.

Moreover, if fixed costs did enter marginal cost when they are temporarily variable, they would enter the marginal cost of a single marginal unit. Up to the last minute before a new plant is used, marginal cost is cost at the margin with the pre-existing plant. After the new plant has been put in use, its cost is fixed and cannot enter variable cost. Thus, long-run marginal cost based upon the assumption that fixed costs enter marginal cost when temporarily variable would be highly discontinuous and/or very uneven. Hence, the smooth long-run marginal-cost curves so often seen in books on imperfect and/or monopolistic competition cannot be based upon this assumption. They imply that fixed costs are continuously variable, which is clearly not true.

To this reasoning some may reply that smooth long-run average and marginal-cost curves are possible and valid because lumpy fixed costs can be scientifically allocated to all individual units of output. We do not believe this is possible. The allocation of fixed costs is quite arbitrary. Neither accountants nor economists have ever been able to agree upon a unique method of allocating lumpy costs. This is inevitable because by definition such costs are not continuously increased as output grows. Hence, an allocation which makes them appear to increase continuously must be arbitrary as well as misleading.

Since fixed cost should never be included in marginal cost, we define the latter as the money cost of producing a single marginal unit with existing fixed capital. It is cost at the intensive rather than the extensive margin of output and therefore never includes land rent, quasi rent, or any other surpluses unless they have been converted into variable costs by contract.

Every producer has an intensive margin, and is or should be producing a marginal unit at or near this margin. It is an error to distinguish between marginal producers and others for all are or should be marginal producers. We may speak of marginal production, but not of marginal producers.

We have now explained why for our purpose, the study of the problem of ideal price-output determination, marginal cost should be defined as cost at the margin rather than as an increment in cost and so as to include only continuously variable costs. One further point, one which is much less important and much more debatable, must be made. We are convinced that for our purpose marginal cost should be defined so as to exclude optional costs.

Optional costs are variable rather than fixed, but they do not vary with output. For instance, it is always possible to increase output without more advertising, and the additional output can always be sold by reducing prices. Hence, advertising is not a necessary marginal cost. The same argument applies to other optional variable costs, such as optional selling costs, gifts to charity, gifts to employees, research costs, etc.

Of course, if contracts making these costs compulsory and variable have been signed, they are no longer optional and do enter into marginal cost. There are other marginal money costs by agreement— royalty payments, rental payments based on volume of sales, etc.— which do not represent marginal real costs. Our definition of marginal cost does not make it a perfect measure of marginal real cost to society. To achieve marginal money costs which measure marginal real costs as well as is possible, the state would have to prohibit the signing of contracts which turn rent surpluses and fixed and optional costs into compulsory variable costs. Moreover, there are many other reforms which would help to make marginal cost, as we have defined it, measure the real social cost at the intensive margin more accurately. We have deliberately excluded this interesting and important problem from the scope of this study, but any such reform would help marginal-cost price-output control to achieve better results.

It should perhaps be noted that our definition of marginal cost is not a *short-period* marginal cost in Marshall's sense. It is often possible to install new tools and equipment in a very short period of time, so that his short-period marginal cost may include some fixed costs while our marginal cost cannot. Moreover, when large surplus capacity exists—a common situation—it is possible to increase output greatly in a short period without incurring any non-marginal costs. The cost of a small short-period increase in output may include fixed costs and the cost of a large increase in output may not. Thus our marginal cost may be either short or long-period cost, or neither.

On the other hand, marginal costs are short-run prices in the sense that they are costs at a given moment, just as market price is always the price at a given moment. No average of costs over a short or long period is a marginal cost. It may be desirable at times to assume that marginal cost equals average marginal cost over a short period, but this is purely a laborsaving step in estimating marginal cost. It does not mean that marginal cost is an average marginal cost.

All marginal analysis is short-run analysis in this sense, but not in Marshall's sense. Hence, all price-output analysis, descriptive as well as prescriptive, should be short-run analysis. The traditional distinction between short-run and long-run price theory is wholly unjustified. It results from a failure to grasp the vital distinction between marginal analysis and total analysis. Marginal analysis cannot deal with fixed costs either in the short or long period.

The effort to create a theory of long-run price determination has resulted not only in the use of the self-contradictory concept of long-run marginal cost but also in the common use of other long-run concepts—long-run price, long-run demand, long-run supply—which have no place in either descriptive or prescriptive price-output theory. All prices and outputs are short-run, and are, or ought to be determined by short-run demand and supply. The fact that a price remains stable over a long period does not make it a long-run price. It is merely a short-run price which is constantly reset at the same level, usually with harmful results. An ideal price would fluctuate so as to balance price and marginal cost in the short run. And an average of different short-run prices is not a single long-run price.

A long-run demand curve shows how much of a good would be sold at different prices if price were stable throughout the period in question. Such price stability is unusual and is always harmful because it makes sales independent of cost fluctuations. A long-run supply curve is based upon the assumption that factor prices remain unchanged, which is rarely true and always harmful when true. It does not show the rate of output at any given time but total output over a long period at various stable prices.

The only way any influence can affect actual market price or output is by changing the short-run demand or supply schedule. There are influences which affect prices continuously over a period of time, and might therefore be called long-run influences, but they do so only by changing short-run demand or supply. Hence, it is idle to study their effect upon long-run demand and supply curves, which have no direct part in price-output determination. Moreover, these long-run curves are not suited to analyzing investment in fixed capital because the latter is not subject to marginal analysis. Hence, long-run supply and demand curves are entirely useless.

One way to make clear the fallacy of long-run price-output analysis is to examine its application to a very long run, a period of a hundred years. Long-run demand and supply schedules and curves for such a period can be estimated though they will obviously be extremely crude estimates. But the price determined by the intersection of these curves is not the price which will, or ought to, exist at any given moment. Nor, on the other hand, is it the average of all prices which will exist during that period. It is literally an arbitrary figure which has no relationship to actual or ideal prices in a dynamic world.

If we gradually reduce the length of the period covered by such long-run analysis, we find that there is no point at which the above conclusions become false. The demand and supply curves may become more accurate, but the result is always an arbitrary price which has no fixed relationship either to the actual or to the ideal price at any given moment.

A number of cost studies have shown that, when production is below capacity, marginal cost is almost stable over a considerable range of output and then rises rapidly when capacity is exceeded. This is not the shape of the short-run cost and supply curves usually shown in textbooks. The gradually rising or falling short-run cost' or supply curves commonly shown are usually long-run curves which rise or fall because they include steadily rising or falling allocations of fixed cost. In other words, long-run analysis has so dominated the price theory of most economists that they even draw their short-run cost and supply curves as if they were long-run curves.

We have said that there are two useful meanings of marginal cost, increment in variable cost and cost at the intensive margin. It is very confusing to call both concepts marginal cost. We believe that increment in variable cost should be renamed.

A few writers have used the term *incremental cost* instead of marginal cost without explaining their reasons. We have rejected this term as a name for cost at the intensive margin because it suggests an increment in cost. For this reason, it might well be used as the sole name for increment in variable cost. It is not a natural verbal correlative for the term *marginal revenue,* but the latter might be replaced by *incremental revenue.*

The relationship of marginal cost, as defined above, to opportunity cost deserves comment. There are at least two different meanings of opportunity cost: (1) the maximum value which could have been created by the best alternative use of the marginal factors, and (2) the highest unaccepted price offer for the marginal unit of output. In the former sense, only reproducible goods have an opportunity cost, and it is about equal to marginal money cost. In the latter sense, both reproducible and non-reproducible goods have opportunity costs, and for reproducible goods these costs should be almost equal to marginal money cost.

The last fact may suggest that the theory of marginal-cost price-output control could be applied to non-reproducible as well as to reproducible goods by treating opportunity cost Number 2 as a marginal cost or by including opportunity cost as well as marginal cost in the basic principle of price-output control. We do not believe that anything would be gained by this. The rule that price should balance sales and output is more basic than the rule that price should equal marginal cost and its application alone would make all prices equal opportunity costs in sense Number 2. The rule of marginal-cost price-output control is required as a supplementary rule only because in the case of reproducible goods it is also desirable to control output so that marginal cost will equal the price which balances sales and output.

MAJOR COROLLARIES OF THE BASIC PRINCIPLE OF MARGINAL-COST PRICE-OUTPUT CONTROL

The general principle of marginal-cost price-output control has nine very significant corollaries: (1) prices should be equal for all customers; (2) separate prices should be charged for all optional services; (3) two or more prices should be used to cover the marginal costs of a good having semifixed marginal costs; (4) different prices should be charged for the first and subsequent units of a good sold in one sale; (5) most prices should vary with marginal costs in regular seasonal, weekly, and/or daily price cycles; (6) price stabilization is uneconomic; (7) the sum of the prices of joint products should equal the marginal costs of the joint products; (8) whenever feasible, wages should equal the marginal productivity of labor; and (9) price taxes should equal marginal costs.

These corollaries have been almost completely ignored by writers on marginal-cost price-output control. The following discussion of them is, therefore, one of the two chief contributions of this book, the other being the distinction between the theories of optimum price-output control and optimum investment in fixed capital.

Each of these corollaries is independent of the others in the sense that it can be individually and directly applied, regardless of whether any of the others have been applied. In most cases no deficit will result from their application. Hence, the most influential argument against marginal-cost control, namely that it causes losses, usually does not apply to them.

These corollaries are economic rules which can only be derived from the principle of marginal-cost price-output control. Hence, a rejection of this principle is a rejection of all of them.

The above list of major corollaries is probably incomplete. It has grown in the author's mind up to the last minute. We expect that other students will perceive other corollaries. But the above list is long enough to show that a large part of prescriptive economic theory can be derived from our basic price-output principle. Price theory is the heart of economic theory.

Equal Prices for All Customers

The principle of marginal-cost price-output control clearly implies that the price of any reproducible price good should be the same to all like customers. This does not mean that customers who are located in different places, or those who buy different quantities, or those who receive different optional services should pay the same price. It does mean that customers who buy the same quantities at the same time and place and receive identical services should pay the same prices because the marginal costs would be the same. Price differences would not represent differences in marginal costs and would therefore conflict with the principle of marginal-cost control. Any form of price discrimination based upon ability to pay is a denial of this corollary.

It follows that children should pay the same price as adults for all goods, including amusement and transportation. Moreover, price discounts to clergymen, soldiers, public officials, needy persons, employees, etc., are all uneconomic. This does not mean that the resulting prices are now too low, for they are usually well above marginal costs, but that the prices paid by all persons should be reduced to the marginal-cost level. In this way, discrimination between persons would be eliminated without raising the prices now paid by favored customers. If the discounts are economically justifiable when enjoyed only by a few, they are much more beneficial when extended to all and increased until prices equal marginal costs. The proper way to help underpaid or needy persons is to raise their income, not to give them price reductions on certain goods.

While price discrimination is never an ideal policy, it may be less of an evil than uniform prices based on average costs. This point is discussed later (pp. 224–25).

Separate Prices for Optional Services

The principle that the costs of optional services—credit, delivery, approval, installation, alteration, etc.—should be covered by separate prices has rarely if ever been stated by economists, partly because of their general aversion to prescriptive economic theory and partly because of their general failure to accept and apply marginal-cost theory. It is a sound principle because the consumer cannot judge whether optional services are worth their cost unless he knows what this cost is and has to pay it. Optional services are separate price goods. They are separate because they are optional, and they are price goods because they ought not to be provided free of charge. Moreover, all buyers not receiving special service pay a price above marginal cost and those receiving special service pay a price below marginal costs if other steps necessary to make prices equal to marginal costs have been taken. Hence, the rule that separate prices should be used to cover the marginal costs of optional services is a corollary of the marginal-cost price-output theory. A violation of the former is consequently also a violation of the latter.

Charging prices for optional services is perfectly feasible under Capitalism as well as under Socialism. It is an important step towards marginal-cost control which need not result in financial loss. Since violation of this corollary may give a competitive advantage under Capitalism, the state should prohibit such violations.

Perhaps the most important application of the rule of charging separate prices for optional services is the rule that freight charges should always be paid by the customer. The basing-point system of prices, which requires all buyers in a given area to pay the same delivered price is uneconomic. It distorts all individual prices by using an average instead of a marginal delivery cost. It prevents the customer from balancing real marginal cost against marginal utility, and induces him to buy more freight service than he would otherwise buy. Since the real economy of locating his plant near his source of supply does not reduce his costs, he fails to locate his plant properly, and, if nearby sources of supply develop later, he has insufficient inducement to buy from them. The net result for the economy as a whole is that much more freight must be hauled in order to produce a given quantity of goods.

Instead of charging separate prices for special services, some firms have long granted special discounts to customers who do not require individual services. The cash discount for prompt payment of a bill is an example. But those who do not pay their bills promptly are really borrowing money from the seller, in addition to buying his goods, and should pay separately for this optional service. Moreover, a cash discount is usually uniform, while customers should pay an interest charge based on the length and risk of the loan. The best solution would be to require all buyers to pay cash and borrow, if necessary, from banks which specialize in estimating risks and charge interest rates which vary with the risk and the period of the loan.

The corollary of separate prices for optional services also rules out free premiums, gifts, and prizes. All such sales promotion aids prevent the prices of individual goods from equaling their marginal cost and are therefore uneconomic. If sales premiums are a price discount instead of a special service, they are barred by the first corollary, for they rarely go to all buyers, and even if they do, they are not of equal value to all of them.

Multi-Marginal Pricing

Certain economic services have two types of marginal costs, semifixed marginal costs and variable marginal costs. Semifixed marginal costs are those which *must* be incurred to serve a customer but which do not vary with the quantity of service rendered him, while variable marginal costs are those which vary with the amount of service rendered. Whenever significant semifixed marginal costs are involved, they should be covered by a separate price independent of the amount of use, and variable marginal costs should be covered by a price per unit of service which varies with these costs. This would not reduce, indeed it would increase, income, and is therefore feasible under Capitalism.

To illustrate the corollary of multi-marginal pricing, we take the case of bank loans. A bank loan involves certain initial marginal costs —investigation, bookkeeping, etc.—which do not vary with the length of the loan, but it involves other costs which vary closely with the length of the loan. These two distinct classes of marginal costs should be covered by separate prices which allocate these costs to the borrowers as accurately as is economical. If this is not done, the borrower will be unable to balance his marginal gain against marginal cost. Whenever significant semifixed marginal costs are involved, they should be covered by a separate service charge so that both buyer and seller can balance marginal cost against marginal benefit more accurately. Since these service charges are essential to ideal pricing, we shall call them "ideal service charges."

Quantity Pricing

We have coined the term *quantity pricing* as a short descriptive name for a fourth corollary of the marginal-cost price-output principle. It too is applicable under Capitalism because it creates no deficit. Quantity pricing means charging a lower price for the second and subsequent units of a commodity sold to one customer at one time. It is quite distinct from price discrimination because under quantity pricing all customers are free to benefit from the lower prices.

The rule that different prices should be charged for the first and subsequent uniform units sold in one sale is a corollary of the principle of marginal-cost price-output control because it states one condition essential to the achievement of prices equal to marginal costs. The marginal cost of selling the second or later unit is much less than the marginal cost of selling the first unit. If the price of the second unit is the same as that of the first unit, one price is not equal to marginal cost.

Price differences between the second and subsequent units sold in one sale would probably cause more trouble than they are worth since the marginal cost differences are negligible for these units. Hence, the theory of quantity pricing does not justify a difference between the prices of the second and later units.

Businessmen have long used quantity discounts to reduce prices on large sales, but such discounts fail to reflect the major drop in costs, that between the first and second units sold at one time, and they often permit a discount based upon the quantity sold over a period of time instead of upon that sold at one sale. Quantity discounts have been used primarily to increase sales rather than to secure a nice balance between marginal cost and price and have been used chiefly by producers and middlemen. In the absence of marginal-cost control, quantity discounts are beneficial since they reduce some prices closer to marginal costs, but they are a lesser evil rather than a sound pricing method. Quantity discounts are particularly unsuitable in the case of retail sales, for retail customers usually buy only a few units of each good, yet it is precisely in retail sales that there is the greatest difference between the cost of selling the first and last unit of the same article in the same sale. Even in wholesale trade, quantity pricing is preferable because it makes it easier for the buyer to determine the net price, i.e., the marginal increment in the total cost, of each additional unit he buys.

There is a close relationship between quantity pricing and multi-marginal pricing. Some of the costs of selling the first unit of an article are semifixed marginal costs, which need not be incurred again when a second unit of the same article is sold in the same sale. Both quantity pricing and multi-marginal pricing reduce the price of the marginal unit without reducing the price of the first unit. Since the corollary of multi-marginal pricing is more general than the corollary of quantity pricing, the latter may be a corollary of the former.

Cyclical Pricing

We have coined the descriptive name *cyclical pricing* to designate the fifth corollary of marginal-cost price-output theory, the corollary that prices should vary directly and proportionately with marginal costs during all regular, and therefore predictable, cycles in marginal costs. The most important regular marginal-cost cycles are seasonal or annual cycles, weekly cycles, and daily cycles. Business cycles also belong in this group if they are considered regular. Economists ordinarily use "cyclical" to describe fluctuations which are a part of the business cycle and do not use it to describe seasonal, monthly, or daily fluctuations, even when these are very regular. Actually, the term *cycle* implies regularity, which is far more characteristic of seasonal, monthly, and daily fluctuations than of the so-called business cycle. The term *business cycle* seems completely inappropriate to those who, like the writer, deny that such fluctuations are predictable.

The idea that prices should vary during each season is not new, but the idea that these variations should be such as to keep prices equal to marginal costs is new and significant. Moreover, many industries —for instance, the automobile industry—which experience significant seasonal cycles in marginal costs do not practice, even to a small degree, cyclical pricing.

Weekly price cycles are customary in a few industries. For instance, movie theaters have long charged higher prices on Saturday and Sunday than on weekdays, but the idea that prices should always equal marginal costs is new, and many industries which ought to vary their prices during the week, notably food stores, have never done so or have even made perverse price changes in order to attract a larger share of business during periods of peak demand.

Regular daily price cycles have been used by theaters, but most firms which ought to use them, notably retail stores, have never done so. It has been argued that one of the chief obstacles to marginal-cost control is the frequency of large erratic changes in marginal costs, but changes in marginal costs due to daily cost or demand cycles are highly predictable. And price changes are not undesirable merely because they are frequent. There has been no serious criticism by economists of the regular changes in prices during the day made by movie theaters.

The great benefit which may be achieved through general use of all types of cyclical pricing is fuller use of existing physical facilities. When the physical facilities of an industry are not fully used during certain periods of the year, week, or day, marginal costs are temporarily low. If prices were reduced to marginal costs at such times, off-peak use of these facilities would increase greatly, and the height of the peaks would be sharply reduced, which in turn would postpone the need for new construction and thus reduce sharply the amount of physical capital required to do a given volume of business.

It is worth noting that the limited and imperfect cyclical pricing now practiced finds no justification or explanation in orthodox value and price theory. Indeed, like price discrimination, it conflicts with this theory. Neo-classical value theorists taught that prices tend to equal the sum of average long-run costs and rent, the average during all periods of each regular cost cycle, not the average during certain periods of the year, week, or day. The literature on monopolistic and/or imperfect competition contains, so far as this critic is aware, no discussion of cyclical pricing, which cannot be explained by the use of long-run marginal-revenue and marginal-cost curves. Only the theory of marginal-cost price-output control can explain the need for cyclical pricing and prescribe the degree to which it should be carried, and thus integrate it into general price theory. The theory of joint costs is inapplicable because goods produced with the same plant at different times are not joint products.

Price Stabilization Is Uneconomic

Individual prices should equal marginal cost. Marginal cost changes frequently, not only in regular cycles but also in an irregular manner due to unexpected changes in individual costs at the margin. Therefore, prices should change frequently, not only as prescribed by the corollary of cyclical pricing but also in order to respond to unpredictable changes in marginal cost. In other words, it is uneconomic to stabilize *individual prices,* to prevent irregular price changes based upon cost changes. This is entirely different from saying that stabilization of the *price level* is uneconomic. In fact we believe that the price level should be stabilized, but that individual prices should not.

If there were no costs involved in changing them, prices should change almost constantly. Since there are price-revision costs (both to the consumer and to the producer) and price-stability costs, these must be measured and balanced against each other. We cannot determine here the point at which these costs balance each other for each good or for the average good, but we are confident that most prices should change at least once a month and that some should change every week. These price changes should be additional to any cyclical price changes.

If all individual prices ought to change frequently, all agreements, contracts, and government regulations which prevent such price changes are harmful. They may benefit individual businessmen by helping them to predict future costs, but they do this by preventing price changes which are socially beneficial. Private gain often conflicts with public gain.

Strictly speaking, the above reasoning applies only to the selling prices of reproducible goods, but the same conclusion applies for other reasons to rent and interest. These costs should always reflect current market conditions. In an ideal society, therefore, long-term contracts for predetermined rent and interest payments would also be prohibited.

The Pricing of Joint Products

Joint products are products necessarily produced together, like cotton fiber and cotton seed, and therefore have common fixed and marginal costs. Products having common fixed costs only are not joint products.

The principle of marginal-cost price-output control implies that the combined price of two or more joint products should equal the marginal cost of producing these joint products, regardless of whether this is above or below so-called average cost. The way in which marginal costs are allocated to the individual joint product should be determined by relative demand. The most practical way to do this is to sell joint products at whatever price they will bring and then increase or decrease their output until the sum of their prices equals marginal cost. If it is possible to vary the proportions between the quantities of joint products produced together, producers should vary these proportions in any way that will yield a profit or decrease a loss and then alter the output of the joint products until any resulting marginal profit or loss has been eliminated.

Marginal Productivity Wage Determination

The eighth corollary is that the wage paid for the marginal unit of work or output should equal the value added to production by that unit of work whenever it is economical to measure and pay separately for marginal units of work or output by individual workers. We shall call this the corollary of marginal-productivity wage determination.

Orthodox economists long taught that wages tend to equal the marginal productivity of labor. This theory was unsound for several reasons. In the first place, it assumed a close approach to perfect competition. In the second place, it assumed universal use of piece rates, for wages can equal the value of the marginal unit of work only when it is possible to measure this unit of work and its output. Wages based upon the amount of time at work can equal *average* productivity but not *marginal* productivity. In the third place, existing piece rates have always been far below the value added to the marginal piece.

The most obvious application of the corollary of marginal productivity wage determination is to piece rates. This application would require a drastic change in present methods of fixing piece rates. In accordance with orthodox piece-rate theory, piece rates are now deliberately fixed so that the worker receives far less than (usually only half of) the value which his labor adds to the raw materials incorporated in the marginal product. The excuse for this method of fixing piece rates is that the employer who introduces piece rates deserves a large share of the gain from the increased output which they stimulate. But the cost to the employer of introducing a piece-rate system is a onetime fixed cost, not a continuing marginal cost. And piece rates now yield the employer a gain much larger than that required to cover the cost of introducing them. If prices are to equal marginal costs, piece rates must be revised so that the rate for the marginal piece is equal to the full value added to this piece, less only the other marginal costs involved. There should be no pure profit to the employer for producing the marginal piece.

Piece rates permit a more accurate determination of marginal costs than do time rates because they make it possible to determine separately the wage cost of the marginal piece. With time rates it is always necessary to average wage costs over a number of units. It follows that if marginal-cost price-output control is desirable, the system of wage payment which alone permits the determination of the precise labor cost of the marginal unit of output has a unique advantage. This is an important new argument in favor of piece rates.

The sudden adoption of sound piece rates might raise the average daily earnings of piece-rate workers by over 100 percent, but they should not be paid wages so high that the demand for piece-rate jobs is larger than the supply of them. To permit control of the daily earnings of piece-rate workers, a rent should be charged for the use of each piece-rate work place. These rents should be raised and lowered so as to keep demand and supply in balance for each kind of piece-rate work place in each plant. Thus, it would always be possible to make piece-rate plants profitable by restricting investment in new piece-rate work places, for this would in time raise work-place rents enough to assure a profit. Since the work-place rents discussed here are essential to ideal pricing, we shall call them "ideal work-place rents."

Price Taxes Should Equal Marginal Costs

Certain taxes should perform the same function as ideal prices; they should limit voluntary consumption to the optimum degree by compelling the consumer to pay a price which measures the full marginal real cost of marginal consumption. Gasoline taxes which make motorists pay the marginal costs of highway use are price taxes. Since price taxes perform the same functions as the prices of reproducible goods, they are subject to the theory of marginal-cost control. Price taxes should equal marginal costs.

It may be argued that the problem of how high price taxes should be is a problem in the correction of money costs rather than a problem

of ideal pricing. This is not an important difference of opinion, however, since either approach leads to the conclusion that price taxes
should equal marginal costs. We believe it is useful to stress the analogy between prices and price taxes since this may help to make clear
both the nature of these taxes and the proper method of determining
them.

DEMONSTRATION OF THE BENEFITS OF MARGINAL-
COST PRICE-OUTPUT CONTROL

In our introduction we noted that the theory of marginal-cost output control is an obvious implication of marginal analysis. This theory
says that price, the best available measure of the social gain from marginal output, should equal marginal cost, the best available measure
of the social real cost of marginal output. The basic reason is merely
that real benefit should be equal to real cost at the margin because
this maximizes welfare. Any attempt to elaborate this argument must
suffer from the difficulties and faults common to all efforts to elaborate
the obvious.

There are two ways of elaborating this brief statement of the obvious positive case for marginal-cost price-output control. First, we
could attempt to state and demonstrate all the assumptions and supporting doctrines—concerning the purpose of economics, the advantages of a price system, etc.—upon which the theory of marginal-
cost control rests. This would require a treatise covering most of the
fields treated in books on the principles of economics. We do not in-
tend to undertake this task here.[3] Secondly, we could assume a large
area of common ground—such as recognition of the need to satisfy
human wants and of the usefulness of money, markets, and prices in
measuring and comparing utility to different persons—and attempt
merely to demonstrate that marginal-cost control is superior to the
major alternatives based upon the same assumptions, especially to so-
called average-cost pricing, as a theory of optimum price and output.
This is the kind of demonstration we shall give.

When the prices of all reproducible price goods balance supply
and demand and equal marginal cost and when the factor prices are

---

[3] We have offered such a demonstration in the *Economic Theory of a Socialist Economy*, pp. 25–324.

properly determined, the marginal value productivity of each variable agent is the same in all uses in plants producing price goods. On the other hand, if some prices are above marginal costs, and others not, there must be one or more agents whose marginal productivity is higher in the plants producing goods with prices above marginal costs than in other plants, and a transfer of some of these agents to the former plants would increase productivity. This transfer should proceed until the marginal productivity of each variable agent is the same in all uses. The resulting achievement of optimum productivity would raise the sum of rent, interest, and wages without requiring more thrift or work. It would increase the real national income produced by a given supply of the factors.

Orthodox economists have long taught that under perfect competition, the allocation of the agents of production is such as to make their marginal productivity equal in all uses, and most have unjustifiably assumed that enough competition and factor mobility exist in the real world to make this principle a fair description of what happens in it, without realizing that, *if this were true, prices in the real world would approximate marginal rather than so-called average costs.* The marginal productivity of a productive agent in different uses cannot be the same if some prices are above marginal costs. Yet none of the critics of marginal-cost control have explicitly rejected the theory that the marginal productivity of the factors should be the same in all uses.

The positive case for marginal-cost price-output control can also be presented in a different way. Marginal costs are the best available measure of the additional real cost of producing the marginal unit. Market prices which balance supply and demand are the best available measures of the real benefit of this unit to consumers. Hence, when price is above marginal cost, the production of one more unit creates net welfare. The function of economic theory and policy is to maximize net welfare. Therefore, the output of each price good should be raised or lowered until marginal cost is equal to a price which balances supply and demand.

If the rise in output is achieved by the use of newly created factors in production, there will be no simultaneous contraction of output in other industries, so that there will be no basis for claiming that such contractions of output reduce the net welfare created by the production of other goods. If the rise in output is made possible by a shift of existing factors from other industries, this shift could not reduce welfare because the factors would be shifted from marginal uses in which they yield no significant net benefit to marginal uses in which they would yield such benefits. As we have already shown, these factor shifts would increase the productivity of the factors shifted.

Both of the above proofs of the benefit of marginal-cost price-output control make use of partial rather than general optimum analysis, and may be criticized for this reason. The simultaneous general application of the conclusion, based upon this partial analysis, that prices should be reduced in all cases where they are above marginal costs would cause some prices which should be raised to be temporarily lowered, since the initial price adjustment would be based upon current rather than eventual marginal costs. If general optimum analysis were possible, it could avoid such mistakes. *But the vital fact is that general optimum analysis is never able to tell how all, or any, prices should be fixed in the real world.* It may do this for relatively simple assumed cases but not for the real world. On the other hand, the type of partial optimum analysis applied above may be easily and quickly used by any manager to determine how to take those steps which, if taken by other managers also, would eventually bring all prices as close as is desirable to their optimum level. This would involve initial adjustments which would have to be corrected, but continuing price adjustments are not a new or impractical procedure. *A general optimum can be approached or achieved only by means of many partial adjustments, and the only useful guide to such adjustments is partial optimum analysis.* The formal elegance of general optimum analysis has so dazzled some economists that they have failed to realize that its role is a very minor one compared to that of partial optimum analysis.

Thus far in this section we have confined ourselves to stating and defending the positive case for marginal-cost control and have ignored the negative case based on the defects of average-cost pricing. The impossibility of using so-called average costs to determine ideal prices, however, is a very significant and relevant consideration. We have already noted many of the defects of average-cost pricing in Part One and shall only state here the basic point that, since every good has many average-cost curves, average costs cannot determine a unique ideal price.

There are two reasons why every good has many different average-cost curves: (1) different goods produced in the same plant at the same time have common fixed and variable costs which can be allocated in many ways, and (2) units of the same good produced in a plant at different times have common fixed costs which can be allocated to these individual units in many different ways. We shall explain these reasons briefly.

Nearly all goods are produced by multi-product plants and/or multi-product firms. In such cases it is possible to allocate common costs to individual products in literally innumerable different ways and none of these ways is the right way. Every model of a product is a different good, and common costs often exceed 50 percent of total costs. For instance, a railroad provides many different services, and the common costs of these services are greater than their marginal costs. As a result, there are millions of different average-cost rate structures which may be used by a railroad to try to cover its total outlays, and it is impossible to prove that any one of these rate structures is ideal. The same thing is true of a one-man firm producing only two products. Thus, existing prices, which cover total rent and costs, are, within certain, often wide, limits, purely arbitrary administered prices.

In the second place, all fixed plant is used to produce different units of the same good at different times. Some fixed capital lasts for fifty years. There are many ways in which the costs of such capital can be allocated to units produced at different times, and there is no method of determining which of these ways is the best way. For instance, when output falls, do fixed costs per unit rise, fall, or remain constant?

The net result of these two vital facts is that there is no possible way of using *average* costs to determine *ideal* prices. The government agencies which have so often pretended to do so have in fact merely used average costs to limit over-all profits. In general, they have approved the price structures existing before regulation began, and any changes made in the relative prices of individual goods have been, of necessity, entirely arbitrary. Only the marginal-cost curve is determinable. Only by the use of marginal-cost curves is it possible to set ideal prices.

PRICE CONTROL VERSUS OUTPUT CONTROL

Our basic principle of price-output control is that either price or output should be directly controlled so as to make price equal marginal cost. We shall now explain when it is better to control price directly and when it is better to control the volume of output. This is only a problem of relative feasibility since both types of control have the same results when they are equally practical.

In the first place, direct price control is much more practical than output control in determining the ideal output of services. Direct control of the output of services would require direct control of the persons receiving these services since services are produced and consumed at the same time. For instance, to increase directly its output of haircuts, a barber shop would have to compel customers to come and get haircuts whether they wished them or not. It is obviously much better to change the price of haircuts and leave customers free to buy them when they feel like it. This is true under both Capitalism and Socialism. Such logic applies not only to the so-called service industries (laundries, barber shops, repair shops, etc.) but to all industries which provide a service, including most utilities and all retail stores. Direct control of output is desirable only in the case of tangible goods which can be stored until they are sold. While retail stores sell such goods, they really perform only the service of making them available to consumers when and where they please. They do not create tangible goods.

In the case of storable tangible goods in adequate supply, price control is more practical than output control under Capitalism but not under Socialism. Under competitive Capitalism, there is a relatively large number of products (due to product differentiation) and firms (due to competition), and the managers of these firms all have a strong profit motive to evade price-output control. For these reasons, complete marginal-cost price-output control may not be practical in many industries under Capitalism, especially those with many firms producing nonstandardized goods. However, price control is more apt to be feasible than output control because price control does not require separate regulations for each firm. When goods are, or can be, standardized, a single price regulation can apply to all firms producing the goods in question.

Under Socialism, on the other hand, the variety of tangible goods would be sharply reduced and their production would be concentrated in fewer and larger plants. This would make the determination of ideal outputs for each tangible good in each plant much more feasible than it now is. Moreover, since these plants would be state owned and their managers could not profit from raising prices and

reducing output, the determination of ideal prices and outputs according to the theory of marginal-cost price-output control could be en-
trusted to them. It would be better for them to regulate output than
to regulate price. Price should always balance supply and demand.
Socialist managers might be tempted to fix price above or below this
level in order to make it equal marginal cost if they were instructed
to fix price at the marginal-cost level. Hence, it would probably be
better to have the prices of tangible goods fixed so as to balance supply
and demand by independent pricing experts and then to instruct
plant managers to increase or decrease the output of each good until
marginal cost equals price.[4]

Two special cases in which such a separation of price and output
control is especially needed may be cited. When a good spoils rapidly
and cannot be economically preserved, it should be sold before it
spoils even if this requires that price be lowered far below marginal
cost. On the other hand, if a tangible good is in such short supply—
due to war, fire, crop failure, etc.—that a price equal to marginal
cost would exhaust stocks before they could be replaced, price should
be well above marginal cost. In such cases, direct control of output is
preferable to direct control of price as a means of making price equal
marginal cost, under either Socialism or Capitalism.

Finally, direct control of price in order to achieve prices which
balance marginal costs is impossible in the case of joint products under
Socialism and Capitalism. It is not possible to allocate joint costs to
individual joint products. Hence, it is necessary to control output
rather than price directly.

MARGINAL-COST PRICE-OUTPUT CONTROL AND ECONOMIC PLANNING

The word planning has many meanings—from city planning to the
budgeting of income and expenses by a single firm—but the common-
est meaning is planning of output, not necessarily in the same way as
it is done in the USSR, but at least in an effective and arbitrary manner. Guessing at the output which would result from optimum prices
is not planning but estimating, predicting, or budgeting. Such guessing is, of course, possible and desirable under marginal-cost control,

[4] This point is discussed more fully in our *Economic Theory of a Socialist Economy*,
pp. 76–79.

but economic planning in its most common sense is incompatible with such pricing.

If a price equal to marginal cost is the ideal price, planning to sell goods at a different price is uneconomic. If an output which makes price equal marginal cost is the ideal output, planning to produce a different output is uneconomic. Moreover, it is impossible to determine in advance what prices will equal marginal cost, or what outputs will result in prices equal to these costs. Hence, planning price or output in the future is always inconsistent with marginal-cost price-output control.

This argument against economic planning applies with equal force to rationing, price control, and any other form of economic regulation which would prevent prices from equaling marginal costs or outputs from responding properly to prices which equal marginal costs.

Socialist thinkers have been primarily responsible for the current vogue for planning among nonsocialists, and the idea of planning is so strongly entrenched among Socialists that it may take several decades to persuade them to abandon it. But the recent recognition of the advantages of the free price system and marginal-cost control under Socialism may in time lead to an abandonment of the idea that price and/or production planning is desirable under Socialism.

THE EFFECT OF MARGINAL-COST PRICE-OUTPUT CONTROL ON PROFITS

Most writers on marginal-cost price-output theory, including the author, have claimed that the general application of this theory must result in large deficits, sometimes called negative rent, because of the prevalence of decreasing costs. In fact, it is optimum investment, or an approach to it, not optimum (marginal-cost) price-output control which necessarily results in such deficits. If investment in a given industry is sufficiently limited, the output can be sold at a profit even when prices are equal to marginal costs, for marginal costs will be above so-called average costs. Only when investment in fixed capital is increased until marginal cost falls below average outlay does marginal-cost control necessarily result in continuing losses.

Fixed capital is durable and should often be constructed in large lumps. If new investment in such capital is properly planned, marginal cost will usually be temporarily below average outlay immediately after a construction project has been completed. This will clearly be true in decreasing-cost industries. As time passes after such a project, demand and sales will grow and fuller use of existing plant capacity will gradually raise marginal costs. If the most economical unit of addition to fixed capital is large, it may be wise to wait until marginal costs are well above average outlay before expanding plant capacity, even in decreasing-cost industries. In other words, optimum investment may result in alternating periods of net losses and net profits. It may also result in continuous losses.

By contrast, marginal-cost control alone need not result either in recurring or in continuous losses. If applied first when excess capacity exists, it would result in losses only until capacity became scarce enough to raise prices above average outlay. Thereafter, it would result in continuous profits, in the absence of new investment sufficient to cause losses. Hence, we shall discuss these losses and the best ways to finance them in the chapter following, on optimum investment.

The fact that the adoption of marginal-cost price-output control need not result in continuing deficits does not mean it would not reduce many prices or increase many outputs. The degree to which such control would change prices and outputs does not depend upon the prevalence of decreasing costs, or upon the amount of the resulting deficits, but upon the prevalence of conditions under which marginal cost is below average outlay and the average amount of this difference.

WHY MARGINAL COSTS ARE USUALLY BELOW AVERAGE OUTLAY

The importance of the theory that price should equal marginal cost rather than average outlay (so-called average cost) depends upon the frequency and degree to which marginal costs now fall below average outlay. Orthodox economists have rarely denied that prices should equal marginal costs when these costs exceed average outlay. But they have nearly all denied or ignored the equally valid theory that prices should equal marginal costs when these costs are below average outlay. Hence, the seriousness of their error depends upon how often and how much marginal costs are less than average outlay.

Although appropriate limitation of investment could easily raise marginal cost above average outlay in all industries,[5] *we believe that marginal costs are now below average outlay nearly all of the time in the great majority of industries.*[6] In this section we shall briefly describe the five major reasons for this condition. The five reasons are: (1) surplus capacity, (2) optional variable costs, (3) free optional services, (4) unsound piece rates, and (5) multi-unit sales. *The condition of decreasing costs is not a reason.*

A plant is operating at capacity (its ideal level of output) when all its selling prices (for the first unit sold in each sale, for the subsequent units, for all optional services, etc.) equal marginal cost and when total income equals total necessary costs and rent (including fixed capital costs, but excluding research, and other optional costs). When output is below capacity, surplus capacity exists and, if income covers costs and rents, one or more marginal costs is below the relevant price.

The chief reasons for the existence of surplus capacity are: (1) the so-called business cycle, (2) the custom of one-shift operation, (3) seasonal fluctuations in demand, (4) regular daily and hourly fluctuations in demand, (5) unpredictable declines in the demand for specific goods, (6) the mistakes of promoters and investors in planning capital expansion, (7) duplication of facilities resulting from monopolistic competition—two or more gas stations at a corner, (8) output reductions due to the sudden creation of monopolies, and (9) the incomplete divisibility of some capital instruments.

Surplus capacity is a very common condition. During years of business recession, depression, and recovery, it exists in nearly all non-extractive and some extractive industries. During boom years, it exists during off-season periods in all industries with seasonal fluctuations. At the height of the season in boom years, surplus capacity exists during those days of the week or hours of the day when the volume of output is below capacity. For instance, in Washington, D.C., at the peak of the boom in the Second World War, movie theaters had large surplus capacity from 9 to 12 A.M. Firms which operate only one or two shifts a day can often increase their output substantially with-

[5] In retail stores it is impossible to raise the marginal cost of selling one more unit of the same good to the same buyer in the same sale above the cost of selling the first unit, but it is easy to raise the marginal cost of selling the first unit above the average outlay for selling first units.

[6] As explained earlier, average outlay may be determined in various ways, each of which gives a different result. We believe, however, that this thesis is valid regardless of the way in which average outlay is calculated.

out raising marginal costs above average outlay. When this is possible, they have large surplus capacity.

The second reason why marginal cost is usually below average outlay is the existence of optional variable costs, like advertising, which enter into average outlay but not into marginal cost as we have defined it. Since optional variable costs are optional, their continuance could be prohibited by the state even under Capitalism. Hence, they are not a necessary element in average outlay (see pp. 258–59 below).

The third reason why marginal costs are usually below average outlay is the common custom of providing without charge optional services having significant independent marginal costs. For instance, if retail prices are high enough to cover free alterations, credit, delivery, and repair service, they are considerably above the cost of selling to customers who do not require any of these services. This reason could easily be eliminated by requiring sellers to charge separately for optional services.

The fourth reason why marginal costs are usually below average outlay is that piece rates paid for the marginal unit of output are nearly always far below the value added to this unit by the worker. Since the marginal cost of a good produced under piece rates includes, and is partly determined by, the rate paid for the marginal unit produced, such piece rates result in marginal costs which are significantly below both market prices and average outlay.

The fifth important reason why marginal costs are usually below average outlay is that whenever a multi-unit sale is made, the marginal cost of selling the second and each subsequent unit in this sale is much less than the cost of selling the first unit. Since selling costs are a large part of total costs, these differences in selling costs are quite significant.

VIII

THE PURE THEORY OF
OPTIMUM INVESTMENT IN
FIXED CAPITAL

INTRODUCTION

IN THIS BOOK we are primarily interested in the theory of optimum price and output with existing fixed capital. We have found, however, that most writers on it have confused it in part or in whole with the theory of optimum investment in fixed capital. One of the chief purposes of this study is to disentangle these two theories. We have just stated the theory of marginal-cost price-output control as a distinct theory. In this chapter we shall further stress the separateness of these two theories by stating briefly the theory of optimum investment in fixed capital as an entirely independent idea.

The theory of marginal-cost price-output control is an application of marginal analysis. Like all forms of marginal analysis, it assumes the existence of continuous margins and compares very small quantities at the margin. When the quantities involved are large and indivisible, marginal analysis is inappropriate. Investment in fixed capital is usually such a case. The cost of a new plant or machine which will last for years cannot be balanced against the utility of one, or a small number of, units of output, which may be produced and sold in a day or a week. To evaluate the economic wisdom of such investments, we must abandon marginal analysis and compare total costs with total returns, including consumers' surplus, over the entire life of the investment.

On the other hand, no new theory is needed to guide optimum investment in variable capital, which is both divisible and liquid. The costs of liquid capital are marginal costs. They fall as well as rise with the volume of output. If the output of a good is decreased or increased until marginal cost, including the cost of using variable capital, equals market price, investment in liquid capital will be at the optimum level. In other words, the theory of marginal-cost price-output control solves the problem of optimum investment in liquid capital as well as the problems of optimum output and price.

There are several reasons why so many economists have thought that the theory of marginal-cost price-output control is also a theory of optimum investment. First, investment is needed only to maintain or increase output. Hence, a theory which prescribes the ideal output seems also to prescribe when new investment is needed. Secondly, the theory of marginal-cost price-output control does solve the problem of optimum investment under perfect competition, because all capital is variable then, and Capitalist economists tend to overlook or minimize the difference between perfect competition and the real world in order to strengthen their defense of Capitalism. Thirdly, many proponents of marginal-cost price-output control have thought that fixed capital costs could be treated as intermittent marginal costs. They have failed to grasp or give due weight to the difference between variable and fixed costs. Variable costs can be allocated to individual marginal units of output, but fixed costs cannot. It is plausible to argue that the cost of a new plant is a marginal cost when the plant is required to increase output, but this reasoning is unsound. It ignores the fact that output can always be increased at the intensive margin without a new plant. It overlooks the fact that if a fixed capital cost is treated as a one-time marginal cost, it cannot be allocated to more than one unit. In other words, the entire cost of a new plant must be covered by the price charged for one unit, the marginal unit whose production the new plant makes possible. If it is allocated to the entire output during the life of the new plant, the result is average-cost pricing, and the resulting prices cannot be lowered when excess capacity exists because this would prevent such an allocation of fixed cost.

The theory of optimum investment deals with the practical investment problems faced by the managers of individual plants. It is not a theory of the allocation of capital funds by a central agency. To be useful, it must be the kind of theory that plant managers can understand and apply without unreasonable expense or delay. Hence, it must deal with money costs rather than social disutility, and with money income rather than with social utility, and it must prescribe feasible partial adjustments. The problem of making money costs and prices measure real costs and benefits as accurately as is economical is a separate problem.

The phrase, "invest in fixed capital," is used in a broad sense here. It includes the purchase of existing fixed capital whether or not this increases the total supply of capital in the economy because to the individual firm all additions to its fixed capital are the same and should be subject to the same theory. In other words, we are stating a theory of ideal investment by the firm, not by the nation. Investment in fixed capital also includes replacement and repair of existing facilities.

The theory of optimum investment stated here can be applied not only to all proposed investments in fixed capital but to all proposed lumpy adjustments in factor use, including proposals to buy, sell, rent, or abandon land or existing fixed capital. Marginal analysis is not applicable to such adjustments. Adjustments in the use of variable factors should never be lumpy.

THE BASIC PRINCIPLE OF OPTIMUM INVESTMENT

The basic principle of optimum investment in fixed capital used to produce price goods is that each plant manager should invest in fixed capital whenever this promises cost savings on the current output and/or new revenue and consumers' surplus from additional output, the sum of which during the life of the new capital will exceed the total costs of securing and using it, excluding price-increase costs but including interest, depreciation, etc., on the fixed capital and the direct variable costs required to use it.

We have tried to state the theory so as to make it clear that the effects of an increase in output on both the income from and the costs of producing the base output should be ignored. Neither the fall in this income nor the rise in these costs represent any real change in welfare or cost. Changes in money income and cost are useful in the control of output and investment only when they measure real benefit and real cost. The only income which reflects real benefits from new investment is the income from additional output, or the savings on current output. The only expenses which reflect real costs are the interest on the additional capital and the costs of any other additional factors used to increase output. The only consumers' surplus which reflects additional real gain over and above that measured in money income or savings is the consumers' surplus on the additional goods produced as a result of the new investment.

The measurement and use of consumers' surplus is essential to the rational control of all investment which must or ought to be made in large lumps. As long as investment can be made in suitably small units, it is possible to secure the ideal use of each unit by assigning it to the use in which it earns the largest monetary return, but when investment must be made in large units, it is necessary to measure consumers' surplus and add it to the monetary return in order to determine the full benefit from the investment.

Terms like large and small are very indefinite. Actually it is not the absolute size of the investment but its proportion to total investment in the industry (narrowly defined) which is significant. An investment which makes possible the provision of a new good, or an old good in a new market, usually has a very significant effect upon consumers' surplus while an equally large investment which permits a 1 percent increase in the output of an old good has a very slight effect upon consumers' surplus. Thus the first toll bridge over San Francisco Bay yielded a very large consumers' surplus, and was therefore socially desirable long before it was profitable, but the construction of a tenth bridge over this bay would yield a consumers' surplus relatively small by comparison.

When there is no charge for the use of a new investment, as in the case of free bridges, the entire benefit takes the form of consumers' surplus. Hence, those who deny the existence or measurability of consumers' surpluses must, if they are consistent, deny the possibility of determining whether such investments are desirable.

It will ordinarily pay to increase output from existing facilities well above the normal capacity level, in order to keep marginal costs equal to the selling price, before demand becomes large enough to justify a large lumpy investment. There are many economies both in building and in operating larger plant additions. To permit the construction of larger plant additions without creating excessive surplus capacity, it is desirable both to operate old plant above its ideal capacity for some time and to build plant additions large enough to create surplus capacity for some months or years after their construction. For the same reason, inventories should be built up after the construction of a new plant and run down before the construction of a plant addition.

After the new plant has been constructed, operations in the old plant should be reduced. New capacity is usually low-cost capacity because of technological progress, but even if there is no difference in efficiency, output in the old plant should be reduced at least to its ideal capacity to minimize average costs. This means that a part of the output of new plant should serve merely to replace output from existing plant and lower the costs of producing it. The resulting savings must be treated as one of the benefits of new fixed investment. They will consist entirely of savings in variable costs, for a reduction in the output from existing plant does not change fixed costs.

The adoption of marginal-cost price-output control and all its corollaries should precede the application of a policy of optimum investment. If some or all prices are above marginal costs, the use of existing plant is below the ideal level. Until price has been reduced to marginal cost and output from existing plant has been correspondingly increased, no one can tell what this output and the related marginal cost will be. This data is essential for judging the wisdom of proposed investments.

The theory of optimum investment applies to fixed investments required to produce a new kind of good. It implies that such investments should be made only when they promise to yield consumers' surplus and a money income which together, over the life of the new investment, will exceed the money costs of the investment. But it does not imply that all investments required to produce new goods which meet this criterion are economic. The production of new goods is economic only when it is also consistent with the theory of ideal simplification.

Our investment theory also applies to the abandonment of existing fixed capital. In order to decide whether to discontinue the maintenance of a large lump of fixed capital, one must estimate and compare the total gains and costs over the remaining life of this capital, including loss of consumers' surplus but not obsolescence. Obsolescence should be ignored because it is a fixed cost. Only variable costs can be affected by a decision to continue or discontinue use of existing fixed capital. While marginal analysis should not be used to judge the wisdom of abandoning plant capacity, it should be used to determine whether to cease using such capacity at any given time, for this can be done by small marginal reductions in output, and output can be resumed by small marginal quantities at any later time.

The theory of optimum investment in fixed capital rules out arbitrary economic planning of investment. If investment is to achieve an ideal level in each firm and industry, it must be guided by the theories of optimum investment and optimum price-output control. Arbitrary plans would conflict with the application of these theories. It is impossible to determine in advance how these theories would decide future problems, and, if it were possible, such predictions would not be arbitrary plans but estimated budgets. An economic plan controls investment; it is not a mere estimate as to the effects of market forces and other factors upon investment.

DEMONSTRATION OF THE THEORY OF OPTIMUM INVESTMENT

The application of the proposed theory of optimum investment in fixed capital would tend to maximize net welfare or want-satisfaction. The money costs of additional factors are the best available measures of real cost. Money income is usually the best available measure of real want-satisfaction. In the case of lumpy investment, it must be supplemented by an estimate of consumers' surplus because the marginal unit of investment is large enough to yield a significant consumers' surplus on, as well as a money income from, the additional output.

The sum of consumers' surplus and money income from additional output is the best measure of the welfare created by the additional output. To get a measure of the total benefit from the investment, we must add to this sum the savings in variable costs on the base output, for they are the best available measure of the real savings on this output. If the estimate of the total benefit is larger than the estimate of the money cost, the proposed investment is economic; if not, it is uneconomic, because the quantities compared are the best available measures of the total real benefit and total real cost involved.

It is, of course, true that money income and money costs are not perfect measures of real welfare and real costs. But to conclude on this ground that they should not be determined and balanced against each other amounts to saying that rational calculation is never desirable because it can never be perfect. The sensible conclusion is that the pricing system should be improved continually but that at any given time it should be used in its necessarily imperfect present condition. The adoption of the policy of optimum investment would itself make one money cost, interest, a better measure of real cost because it would result in a more productive allocation of capital, which would raise interest rates. And marginal-cost price-output control would make other money costs better measures of real costs.

Optimum investment alone cannot maximize welfare. Optimum pricing, optimum wage determination, optimum taxation, optimum distribution of wealth, and numerous other optimum conditions are needed to achieve the closest practical approach to maximum want-satisfaction. However, this is not a reasonable argument against efforts to achieve any of these ideal conditions. They are all ends towards which we must strive, not present or possible conditions. In the real world, all progress is achieved by individual steps towards such goals, not by the miraculous achievement of any general optimum.

When first generally applied, the policy of optimum investment would increase the outputs and lower the prices of certain goods. This would change the demand curves for all goods. It would also raise factor costs and the cost curves for all goods. These facts may suggest that our demonstration of the theory of optimum investment is invalid because it ignores changes in producers' surplus everywhere and considers the change in consumers' surplus from only one good, that whose output is increased by the new investment. We believe that this potential criticism is unjustified.

The changes in nominal producers' and consumers' surplus in other industries do not represent a loss of real welfare. Instead they are evidence of a significant increase in such welfare. To illustrate, let us assume that a proposed investment will increase the output of radios, lower the demand curve for oranges, and enable workers in orange orchards to obtain higher wages. Do the oranges still consumed give less pleasure per orange, as implied by the fall in the demand curve? Do workers work harder as implied by the rise in the cost curve? The answer is no in both cases. The demand and cost curve movements do not indicate any change in the net welfare obtained from the production and consumption of the oranges still produced. There is a small nominal loss of producers' and consumers' surpluses from the oranges no longer produced and consumed, but this too represents no loss of real welfare. Output is reduced at the margin, where nominal producers' and consumers' surpluses are negligible, and output would not be cut unless the shifted factors were more productive in the new use than in the old.

In the above analysis we have assumed that producers' surplus is a positive quantity and consists largely if not entirely of land rent, in other words, that it is represented by the area above the marginal-cost curve and below a horizontal line through the intersection of the demand and marginal-cost curves. In fact, however, this common definition of producers' surplus is narrow and illogical. Land is not a producer, and the real producers—workers, savers, etc.—also earn surpluses which are not included in marginal cost and not represented by the area above a rising marginal-cost curve. All factor income above that needed to keep factors on the job is a surplus. Since optimum investment increases the productivity of all the factors without increasing equally the real effort or sacrifice of producers, it must increase total producers' surplus in this broad sense of the term, whether or not it also increases total land rent.

But if new investments prescribed by the theory of optimum investment increase producers' surplus in the broad sense of this term, should not the effect of a lumpy investment in a given plant on the producers' surplus created by that plant be estimated and used in the same way as the consumers' surplus on the additional output? The answer is no since there is no way of measuring the effect of an investment in fixed capital upon producers' surplus broadly defined. The usual graphic presentation of producers' surplus is of little help because (1) it shows only a small part of total producers' surplus, namely land rent and quasi rent, and (2) it shows this much only in increasing-cost industries. Optimum investment would increase output chiefly in decreasing-cost industries. There would usually be a net deficit rather than a surplus.

THE DEFICITS DUE TO OPTIMUM INVESTMENT

The Nature of These Deficits

Optimum investment in decreasing-cost industries would normally result in continuing, but not necessarily continuous, deficits if prices were lowered to marginal-cost levels. This is a truth by definition, for a decreasing-cost industry is one in which new fixed investment permits an increased output at lower average outlay.[1] And marginal cost falls much more than average outlay when plant capacity is increased by new fixed investment. Such an investment should be delayed until scarcity of fixed capital and/or growing demand has forced marginal cost relatively high, and should be large enough to result in surplus capacity which would make marginal cost relatively low after the investment has been made.

Although continuing deficits are the inevitable result of optimum investment in fixed capital in decreasing-cost industries if the theory of marginal-cost price-output control is applied after each new investment has been made, they need not result from the application of this theory. If fixed investment in decreasing-cost industries were suitably limited, the quasi rent from their fixed capital could be raised high enough to make them profitable even when prices equaled marginal cost. The shortage of fixed capital would raise marginal cost to or above average cost. If a loss results from marginal-cost control in decreasing-cost industries, therefore, it is due to carrying investment in fixed capital beyond the level which makes marginal cost equal average outlay.

Investment in fixed capital in most decreasing-cost industries has probably already been carried well beyond the point which makes marginal cost equal average outlay. Thus the sudden general introduction of marginal-cost price-output control would result in large temporary losses. But these losses would be due to previous investment in fixed capital, not to marginal-cost control, and could easily be eliminated without abandoning marginal-cost control merely by suitably limiting future investment.

The term *negative rent* has been used as a name for the deficit which would result from marginal-cost price-output control by some who believe such control also solves the problem of optimum investment. We have noted the fallacy in the last belief, developed on independent theory of investment, and argued that it is only the application of the latter which would result in large continuing deficits. The question now arises as to whether the deficits due to optimum investment should be called negative rent. We believe that they should not be so named.

The chief reason for calling these deficits negative rent is that, like

[1] To be consistent, we should rename *decreasing-cost* industries *decreasing-outlay* industries, but we are afraid to introduce any more new terms.

land rent and quasi rent, they are quantities which result from fixing a price equal to marginal cost. They should never enter into marginal cost. They should result from, but have no influence upon the determination of price and output. This reasoning may suggest that the only difference between land rent and quasi rent, on the one hand, and the continuing deficits due to optimum investment, on the other hand, is that the former are positive quantities (surpluses) while the latter are negative quantities. But actually there are other vital differences which make the use of the same term, rent, to describe both quantities misleading. For instance, land rent accrues to landowners, and quasi rent to owners of fixed capital, and the firm which uses land and capital may not own them. The deficits due to optimum investment can accrue only to the firms which practice such investment. Moreover, these firms may pay land rent and quasi rent and have a deficit due to optimum investment at the same time, which shows that positive and negative rent do not cancel out. In such cases, the payment of positive rent increases the private deficit. The net social deficit is the difference between positive rent and the deficit to the firm. But it is confusing and illogical to define as negative rent a quantity which often includes positive rent. The basic trouble is that positive rent arises in all firms whether or not their operation results in profits or loses, while so-called negative rent arises only in firms which lose money. Hence, positive rent is not the opposite of negative rent and the latter term is inappropriate.

The Size of Deficits Due to Optimum Investment

Both the importance and the difficulty of achieving an ideal volume of fixed investment in all price-goods industries depend upon the amount and prevalence of the deficits which would result from optimum investment, assuming optimum pricing. If optimum investment brought about only small changes in the distribution of fixed capital among industries, it would be a minor reform and would create only small deficits. On the other hand, if it resulted in large changes in such capital distribution, it would be a major reform and would result in large deficits. We believe that this reform is very important, that it would cause great changes in capital distribution and, as a result, large deficits.

Optimum investment in fixed capital would result in substantial shifts of capital and large deficits because there are many industries subject to decreasing costs. It is optimum investment in decreasing-cost industries which gives rise to deficits. The greater the number and size of such industries and the steeper the rate at which their costs decrease with additional investment and output, the larger the deficits. Hence, if we wish to gain even a rough idea of how large the deficits due to optimum investment in our economy would be, we must investigate the number and importance of decreasing-cost industries and the rate at which their costs decrease.

Both Marshall and Pigou thought that most firms and industries are subject to decreasing costs. Marshall wrote that:

The general argument of the present book shows that an increase in the aggregate volume of production of anything will generally increase the size, and therefore the internal economies possessed by such a representative firm; that it will always increase the external economies to which the firm has access; and thus will enable it to manufacture at a less proportionate cost of labour and sacrifice than before.[2]

Pigou quoted this statement with approval.[3] The great majority of English-speaking economists, however, deny the predominance of decreasing costs. In most textbooks, all long-run cost curves turn up in time to intersect the demand curve at a point (price) which will yield a profit, and the text usually presents the same view.

We could try to support Marshall and Pigou by listing and explaining the numerous advantages of large-scale production, but this has been done reasonably well by many authors. Indeed, some textbooks which ignore or minimize the importance of decreasing costs in their discussion of price theory contain good explanations of the advantages of large-scale production in separate chapters.

As long as a single real or alleged disadvantage of large-scale production remains, it will be possible to claim that this disadvantage becomes so great as output grows that in time it offsets all the advantages and causes the so-called average-cost curve to turn up.[4] Whether the curve turns up soon enough to serve as an argument against monopoly is usually ignored. The only way to answer this dubious claim is to cite suitable quantitive data.

---

[2] Alfred Marshall, *Principals of Economics*, 8th ed (New York, 1948), p. 318.

[3] Pigou, "An Analysis of Supply," *Economic Journal*, XXXVIII (June, 1928), 252.

[4] Thus Edward Chamberlin merely asserts that the "increased difficulties of coordination and management" must cause an eventual upturn in the cost curve, but offers no evidence. *Theory of Monopolistic Competition*, 4th ed. (Cambridge, Mass., 1940), pp. 206–7.

The National Bureau of Economic Research collected data on so-called average costs by size of firm for a variety of industries and published its findings in *Cost Behavior and Price Policy* (1943). In most industries, these costs were found to decrease sharply with rising plant size and the decline in costs continued through the entire range of plant size. In some cases, however, costs reached a minimum and then started to rise.

Another, though less direct, approach to this problem is to use data on profits by size of firm. The Treasury Department has published such data, derived from income tax returns, for each year since 1933. In spite of the fact that the economists who have studied this profit data have usually been biased in favor of the contrary conclusion, most of them have found that there is a very significant positive correlation between profits and size. Thus W. L. Crum finally conceded, "My findings clearly show that, on the average, large enterprise in all or nearly all broad lines of industry, and in different stages of the economic cycle is more profitable than small enterprises." [5]

Both costs and profits are, of course, affected by many factors in addition to the economies or diseconomies of large-scale production. For instance, if small firms paid lower wages than large firms, as they apparently do, their unit costs would be lower and their profits would be higher than those of large firms, other things being equal. Profits are also greatly influenced by the level of selling prices, and large firms apparently grant consumers lower prices than small firms. Several studies have demonstrated that chain stores sell for lower prices than small independent stores, and the steadily growing public preference for manufactured products produced by large firms like Westinghouse and General Electric is probably also due in part to lower prices as well as to advertising.

One reason why businessmen and economists fail to perceive the prevalence of decreasing costs is that any individual firm, large or small, must usually incur additional selling expenses in order to take business away from its competitors, and this makes the additional business unprofitable. But optional selling costs are not necessary costs. They need not exist under Socialism, and could be largely ended by legal prohibition under Capitalism. Hence, they do not prove that

[5] *Corporate Size and Earning Power* (Cambridge, Mass., 1939), p. 7. After making his first investigation of the profit size-of-the-firm correlation (that covering 1931) and finding to his surprise that it was positive, W. L. Crum had remarked, "It is very doubtful if this rule as to profits holds under normal conditions."

the firm is subject to increasing costs. They demonstrate the absence of perfect competition, not the absence of decreasing costs.

There are, of course, other arguments both for and against the thesis that most firms are subject to decreasing costs. To treat the subject comprehensively would require another book.[6] In our opinion, however, the logical and statistical evidence cited above strongly supports our thesis. It is certain, in any case, that the arguments offered to support the opposite conclusion are extremely inconclusive, and their unquestioned acceptance by the great majority of economists suggests a bias in favor of arguments which can be used to defend competitive Capitalism.

[6] For a recent study concluding that most British industries have decreasing costs, See L. Rostas, *Productivity, Prices, and Distribution in Selected British Industries* (Cambridge, 1948).

IX

METHODS OF

FINANCING IDEAL DEFICITS

INTRODUCTION

In CHAPTER VIII we explained that a combination of optimum investment and optimum price-output control would result in large continuing deficits in decreasing-cost industries. To distinguish these deficits, whose existence is necessary to the achievement of ideal price, output, and investment, from other deficits, we shall call them ideal deficits. If ideal investment and price-output policies are to be adopted, some practical method of covering these deficits must be found.

When population is at an optimum level with respect to both natural resources and capital,[1] the total ideal deficit is just equal to the sum of rent and interest. This significant relationship, first noted by J. E. Meade (see pp. 62–63 above), follows from the fact that, when an optimum population exists, wages equal both the average and the marginal product per worker and thus absorb the entire national income, leaving nothing for rent or interest. If the marginal product of labor were either above or below its average product, it would be possible to raise or lower average income by increasing or decreasing the population, and this would prove that population was below or above the optimum level, the level which maximizes average income.

Every increase in population above the optimum level increases land rent, quasi rent, and interest because it makes land, fixed capital,

[1] The fact that the size of the optimum population in an advanced state depends more upon the quantity of capital than upon the quantity of land is commonly overlooked.

and liquid capital relatively scarcer. It requires a greater expansion
in the output of increasing-cost industries than in the output of
decreasing-cost industries. It may increase the total ideal deficit, but
it will increase rent and interest more. Hence, the total ideal deficit is
less than the sum of rent and interest in states which are overpopulated
as nearly all countries, including the United States, are. Thus our
problem in this chapter is to suggest methods of financing deficits
which total less than the sum of interest and rent.

There are a variety of methods of financing ideal deficits. They
may be divided into two classes—those which may be used by the
state and those which may be used by individual firms, whether privately or publicly owned. State financing of deficits is decidedly preferable, since it alone permits the full achievement of optimum output
and investment, but the methods of financing ideal deficits open to
individual firms are either already politically feasible or are likely to
become so long before state financing and therefore deserve discussion as transitional steps towards optimum output and investment.

Financing by the State

The chief methods of state financing of ideal deficits are: (1) the use
of interest and rent, (2) the creation of new money, (3) the use of tax
revenues now used to pay interest on the national debt, (4) the cur-
tailment of other expenditures, and (5) taxation.

In a fully socialized economy, most rent and interest should accrue
to the state and might be used to cover the negative rent. In advanced
states, 20 to 30 percent of the land and capital is already owned by the
state. However, the revenue from this property is now being used to
meet other state expenses, and this is likely always to be true. Moreover, a fair price should be paid for additional property taken over by
the state. Even under Socialism, therefore, the achievement of optimum price, output, and investment would require either additional
revenues sufficient to cover all ideal deficits or an equal reduction in
other expenditures.

The second method of state financing of ideal deficits, the creation
of new money, would provide a much smaller sum, but it is a source
of revenue not now in use. At present the United States requires a
3 or 4 per cent annual increase in the quantity of money, broadly defined, in order to prevent deflation. This new money is now provided
by private banks, largely in the form of demand deposits created to

make new loans and investments. The total quantity of money now in existence in the United States is well over $100,000,000,000. If the state assumed the function of creating all new money, it could not only assure a stable growth of the money supply, thus greatly reducing the severity of depressions, but would also secure an additional net income of four to five billions a year which could be used to finance ideal deficits.

The third method of state financing, the use of funds now required to pay interest on the national debt, is likewise of minor importance, but is also an unused and therefore available method. The domestic national debt of any state could be eliminated by means of a capital levy. Such a levy does not change the amount of real wealth, and is therefore a small burden on the economy.[2] It has been ably defended by other writers, but we shall not repeat their arguments here. The elimination of the American national debt would free for other uses about seven billion dollars a year now used to meet interest payments. It would also make available any funds now used to reduce this debt.

The fourth method by which the state might secure funds to cover ideal deficits is to reduce other expenditures. It could be used under either Capitalism or Socialism. This is no place to offer a detailed discussion of the need for existing government expenditures. We may point out, however, that the largest single expenditure, that for the armed forces, may be very greatly reduced by the organization of an effective world government before the end of this century. This alone might save the United States fifty billion dollars a year, which could then be used to cover ideal deficits.

Taxation, the fifth method of state financing, would probably be the most important under either Capitalism or Socialism. Any proposal that taxes should be levied or increased in order to cover ideal deficits under Capitalism is certain to be met with the argument, among others, that additional taxes would be an added burden on private enterprise and would discourage businessmen. The effect of these taxes would depend, of course, upon their nature. If they fell on the net profits of businessmen, they might discourage enterprise and investment, particularly in view of the high level of such taxes at present. But other kinds of taxes are available. For instance, a poll tax

[2] If offset by the reduction in progressive income taxes made possible by ending interest payments, it is not even a burden on property owners. However, when used to reduce interest payments on the national debt, it is a burden on property owners, but it is an ideal burden because it does not reduce the future reward for work and thrift.

sufficient to cover ideal deficits would not affect businessmen or business profits, and therefore could not reduce private enterprise.

A more plausible argument against additional taxes to cover ideal deficits is that they would increase the burden of taxes to intolerable levels. This argument, however, has been used against new taxes for generations, and taxes are far higher today than they were a century ago, both absolutely and as a proportion of income. Experience suggests that there is no specific limit at which taxes become intolerable but rather that this depends largely upon the desire of taxpayers for the services and benefits made possible by their taxes. Thus, if they can be convinced that optimum investment would increase average real income after taxes, they would probably be willing to pay the taxes necessary to make it possible.

It would be easy at this point to turn the argument about ideal output and investment control into an argument as to whether voters can be taught to desire them. But this is a book on economic theory, not a book on popular education or social psychology.

Returning then, to the question of whether voters *should* approve of such taxes, we must emphasize that taxpayers who financed ideal deficits would receive a real benefit more than sufficient to compensate for the burden of suitable taxes. If the burden of the taxes required to cover ideal deficits, including collection costs, were greater than the benefits of optimum price-output control and investment, these policies would be uneconomic; they would not increase the social dividend. Every argument in favor of them is therefore an argument against the idea that taxes needed to cover ideal deficits are a burden. Critics who ignore these arguments, and merely claim that optimum investment is not feasible because the taxes needed to realize it would be too burdensome, have failed to grasp this.

Another plausible argument against the use of taxes to cover ideal deficits is that they would fall on some persons who would derive no benefit from the policies which create these deficits, or less benefit than the cost to them in taxes. Almost all social reforms and technological advances injure some persons. The abolition of slavery seriously injured slave traders and slaveowners. Prohibition sharply reduced the value of distilleries and breweries. The invention and introduction of the automobile injured harness manufacturers and many others. The argument that ideal price-output control and investment, and/or the taxes required to support them, would injure the minority is not

a sound argument against them, for, if it were, all social and technological change should be prohibited. Moreover, the number of persons
who would be injured by these ideal policies and/or the associated
taxes is small, because the benefits would be spread throughout the
entire economy. All retail prices would be reduced, and nearly all
wages would be raised. This answer assumes general adoption of the
policies in question. It is, of course, true that if either policy were
applied to a few local industries only and if the taxes to cover ideal
deficits were levied upon the entire country, a minority would benefit
and a majority might suffer. The obvious solution to this problem,
however, is not to abandon the policy but either to extend it to the
nation as a whole or to restrict the taxes covering the ideal deficit to
the areas enjoying the lower prices.

We have already pointed out that the theory of marginal-cost price-
output control implies that all taxes which distort marginal costs are
bad taxes (pp. 85, 131). Obviously, therefore, the taxes used to finance
ideal deficits should not affect marginal costs. They should certainly
not be sales or excise taxes because such taxes directly increase marginal costs. All taxes which enter marginal cost should represent and
measure real marginal costs not represented by other marginal money
costs.

Corporation income taxes are a bad means of covering ideal deficits
for several reasons. By reducing the net income from new investments
by corporations, they prevent many desirable investments and reduce
the marginal productivity of capital. In the United States today (1952),
they appropriate over half of the income from new corporate investments and thus reduce the marginal productivity of corporate capital
by more than 50 percent. In addition, income taxes on corporations
discriminate against the most efficient form of business organization,
against large-scale production, and against the most profitable and
efficient companies. Such taxes are politically popular because they
seem to fall largely on rich stockholders, but they are in fact largely
passed on to the average consumer in the form of higher prices.

Personal income taxes have some, but much less serious disadvantages. By reducing the income from marginal work they reduce slightly
the amount of work done when the worker is able to control his
hours of work or when he is paid by piece rates. However, these effects
are usually small, and they may be offset by desirable effects upon inequality of income, especially under Capitalism. In any case, personal

income taxes are much preferable to sales taxes as a means of covering ideal deficits.

The ideal taxes for covering ideal deficits are those which do not vary with either output or income. In this class are poll taxes, estate taxes, gift taxes, taxes on land rent, and taxes on pure profits. Taxes on tolerated but disapproved activities (gambling, drinking, smoking, prostitution, etc.) are also suitable since the resulting fall in output is probably beneficial.

Poll taxes have one significant defect when the distribution of income is perfect or when there is too much inequality of income; they increase the inequality of net income after taxes. On the other hand, taxes on estates, gifts, land rent, and pure profit reduce the inequality of income. Hence, it would be possible to combine poll taxes with other ideal taxes in such a way as to avoid any net regressive effect on personal income. However, the distribution of income in most countries is still much too unequal. Therefore, until undue inequality has been largely eliminated by other means, progressive personal income taxes would probably be more desirable than poll taxes as a means of covering ideal deficits. With the exception of poll taxes, however, the taxes which do not affect marginal cost or output are superior to progressive personal income taxes, for they reduce inequality of income without affecting the marginal costs or outputs of individual goods. If a capital levy is considered a tax, it also belongs in this group of taxes most suitable for covering ideal deficits under Capitalism. Moreover, the creation of new money is an ideal means of covering these deficits because it does not distort the marginal cost and output of individual goods.

Under Socialism, a combination of poll taxes and personal income taxes would probably be the best method of covering ideal deficits. Personal incomes would presumably be directly fixed at ideal levels by employing agencies. Hence, it would be necessary to offset the regressive effect of poll taxes. Since taxes on inheritance, gifts, land rent, pure profit, and capital would not be available, progressive personal income taxes should be used to offset this regressive effect.

Financing by Individual Firms

If the state is unable or unwilling to raise the funds required to cover ideal deficits, or if the payment of state subsidies to those firms which incur deficits is impractical, the benefits of optimum investment and marginal-cost price-output control may be partly achieved by special pricing methods which bring some prices closer to marginal costs and increase output without causing a deficit. These special pricing methods are: (1) the use of nonideal service charges, (2) the use of nonideal work-place rents, and (3) price discrimination.

NONIDEAL SERVICE CHARGES. We have noted that multi-marginal pricing would result in ideal service charges which measure certain semi-fixed marginal costs, such as the costs of meter-reading, periodic bills, etc. These charges would be needed to determine ideal deficits. They are not an optional means which firms could use to reduce or cover ideal deficits determined without them. However, many firms could voluntarily impose nonideal service charges, as independent or supplemental charges, in order to prevent an ideal deficit. If nonideal service charges were high enough, they would permit prices for marginal units of output equal to marginal cost. This would induce customers who paid such charges to use more of the service in question, which would bring output closer to the optimum level which ideal price-output control and investment alone can achieve.

There are two main types of nonideal service charges, charges per period of time and charges per visit to a store or restaurant. The former would prevent a few potential consumers from buying any service, and this minor disadvantage must be balanced against the major advantage of persuading all who pay the service charges to consume the ideal amount. Charges per visit would not cause any consumers to refrain from consumption altogether, but they would prevent all consumers from making as many visits as they otherwise would to stores, restaurants, etc. They would buy more at each visit, but their total consumption would be below the ideal or free-choice level. Since they would visit stores less often, they would have less opportunity for "impulse" buying. And on their less frequent visits to restaurants they could not eat more meals per visit. Nonideal service charges cannot result in ideal outputs. However, both kinds of nonideal service charges would result in outputs much closer to the ideal level than so-called average-cost pricing would. The latter not only causes some consumers to buy nothing of certain goods, but also persuades every consumer to buy too much or too little of every good he buys because the price charged for the marginal unit is always too low or too high.

The combination of flat service charges per period of time with use rates equal to marginal costs is particularly suitable for public utilities, and there are other possible uses—for instance, use by private clubs, whose flat membership fees might cover all non-marginal costs. Cooperatives of all kinds could cover non-marginal costs by high membership fees and then sell all goods and services at marginal cost. This is an important but unrecognized advantage of cooperation.

The combination of a flat charge per person per visit with prices equal to marginal cost for each unit is suitable for retail stores, restaurants, circuses, pool halls, and most other places visited by customers. Night clubs which charge a cover charge plus a separate charge for each dish or drink ordered already use nonideal service charges. Though their prices for food and drinks are now above the marginal-cost level, their price system could easily be revised so as to achieve both private profit and food and drink prices equal to marginal costs.

NONIDEAL WORK-PLACE RENTS. As explained in our discussion of marginal productivity wages, ideal work-place rents are essential to ideal price-output control. They are needed to determine ideal deficits and are not an optional method of reducing or financing such deficits. However, work-place rents could be raised above the ideal level in order to prevent deficits. This method of avoiding ideal deficits is much inferior to taxation, but it is much superior to so-called average-cost pricing as a means of covering costs not covered by ideal prices.

Work-place rents above the ideal level would result in some work places remaining idle, but average-cost price-output control has the same effect to a greater degree, and the combination of high work-place rents and ideal piece rates would greatly increase the output per occupied work place. In other words, if a private firm must choose between excessive work-place rents and piece rates equal to average labor productivity as a means of avoiding losses, it should choose excessive work-place rents as the lesser evil.

PRICE DISCRIMINATION. Price discrimination is charging differing prices to different people for the same good when cost differences do not justify the price difference. It conflicts with the first corollary of marginal-cost theory, the rule that prices should be equal for all customers. Nevertheless, price discrimination may at times be a lesser evil. When it is not politically feasible for the state to finance ideal deficits, price discrimination may be more economic than either a limitation of investment below the optimum level or so-called average-cost pricing because it achieves a closer approach to the ideal output which would result from optimum investment and price-output control.

Suitable price discrimination increases output by reducing prices for some consumers below average costs. If the demand of various consumer classes differs in elasticity and discrimination is technically feasible, as in the case of railroads and public utilities, it may raise physical output closer to the ideal level without burdening those customers required to pay the highest rates. Indeed, it may even do so with a reduction in their rates. By increasing the number of persons paying a share of the overhead costs, it may permit lower prices for old as well as for new customers. But it may be desirable even when it increases prices to some old customers.

This argument has been used so often to justify price discrimination by the railroads that it requires no detailed demonstration here, but one new point needs to be made. Before the development of the theories of marginal-cost price-output control and optimum output, there was no known solution to the problem of optimum output and hence no means of demonstrating that the increased output made possible by price discrimination is nearer the ideal output than that which results from average-cost pricing. Now that these theories have been stated, however, it is clear that price discrimination permits only an approach toward, not an achievement of, the optimum level of output. At present, this approach is rarely very close to the optimum level because price discrimination usually reduces the lowest prices only a part of the way to the marginal-cost level, and because it permits only a small minority of all consumers to buy at these minimum prices.

X

THE APPLICATION OF
MARGINAL-COST PRICE-OUTPUT THEORY

INTRODUCTION

IN THIS CHAPTER we shall explain the application of the general theory of marginal-cost price-output control to individual prices and outputs. A full discussion of this subject would, if course, require many volumes, and we believe that many volumes will be written on it. We shall confine ourselves to a brief statement of the application of this theory to those prices and outputs which would be most affected and to those on which the effect is least understood.

As we have noted, the theory of marginal-cost control is distinct from the theory of optimum investment in fixed capital. Marginal-cost control may be practiced with or without optimum investment, although the latter requires the former. Hence, it is not necessary to explain the application of the theory of optimum investment in this chapter. We shall discuss it occasionally, primarily to stress the difference between optimum price-output control and optimum investment, but these references are not essential to our argument.

It is worth repeating at this point that the practical application of any price-output theory to specific cases can only be guided by partial optimum analysis. The theory of a general optimum is useless for practical purposes, regardless of how mathematically elegant it may be, because it does not tell us how individual prices, and outputs should be determined. Therefore, we shall rely entirely upon partial optimum analysis.

Marginal-cost price control is much more suitable than marginal-cost output control for all industries producing services—including railroads, utilities, and retail stores—under Socialism as well as under Capitalism. Moreover, such price control is probably more suitable for most other industries also under Capitalism. In this book, we are especially interested in demonstrating the wide applicability of marginal-cost price-output theory under Capitalism, both because this has been neglected by other writers and because we have discussed its applicability under Socialism in detail in another book. For these reasons, we shall devote this chapter largely to the application of the theory of marginal-cost price control.

The basic principle of marginal-cost price-output control and its nine corollaries apply to all price goods. A comprehensive discussion of the application of marginal-cost theory would require an explanation of how the basic rule and each of its corollaries should be applied to each price good in each industry. To save space, we shall discuss only representative prices and outputs in certain industries, and we shall only explain the application of the most relevant corollaries.

THE APPLICATION OF MARGINAL-COST PRICE-OUTPUT THEORY TO INDIVIDUAL PRICE GOODS

There are two ways of bringing outputs closer to ideal levels. One is to control individual prices and outputs so as to bring individual prices closer to marginal costs and the other is to adopt reforms which simultaneously bring *many* prices closer to marginal costs. In this section, we shall explain, by industries, how *individual* prices or outputs should be controlled.

Railroad Rates

Most writers who have tried to apply the theory of marginal-cost price control to railroads have stressed the fact that railroads are notably subject to decreasing costs and have concluded that for this reason alone rates equal to marginal cost would be far below the so-called average-cost level. However, they have been talking about long-run marginal cost, and rates should equal current marginal cost. Optimum pricing alone would indeed reduce rates sharply, probably by two thirds, as long as excess capacity prevailed, but since rolling stock is insufficient to handle a large increase in traffic and since some of it wears out every year, it would not be long before marginal cost rose above the so-called average-cost level if no new rolling stock were purchased. Hence, marginal-cost price control alone would result in temporary deficits only. However, optimum investment in fixed capital is also desirable, and together with marginal-cost control would probably reduce railroad rates well below the present level and result in large continuing deficits.

The initial fall in the rate level which would result from the introduction of marginal-cost control is not the most important rate change which would follow. Much more important, for instance, is the fact that freight rates would be based upon the marginal cost of transport rather than upon the value of the good being shipped. Freight rates are now based upon the value of goods, which is thought to represent ability to pay, because this enables railroads to discriminate between shippers. Shippers of the most valuable goods are required to pay rates more than ten times as high as shippers of the least valuable goods, and a large thick commodity classification book must be consulted by every shipper to determine which discriminatory rate his goods are subject to. Basing rates on the value of the shipment instead of upon the cost of the service is a clear violation of the first corollary of marginal-cost control, the rule of equal prices for all customers. Shippers buy ton-miles of transport, not ton-miles of shoe transport or ton-miles of hat transport. The price for this basic service should be the same to all customers. There are, it is true, different classes of transport (fast, slow, refrigerator car, cattle car, etc.), and rate differences based upon cost differences are required by marginal-cost price-output theory, but rate differences based only upon differences in the value of the good shipped conflict with the first corollary.

Many other railroad pricing policies would be changed by the application of the first corollary. For instance, it is now customary to grant special low rates to urban commuters because it is believed their ability or willingness to pay is low. However, the mean marginal costs of hauling commuters, who travel during the hours of peak demand, is much greater than the costs of hauling passengers who travel during off-peak hours, and therefore they should pay a higher rather than a lower rate. Indeed, there should be no separate classification for commuters, some of whom travel during off-peak hours. If any classification is used, it should be a classification into peak and off-peak hour passengers.

A similar criticism is valid against all rate reductions for excursion and vacation trips, usually made during months of peak passenger demand, and for all reductions on round-trip rates. The marginal costs of transportation, other than ticket-selling costs, are not affected by the fact that a man buys a round-trip ticket instead of two one-way tickets. And if it is desired to reduce ticket-selling costs, the same rate reduction should be granted to a man who buys two one-way tickets.

Special fares for ministers, children, soldiers, etc., also violate the first corollary. In general, all fare and freight rate differences which do not represent marginal cost differences are contrary to the theory of marginal-cost price control.

There are two classes of marginal costs of freight movement: (1) marginal terminal costs—all marginal costs incurred before freight leaves the home terminal and after it arrives at the end terminal (spotting and picking up cars, accounting costs, etc.), and (2) marginal line-haul costs—all marginal costs of moving freight between terminals. Both are significant costs of every freight movement, and neither varies with the value of the shipment.

Although marginal line-haul costs do not vary with the value of the freight, they do vary with the nature of the railroad line. It costs more to pull cars uphill than down, over single-track than over multi-track lines, and over rough light rails than over smooth heavy rails. The basic rule that price should equal marginal costs means, therefore, that line-haul charges should differ, as marginal costs differ, on various sections of railroad line.

If the differences in marginal line-haul costs on different sections (defined as the distance between the two nearest terminals) were great enough and if there were no costs of determining and using different line-haul charges for every section of every rail line, these numerous charges should be determined and used. Probably the differences in line-haul costs are small enough and the costs of determining and using them are large enough to justify grouping all sections into five to ten cost classes and using a uniform line-haul charge for all sections in each cost class. All routes (combinations of sections) should also be classified into these cost groups on the basis of the average line-haul cost per mile for the entire route.

Similar reasoning applies to terminal charges. The cost of terminal service depends upon the type of service and the efficiency of the terminal. These costs should be determined and grouped into cost classes, and the rates for all terminal services in each class should be uniform. The freight charge for each carload should include two terminal charges, each calculated by the use of a cost classification of terminal services and a list of charges for each class of terminal service.

Line-haul charges should be stated per gross ton-mile. In other words, the entire gross weight of the loaded car, including the weight of the car itself, should be used. It is impossible to haul freight without hauling a freight car, and costs vary with the total, not the net, weight.[1] Rates based on gross weight would encourage fuller loading of cars. To determine the cost of a carload shipment, a shipper should add the weight of the empty car to the weight of his freight. Hence, the rate book should state the weight of each kind of empty car.

The second corollary of marginal-cost price-output theory, the rule of separate prices for optional services, should be applied to all of the numerous optional services rendered by railroads. If goods are stored, processed, reshipped, reconsigned, specially protected, moved at special speeds, or in any other way given optional services, the railroad should make a separate charge for this service and this charge should approximate the marginal cost of rendering the service. It was once common for railroads to perform certain optional services free for preferred customers instead of granting them the personal price discounts outlawed by the ICC. Other optional services, like pickup and delivery, are now performed free of charge. This is all contrary to the second corollary.

The third corollary, multi-marginal pricing, requires that semifixed marginal costs be covered by separate prices. Terminal costs are semifixed marginal costs. They are independent of the amount of transport service rendered in the sense that they do not vary with the distance freight is moved, but they can be allocated to individual units of service. Hence, it would be desirable to charge a separate price for them. In other words, all freight bills should include at least two separate charges, terminal charges and line-haul charges. Since terminal costs alone are over half of total marginal costs, the result of the application of multi-marginal pricing would be to make total charges per mile much lower for long hauls than for short hauls.

The fourth corollary, quantity pricing, is also applicable to railroad

[1] If a railroad has cars of different empty weight which can hold the same net weight, the charge should be based upon the weight of the last car used, probably the heaviest car, for new cars are lighter than old cars of the same capacity.

rates. Line-haul costs do not vary with the number of carloads shipped by a single shipper, but terminal costs do. It is much easier to pick up ten loaded cars from one company than to pick up ten cars from ten scattered spur tracks. Therefore, terminal charges should decline as the number of cars offered for shipment by a single shipper at a single time from a single plant increase. Further economies result from the shipment of two or more cars to a single consignee at the same time since it costs little more to spot two cars instead of one on the consignee's spur track. Therefore, terminal charges should be still lower when two or more of the cars subject to the above discount are consigned to the same consignee. These charges should reach their minimum for an entire trainload from one shipper to one consignee.

We turn next to the applications of the fifth corollary, cyclical pricing. The marginal costs of railroad operation fluctuate cyclically due to seasonal changes in the volume of traffic, which cause seasonal unemployment and/or scarcity of labor and rolling stock. When the quantity of rolling stock becomes short, trains should move faster, and labor should work overtime. Such measures raise peak marginal costs above off-peak marginal costs. Since marginal costs fluctuate seasonally, often to a marked degree, railroad rates should also move in regular seasonal cycles. This would persuade shippers to reduce their shipments during peak periods and increase them during off-peak periods and thus bring about a fuller use of existing facilities, a reduced need for new capital, and lower average costs.

As the volume of freight grows, due to seasonal or secular factors, the first physical bottleneck is usually the fixed supply of freight cars of each type. No charge should be made for the use of a given type of freight car as long as the supply of them exceeds the demand at the terminal. When cars must be imported from other terminals, the costs of importing them become marginal costs and should be added to freight rates. When cars are short all over or the cost of importing cars is excessive, the supply of and demand for each type of car should be brought into balance in each terminal area by charging daily car rentals (demurrage rates). This rental charge should cover at least three, and sometimes four, time periods: (1) the necessary time the car is on the shipper's spur track; (2) the average time (not the actual time) required by the desired haul; (3) the actual time the car is on the consignee's spur track until he reports it ready for release; and (4) if the movement of the loaded car is in the prevailing direction for such cars, the average time required to return the car to its point of origin. The rent per day for each type of car should be just high enough to balance the supply of and the demand for each type of car. The current practice of charging demurrage rates above marginal cost whether or not cars are in short supply is clearly contrary to marginal-cost price-output theory.

On any given railroad route there is usually more traffic in each kind of car in one direction than in the other. When this is true, the marginal cost of hauling freight in one direction includes the cost of hauling the empty car back. This cost may be reduced by using the car to haul freight part of the way back, either on the same route or on some other. Shippers in the prevailing direction should always pay all costs of the return trip not covered by those who use the cars on part or all of the return trip. Shippers (and passengers) against the prevailing direction should pay only the additional costs due to their use of cars which must be returned empty anyway, so long as rates this low do not result in the use of all empty cars. When all empty return cars are used, rates on the return trip should be raised and rates on the trip out should be lowered so that the demand for cars of each type both ways is equal and so that the sum of the rates in both directions just covers the combined marginal costs of the round trip. This is an application of our sixth corollary, on the pricing of joint products.

When the prevailing direction of traffic is subject to regular seasonal changes, the cost of returning empty cars must be weighed against the cost of leaving them unused until they are needed to carry freight in the opposite direction. If there is a surplus of cars, there are no marginal costs of idleness. At such times, therefore, cars need not be returned until they are needed to carry freight on the return trip, and the original shipper need not be required to pay any part of the costs of returning an empty car. However, this reasoning is valid only if the freight moved in the type of car in question is equal in both directions for the seasonal cycle and if there is a surplus of cars at both terminals throughout the season. These conditions are likely to be rare. The general rule that shippers should pay part or all of the costs of returning empty cars is therefore usually valid.

Some car costs, notably wear and tear caused by use (not by the weather), are marginal costs even when cars are in excess supply. These pure marginal costs should be included in marginal line-haul and/or terminal costs.

We have now explained some of the applications to railroad rates and passenger fares of six of the nine corollaries of the principle of marginal-cost control. We shall not discuss the application of the other three because either they are inapplicable or their meaning is reasonably clear. Piece rates are difficult to apply to railroad work, but they ought to be used wherever they are economical, and when they are used, the pay for the marginal unit of output should equal the full value of that unit. The sixth corollary, which condemns price stabilization, is applicable to all prices of reproducible price goods. The ninth corollary does not apply to any prices. It is applicable only to price taxes, which are not discussed in this chapter.

Since railroads must supply marginal service in car lots, the marginal supply unit is often larger than the marginal demand unit. This is always true for less-than-carload freight and for passenger service. Hence L.C.L. freight rates and passenger fares should equal mean marginal costs (the average variable cost per demand unit of adding one supply unit), not marginal cost (see pp. 74, 151 above).

Railroads are now owned by the state in nearly all advanced nations. Thus private ownership is no obstacle to the application of the theory of marginal-cost price control to railroad rates in most countries. In the United States, where private ownership prevails, the railroads have been closely regulated by government agencies so long that it should be possible to require railroads to adopt marginal-cost price control if the government were to assume responsibility for the resulting loss of net income.

A large part of the above discussion of railroad rates obviously applies also to the rates charged for highway, airway, and water transport.

Highway and Canal Tolls

Modern paved highways represent heavy fixed investments. Their total cost consists largely of: (1) interest, and (2) maintenance made necessary by exposure to the weather. Only a minor fraction of total costs is due to use. Moreover, virtually all wear and tear caused by use is probably due to a very small number of users, those operating heavy trucks and busses. Private passenger cars and light trucks cause no significant wear. Once a highway has been built, there is no point in restricting its use by such cars. Since toll charges always restrict use, and, in addition, cause both inconvenience to those who pay them and collection costs to those who collect them, owners of light cars should not be required to pay tolls unless this is necessary to prevent undue congestion, a rare situation on toll roads. If tolls are needed to reduce congestion, they should be imposed only during hours of peak use.

When heavy trucks and busses cause significant marginal wear to highways, they should be required to pay a toll or price tax roughly equal to the marginal cost involved. Gas taxes might serve this purpose if the loaded weight per wheel were properly restricted and this restriction were enforced.

The large gas taxes now collected are uneconomic because they compel small car owners to pay a price for highway use which is far above the marginal cost they cause. It would be much better to raise an equal sum by fixed annual car license fees. Income and poll taxes would be still better because they would not fall on the price of any specific good. In other words, gas taxes in excess of marginal costs are bad because they reduce highway use below, and raise the use of other goods above, the ideal level, while income and poll taxes are good taxes because they do not influence significantly the nature of consumption.

The common argument that tolls should be used to finance new highways and other projects because they cannot be financed in any other way is political rather than economic. If consumers can pay tolls, they can pay taxes, and the collection of taxes involves less inconvenience to the public and lower collection cost to the state than does the collection of tolls.

Once a canal has been built, marginal use costs little. If there are no locks and no congestion, marginal costs may be negligible, in which case no tolls should be charged. If there are locks, but no congestion, tolls should cover only the marginal costs of lock operation. When congestion develops, tolls should be raised until they reduce traffic to the ideal level.

Panama Canal tolls now (1950) amount to $14,000 per round trip for a C-3 freighter, the equivalent of a month's wages for the crew of forty-five. These tolls cover the full average costs of civilian and military use of the canal. The marginal costs of civilian use are probably less than 5 percent of the tolls. If civilian tolls were reduced to this level, far more use would be made of the canal, and much more benefit obtained from it. Moreover, since the canal was constructed primarily for military reasons, the general taxpayer should pay all non-marginal costs as well as the marginal costs due to military use.

Panama Canal tolls should, of course, ignore the value of the cargo and the size of the ship except when these affect marginal costs. They should be based solely on marginal costs unless congestion threatens.

The chief marginal cost of using the Panama Canal is the cost of operating the locks. This cost is little greater when two, three, or four ships use the locks at the same time than when one ship uses them. Hence, ships which are able and willing to go through the locks together should pay much lower tolls than those which require or demand individual lock service.

Bridge and Tunnel Tolls

Bridges and tunnels also represent a very large capital investment and cost of maintaining the physical facilities is little affected by the volume of use. Charging a bridge or tunnel toll prevents some desirable use whenever use is below capacity. If the toll is fifty cents, thousands of people who would get some benefit from using the bridge or tunnel, but who estimate the value of this gain at less than fifty cents, or who do not have fifty cents at the time they wish to use the bridge or tunnel, will not use it. As demand is often elastic in such cases, the number of persons who might gain from the abolition of tolls is often large. Once a bridge or tunnel has been built, the greater the voluntary use of it, up to the point of congestion, the greater is the social benefit since more use means more benefit at no cost. And congestion is likely only during hours of peak use, i.e., only during a few hours a day. During these hours, tolls high enough to prevent congestion would be economic if the gains from reducing congestion were greater than the costs of using tolls, including the slowing down of traffic at the toll gates and the total, not marginal, cost of collecting tolls.

Although this argument for free use of bridges and tunnels is less than twenty years old, most highway bridges and tunnels in America are free, probably because of the obvious inconvenience of stopping cars to collect tolls. Moreover, since most of them are now free, it is certainly feasible to make the remaining toll bridges and tunnels free.

Postal Rates

The postal service is an industry with indefinitely decreasing costs. The adoption of both optimum investment and marginal-cost price control would reduce postal rates far below present levels. Optimum pricing alone would reduce postal rates well below existing rates and keep them below these rates for a long time, if not indefinitely, because there is large surplus capacity in the fixed plant of this industry (one-shift operation is customary) and because the chief cost of handling mail is a labor cost, which declines steadily as the volume of mail increases. For instance, a postman who delivered twice as much mail to each address as he does now would need to walk only half as far to deliver his present daily load.

We have already explained that freight rates should be reduced to marginal costs. The railroad rate for carrying mail is now far above the marginal cost of carrying it. Much the same thing is true of air and highway mail-carrying charges.

The American postage rate on first-class mail is three cents, but the marginal cost of handling such mail is probably less than one cent. Hence, the rate on such mail should be reduced to one cent or less. This is so low, the demand for first-class mail service (advertising excluded) is so inelastic, and the cost and inconvenience of printing, selling, affixing, and postmarking stamps are so great that the rate should probably be reduced to zero.

While first-class mail rates are now probably above so-called average cost, rates for second, third, and fourth-class mail are well below average cost, and this is responsible for the continuing postal losses. It is likely, however, that these rates also are well above marginal cost. If so, they should be reduced to marginal cost. Since marginal cost is the same regardless of the contents of a letter or package, the rates should be the same for all mail unless it is decided to carry non-advertising letters free of charge.

The demand for postal service is very much greater during the Christmas season than at any other time of the year. Many extra temporary workers must be hired to handle Christmas mail, and marginal costs are higher than at other times of the year. Postal rates should therefore be higher at this season.

People who change their address and have mail forwarded to a new address impose significant costs on the postal system for which they should be required to pay. A charge equal to marginal cost (perhaps twenty-five cents) should be made for recording a change of address, and an additional charge of perhaps five cents should be made for re-addressing each letter or parcel. In addition, extra postage should be charged for forwarding mail not handled free of charge. These policies would greatly reduce the volume of mail sent to old addresses.

Rapid-Transit Fares

Rapid transit includes subway and streetcar systems, both of which have heavy fixed costs, and bus transportation, which has relatively small fixed costs. Because of this difference in fixed costs, marginal-cost price control would have different effects.

In the case of subways and streetcars, marginal-cost price control would result in great differences in fares between periods of peak demand for service (7–9 A.M. and 4–6 P.M.) and periods of off-peak demand. For instance, in New York City the peak-hour fare might be twenty cents and the off-peak-hour fare might be five cents or zero. During off-peak periods, the fare should be equal to mean marginal costs which are far below average costs at such times. During hours of peak use, on the other hand, fares should be high enough to balance supply and demand without undue crowding. Only experience can show what fares would achieve this result. Such a variation in fares would both increase traffic during off-peak hours and decrease it during peak hours.[2] It would increase the benefits from the use of the existing capacity and postpone the need for additions to this capacity.

It is quite possible that mean marginal costs for streetcar and/or subway transportation during some off-peak hours are so low that transportation should be free at this time. The cost and inconvenience of collecting fares are considerable. If no fares were charged, it would be unnecessary to employ conductors, and delays caused by collection of fares would be eliminated. Passengers are often unable to get on a streetcar until persons ahead of them have paid their fares, and the motorman cannot start his car until all passengers are abroad. On one-man cars, he cannot start until all fares have been paid. In New York City, passengers often miss a subway train because they have to get change at the change booth before they can pass through the turnstiles. The five or ten-minute delay thus caused is far more costly in real terms, with labor worth two dollars an hour on the average, than the marginal cost of subway transportation during off-peak hours.

As previously explained, the fixed costs of urban bus lines are much lower than the fixed costs of streetcar and subway lines. This means

[2] In his *Studies in the Economics of Overhead Costs* (Chicago, 1923), John M. Clark stated that no variations in streetcar fares between off-peak and rush-hour business "would serve any useful purpose in improving the load-curve" (pp. 173–74), but gave no reasons for this surprising conclusion. To us it seems obvious that the use of streetcars in off-peak periods would increase if fares were drastically reduced or eliminated.

that the application of marginal-cost control to bus fares would result in much smaller differences between peak-hour fares and off-peak-hour fares, but there would still be significant differences.

Many rapid-transit systems are already city owned, and the number will increase. In such cases, there is no obstacle to the use of marginal-cost price control except prejudice. The benefits of a rapid-transit system are so widely distributed that there should be little objection to the local taxes needed to cover deficits on transit systems once the real facts are understood. Rapid transit increases real-estate values in all areas served, saves the time and money of all users, reduces congestion on city streets, increases the mobility of labor, and in other ways benefits all city dwellers.

Telephone Rates

We shall discuss the application of the theory of marginal-cost price control to telephone rates separately because the phone industry differs in important respects from other utilities.[3] To simplify our problem, we assume that all central exchanges are fully automatic, even those handling long distance calls.

The first corollary of marginal-cost control, equal prices for all customers, implies that phone rates should be the same for commercial, government, and domestic customers. Rates should differ only with the kind and time of service, not with the class of customer.

The second corollary, separate charges for optional services, means that a price equal to marginal cost should be charged for every call to information, every copy of a phone book, each repair service due to the customer's fault, all optional phone accessories, each listing in the phone book, and all other optional services rendered by the phone company, if the real costs of making such charges do not exceed the benefit from them.

In the larger American cities, phone books contain a thousand very large pages and the marginal cost of printing and distributing them often exceeds a dollar. Many homes and offices require several different directories and/or must replace them before new ones are printed

<hr>

[3] Another reason for a separate treatment is that we wish to explicitly support several rules rejected or ignored by A. Hazelwood in his article "Optimum Pricing as Applied to Telephone Service," *Review of Economic Studies* (June, 1951). He denied the virtues of marginal-cost pricing and tried to apply average-cost pricing to telephone rates. For another recent discussion of ideal telephone rates not reviewed in our history, see D. G. Tyndall, "The Relative Merits of Average Cost Pricing, Marginal Cost Pricing, and Price Discrimination," *Quarterly Journal of Economics* (Aug., 1951), pp. 369–71.

because of hard or careless use. A special charge for each copy of each book would allocate these widely varying costs to those responsible for them and would decrease the demand for books. Those who wish to be listed in the phone book should pay the full cost of setting the type for the directory, as well as all clerical costs of collecting and editing the copy. This might be twenty-five cents per line for the first listing and ten cents thereafter for each reprinting without change. The costs of paper, printing, binding, and delivery should probably be paid by those who receive directories, according to the number they receive, since these costs vary primarily with the number of books needed.

The third corollary, multi-marginal pricing, requires that special charges be made for separate necessary steps in providing a service when the costs of these steps vary independently. Therefore, special charges should be made for connecting a building with a phone exchange or main, for turning service on or off when people move, for rendering bills, and for installing and removing instruments. These services should be charged for separately, at a price equal to marginal cost, because their frequency and cost varies widely from customer to customer.

The fourth corollary, quantity pricing, cannot be literally applied to phone messages, but it suggests that the charge for a ten-minute call should not be twice the charge for a five-minute call. Certainly the marginal costs of a ten-minute call are much less than twice the marginal costs of a five-minute call.

The fifth corollary, cyclical pricing, means that the level of charges for phone calls should usually rise and fall in cycles. With automatic exchanges, the marginal-cost per phone call (including busy and completed calls) is probably constant. However, rates should rise enough to balance supply and demand during peak hours if peak demand exceeds capacity at prices equal to marginal costs. In other words, phone message rates should always either equal short-run marginal cost or be high enough to balance supply and demand. With automatic exchanges and excess capacity the marginal costs of local phone calls are too small to justify measuring their number or duration and making special charges for them. It would obviously be uneconomic to spend two cents to determine charges of less than two cents a call. Assuming unused capacity, it would probably be uneconomic to spend one cent to determine and collect a charge of three, four, or five cents. The fact that this would be profitable to the phone company does not prove it would increase welfare. The additional work involved in charging and collecting prices is worth while only when it prevents a greater loss from excessive consumption, consumption whose marginal cost is above the price consumers would be willing to pay, and this loss is only the usually small difference between marginal cost and marginal benefit. Moreover, the demand for local phone service is relatively inelastic. The average person who has a phone would not use it much more often to make local calls if the charge were reduced from one or two cents to zero. Hence, all local phone calls during periods when capacity exceeds demand should probably be free of charge.

Other Public Utility Rates

In a broad sense of the term, all of the industries we have so far discussed are public utilities. In this section we shall consider the chief remaining utilities—gas, water, electricity, steam, and sewer systems— all of which come under the term public utility in its narrowest sense because, like the telephone industry, they have main lines over or under every street and connections to most houses on each street.

These utilities have large fixed costs and usually operate at a level well below their capacity. Only during a few hours of the day in months of peak seasonal demand does demand approach capacity. Thus their marginal costs are far below average cost 90 percent of the time. The application of the theory of marginal-cost price control to them would therefore result, at least at the start, in a sharp fall in the average rate and, hence, a sharp rise in the use of utility service. For instance, domestic users of electricity might have their electric rates cut from an average of around four cents per kilowat hour to perhaps one cent.

There are some towns where the marginal cost of using water or natural gas is negligible because they are close to large supplies of water and natural gas which would otherwise be wasted. In such cases, no charge should be made for marginal use of water or gas unless this pricing policy requires an expansion of transmission and distribution lines. Even if an expansion in these lines is required, the savings in meter and collection costs resulting from free use may be so great that consumers would be glad to pay for these additional facilities through taxes or fixed service charges in order to continue to enjoy free use of marginal service.

The use of meters to measure water and gas and the rendering of individual bills are much more expensive than most people realize. Meter use costs amount to about 10 percent of total costs, and in many cases to half of marginal costs. The saving from the elimination of meters and other expenses of rendering individual bills would help to compensate for the cost of new distribution equipment required as a result of eliminating charges for water and gas whose marginal cost is negligible at the source of supply.

The first corollary of marginal-cost control requires that utility rates for the same service should be equal for all consumers. This means that domestic, industrial, and commercial users should all pay the same rates. Rate differentials should be based on cost differences, not on the customer's ability to pay.

The second corollary means that all utility customers should be required to pay special charges which cover the marginal costs of all optional services rendered. Among these services are repairs on appliances, installation of extra equipment, relocation of connections or outlets, etc.

The third corollary implies that customers should pay separately for the marginal costs necessary to provide or maintain utility services to them individually, but not a part of the cost of the marginal unit of service. These include the cost of turning service on or off, meter-reading costs, and the costs of submitting periodic bills. They never include any costs of investment in fixed capital.

The construction of a main line by each lot is a fixed investment which is subject to the theory of optimum investment rather than to the theory of optimum price. The capital cost of installing utility mains is really a part of the capital cost of opening a new subdivision. It should be paid by the subdivider, not by the utility, and passed on to each lot buyer, for they are directly responsible for these marginal capital investments. The costs of connecting each house with the street main and installing a meter are a similar investment, one which should be made by the housebuilder, or buyer, not by the utility. This cost depends upon the size of the lot, the level of the lot, closeness of rock to the surface, the size and plan of the house, etc. Since this investment is for the sole benefit of the homeowner and since its amount depends in part upon his decisions, he should pay for it, but it is never a marginal cost.

The fourth corollary, quantity pricing, has no application to utility rates. However, cyclical pricing, the fifth corollary, has important applications. Demand for most utility services goes through regular daily, weekly, and annual cycles, and rates should vary accordingly, unless demand is always short of normal capacity. If demand is below capacity throughout the cycle, there is little if any basis for rate changes since off-peak marginal costs are likely to be about the same throughout the cycle. When demand rises above normal capacity in periods of peak demand, however, marginal costs rise sharply, and rates should rise with them until they balance supply and demand.

The chief obstacle to this form of cyclical pricing of utility services is the difficulty of distinguishing between peak-period and off-peak-period use by small consumers. Most meters merely record total use and do not permit price discrimination according to the hour or day of use, though discrimination by month or season of use is possible. However, clock meters, which distinguish between daily peak and off-peak use, have long been available and may soon become economical for some domestic uses.

The system of pricing utility services which we have recommended might result in large deficits during the first years of its use, even if no new investments were made, and would certainly result in continuing deficits if investment were maintained at the optimum level. Public utilities, however, are already largely owned by the state in most advanced countries, so it would be easy for the state to subsidize them without creating management problems, if taxpayers were convinced of the wisdom of such subsidies and the taxes necessary to support them. In the meantime, the losses resulting from ideal pricing alone, or from both optimum pricing and investment, might be covered by regular periodic fixed charges per customer which do not vary with the volume of use of utility service.

Another compromise or transitional method of partly covering these deficits deserves mention. When excess capacity exists, marginal-cost price control results in deficits to utility stockholders. When inflation occurs, creditors lose real income and equity owners gain both real and money income. If the gains to equity owners from inflation were balanced against their losses from rate reductions, it would often be possible for regulatory authorities to bring utility rates closer to marginal costs without any loss to equity owners. Since inflation recurs periodically, it provides many chances for bringing prices closer to marginal costs under Capitalism.

There is, indeed, evidence that American railroad and utility rates have been so regulated during and after periods of inflation that they were in fact brought much nearer to marginal cost. This occurred because regulatory authorities tried to prevent the equity owners from earning unreasonable profits rather than because they attempted to bring prices closer to marginal cost. In fact, however, the latter result is a better justification for their policy than the former.

Moving-Picture Film Rentals

The cost of producing a new moving picture may be millions of dollars but once the film has been made the marginal cost of making prints and renting them to exhibitors is relatively small. Therefore, the rents charged for prints should be small. All the costs of producing the original negative should be covered by taxation or by some other system of fixed charges.

Since the principle of marginal-cost control applies only to *reproducible* goods, it does not apply to original films, or to any other works of art, but it does apply to film prints and all other reproductions of works of art. When original works of art are sold outright, they should be sold for whatever they will bring, not for prices which equal marginal costs. On the other hand, if reproductions of works of art are sold, they should be sold for a price which covers the marginal costs of reproduction only, even if this results in a heavy loss to the creator of the original work of art. Moving-picture prints, of course, should be rented, rather than sold, in order to permit marginal-cost pricing.

Spending a large sum of money on making a new moving picture negative is lumpy investment in something as durable as most fixed capital. The problem of whether to make such investments is not subject to marginal analysis. It can only be solved by a comparison of total costs with total benefits, including consumers' surplus, over the life of the negative and the prints made from it.

Undue limitation of investment in new films would increase the consumers' surplus earned by old films, but it would not make these old films less unprofitable if prices were ideal. The income from additional use of the old films would merely cover the additional costs due to such use.

If private film producers are subsidized in order to permit them to rent films at rents equal to marginal costs, this should be done in such a way as to offer rewards for producing popular pictures and penalties for producing unpopular pictures. Such a result could easily be achieved by paying total subsidies large enough to cover total production costs but distributing these subsidies among individual producers on the basis of paid attendance at exhibitions of their films. The subsidy paid for each picture would then depend on the popularity of the picture. There would be no guarantee of a profit for every picture or every producer. The ablest producers might earn large profits and the least able might suffer large losses. Moreover, such subsidies would not require any limitation on free entry of new firms into the industry.

If the proposed film investment and price-control methods did not result in the production of enough religious or art films, those who desired more of these films could organize clubs and raise extra funds to further subsidize such films.

The existing system of fixing film rents is bad not only because rents cover average costs but also because they vary with attendance. Thus they turn fixed real costs into variable money costs. If film rents were equal to marginal cost, they would not vary with attendance or the gross income from their exhibition, but only with the wear and tear due to film use.

Theater Ticket Prices

The reduction of film print rentals to the marginal costs of renting such prints would alone result in a sharp fall in the price of movie theater tickets. But this is not enough. Whenever there are empty seats, these prices should be further reduced towards the level of the marginal costs of admitting one more person to the theater, and these costs are very low, if not negligible.

Most of the costs of operating a theater are non-marginal costs. Film rentals equal to marginal costs would not vary with theater attendance. Property taxes, insurance, interest, and the wages of the manager, cashier, ticket taker, and projectionist are all fixed costs. Only the number of ushers hired, the wear and tear on the seats and carpets, and the amount of cleaning work vary with attendance, and then by no means proportionately. Hence, marginal costs are probably less than 10 percent of so-called average costs whenever some seats remain empty. At such times admission charges should be less than 10 percent of average cost.

In the past, attendance at moving-picture theaters has probably averaged less than 25 percent of capacity. Moreover, the number of theaters is less than it would have been if film rentals had been reduced to the level of marginal rental costs. The application of marginal-cost price control to film rentals and theater admission prices would increase attendance at existing theaters by 200 to 300 percent at an additional cost of only 20 to 30 percent. Combined with optimum investment, it would also increase the number of theaters. The moving-picture production and exhibition industries are therefore among those industries whose benefits are most seriously limited by so-called average-cost pricing.

Unlike factories, theaters cannot increase their output at any given time merely by hiring more or better labor and raising their marginal costs. The number of seats is limited, and marginal costs do not increase as this limit is approached. Therefore, prices should be raised above marginal cost whenever this is necessary in order to balance supply and demand. Ideal investment in theaters would not provide enough seats to meet peak demand at prices equal to marginal cost. Since the desire to attend movies varies in strength in a predictable manner from hour to hour each day, from day to day each week, and from season to season during the year, theater prices should vary during the day, week, and year in a regular way. Moreover, these variations should be much greater than they are now. They should keep the theater almost full at all times when price is above marginal cost, but should also prevent waiting for entrance. If patrons want more space, seats should be placed farther apart.

It is customary for theaters to charge different prices for seats in different sections of the theater. Such price differences are not justified by marginal-cost theory, but they may be necessary to balance supply and demand for seats in each section. Existing price differences have not been designed to accomplish this but to expropriate a portion of the consumers' surplus by basing prices on ability to pay.

It is also usual for movie theaters to grant reduced prices to children. This is contrary to the first corollary of marginal-cost control. The marginal costs of providing a seat are as high for a child as for an adult. However, since prices for children are now above marginal costs, the full application of marginal-cost price control would reduce all theater prices below the level now charged for children.

There are a number of ways in which a Capitalist state could induce moving-picture exhibitors to lower their prices towards or to the marginal-cost level. In the first place, it could grant subsidies or tax exemptions to theaters with an average seat vacancy rate of less than 10 percent. This is a relatively feasible method because it does not require the determination of net profits or marginal costs for individual theaters. The average vacancy rate is far easier to determine and check. In the second place—perhaps in combination with the first method—the state might impose special taxes of so much per seat on all exhibitors having an average vacancy rate of more than 10 percent. A third method would be for the state to abolish theater admission taxes, which now (1952) amount to 20 percent in the United States. All sales taxes which do not represent a real marginal cost are economically harmful, but they have especially bad results when they fall on theater tickets. A fourth method would be for the state to pay subsidies equal to a uniform percent of gross revenue to all theaters with a vacancy rate less than 10 percent. These subsidies should be just high enough to persuade the great majority of theaters to achieve the desired low vacancy rate.

Other methods might be suggested and a great deal more might be said about each of the methods already mentioned, but we cannot devote more space to this subject. It is worthy of emphasis, however, that none of the methods proposed would encourage extravagance on the part of exhibitors or reduce their incentive to exhibit the most popular pictures, for each manager would remain free to increase his profits by reducing his expenses and by showing the most popular pictures.

We have not proposed that a Capitalist state should instruct each theater to fix its prices at marginal costs, on the understanding that the state would cover its deficit, because : (1) there are over 15,000 theaters —too many to permit economical state review of deficit calculations; and (2) under Capitalism a subsidy high enough to cover any deficit would remove all pecuniary incentives to economy, efficiency, and the best choice of films. In a Socialist economy, on the other hand, every theater manager would report to an area supervisor who could check upon accounting methods, operating efficiency, and the choice of popular films. Such supervision is not possible under competitive Capitalism, and, even if it were, the supervisors would be interested in private profit rather than social welfare.

Taxation is the ideal source of funds to cover the deficits which would result from renting and exhibiting films at prices equal to marginal cost because it would have the least effect upon theater attendance, but other methods much superior to average-cost pricing are also available. For instance, entrance to moving-picture theaters could be limited to those who had paid an annual license fee to the state, and these fees could be high enough (perhaps $20.00 would do) to cover the over-all deficit in the production and exhibition of films. This would prevent some persons from going to movies at all, and that is why it is a less desirable method than taxation, but once a person had bought a license he would attend movies much more often, and the same investment in producing films would yield a much greater total benefit.

We have discussed only moving-picture theaters in this section because they make up 90 percent of all theaters. Most of the discussion applies also to other theaters and to other types of structures for seating spectators. The marginal cost of permitting people to occupy seats that would otherwise be vacant are so low that the managers of all theaters, ball parks, stadiums, and other stands should reduce their prices enough to achieve almost full occupancy. The more expensive the stage show or spectacle, the greater the social gain from such a price policy.

If it were possible to charge a price for television shows, the prices should equal marginal cost per viewer, which is zero. The government, not the viewer or the advertiser, should pay for all radio and television shows. The elimination of advertising would not only be a boon worth almost any cost but would actually reduce broadcasting costs.

Other Commercial Recreation Prices

Demand for the use of bowling alleys, golf courses, tennis courts, pool tables, swimming pools, and other recreational facilities varies greatly from hour to hour during the day, from day to day during the week, and from month to month during the year. The price for their use should be equal to marginal cost except when demand at such a price exceeds supply. During such times price should exceed marginal cost and fluctuate cyclically so as to balance supply and demand. The price for using a hard-surfaced tennis court should vary from ten cents an hour or less in off-peak periods to a dollar or more per hour during some peak periods, and the price for using bowling alleys should vary from perhaps fifteen cents a line to fifty cents a line. Since pin boys must be employed for off-peak as well as peak use, the prices for using bowling alleys should not vary as much as the prices for using tennis courts. Indeed, the costs of marginal use of hard-surfaced tennis courts are so small, and the costs of collecting small fees are so large, that their use should probably be free during off-peak periods, especially if they are publicly owned.

The prices charged for the use of commercial recreational facilities already vary somewhat according to demand. However, these variations have not been introduced in order to maximize the general welfare but rather to maximize the profits of the owners. Therefore, they rarely if ever even approach marginal costs during off-peak hours. Marginal-cost price control would drastically reduce the prices now charged during off-peak periods.

It is probably not practical to apply marginal-cost control to privately owned recreational facilities, since they are numerous and usually small, but many recreational facilities are already publicly owned and the number is increasing steadily. Marginal-cost price control could be applied to such facilities now.

Book and Periodical Prices

Books are printed in lots (editions or printings) and the marginal cost of printing one more book is the cost of adding one more unit to a lot. It does not include any of the costs of writing the book, editing it, setting it up in type, etc. It includes only the costs of the additional materials and labor required to print and sell one more copy, and is usually a small fraction of average outlay. Even when the costs of writing a book, which average over half of total cost, are ignored, the marginal costs of clothbound copies are less than 25 percent of average costs. In the case of paper-bound books printed in small editions, marginal costs are a still lower proportion of average costs, for binding costs are a large part of the marginal cost of clothbound books.

The application of marginal-cost output control to books would probably reduce the price of the average clothbound book by 70 to 80 percent, and the price of most paper-bound books by 80 to 90 percent, assuming no royalties are paid to authors. Cheap paper-bound reprints now selling for twenty-five to fifty cents would not be so seriously affected, but they make up an extremely small fraction of the total number of titles published. Such price reductions would result in a vast increase in the number of books sold, and the higher the quality of the book, the greater would be the increase in sales, on the average. Every additional book sold would yield a real benefit greater than its real cost. The book publishing industry is one of those whose output would be most increased by the adoption of marginal-cost output control. The same reasoning applies to periodicals not financed in large part by advertising—for instance, to the learned journals.

Since books and learned journals are one of the chief aids to both education and research, the application of marginal-cost output control to them would do much to improve the educational level of the people and to speed up the rate of social and technological progress. The combined budget of the publishers in question is so small that these notable results could be achieved at a relatively small cost.

The above estimates of the differences between average and marginal costs in book publishing assume that author's royalties are not a marginal cost. This conflicts with our definition of marginal cost. Author's royalties are actually a marginal money cost, since they are now necessary costs at the margin. However, they represent no real marginal cost. Once an author has written a book, the publication of it causes no further real cost to him. Hence, there should be no royalty payment for the publication of marginal copies.

It is, of course, necessary to reward authors for their work. Magazines and newspapers do this by buying stories and articles outright or by hiring writers on a salary basis. These methods make the author's compensation an overhead cost which does not vary with the number of copies printed and would therefore not affect prices based on marginal costs. Under marginal-cost output control this method of paying authors would greatly increase the resulting deficit,[4] but it would be very beneficial.

Both the decision to write a book and the decision to publish it have much in common with decisions to make new investments in fixed capital. They involve large lump sums rather than small marginal adjustments, and both result in a significant consumers' surplus. In the past, failure to give due weight to consumers' surplus has reduced the number of titles published far below the optimum level. On the other hand, once it has been decided to publish a book, the problem of the ideal size of each printing is subject to marginal analysis and the theory of marginal-cost output control. Each printing should be just large enough to permit the sale of the last copy at a price equal to its marginal cost, which is much less than the average

---

[4] The above comments on copyright royalties apply with equal force to patent royalties. The use of all new patents should be free of charge since royalties represent no real marginal cost.

cost. Every new printing should therefore result in an additional deficit. As in the case of investment in new films, the sole return on the investment should be the consumers' surplus.

A special type of price discrimination is commonly practiced by publishers of a best seller. Prices of new books are kept at a fairly high level until the most intense demands have been met, and then the price is reduced below average cost to widen the market. Often slightly cheaper reprints or new editions are sold at much lower prices. Such discrimination increases the real benefit from the author's and publisher's original investment and is much preferable to straight average-cost pricing, but it does not permit the maximum benefit, achievable only by means of marginal-cost output control.

Although advertising is largely an economic waste and raises the average costs and prices of advertised goods above marginal cost, advertising in periodicals permits the sale of many of them at prices fairly close to or even below marginal cost. A typical hundred-page book sells for $1.50, but a hundred-page magazine with much bigger pages and many expensive illustrations, like *Life,* sells for twenty cents, a price which may be below marginal cost. Thus the application of the theory of marginal-cost control to periodicals containing large amounts of advertising would have relatively little effect upon their price and circulation.

Retail Markups

A retail price includes the producer's selling price and the wholesaler's markup. Only the retail markup, perhaps 40 percent of retail price on the average, is the price of the service performed by the retailer. Since it is the price of a *service,* it is subject to the theory of marginal-cost *price* control. Retail markups would be affected in several significant ways by a full application of this theory.

In the first place, application of the basic principle of marginal-cost control would reduce markups and create deficits. Most retail advertising and some other retail selling costs are neither marginal costs nor investment costs. They are in fact inconsistent with both optimum pricing and optimum investment. But even if they were eliminated, the marginal costs of retailing would be much below average cost because monopolistic competition has resulted in a large excess fixed retail capacity. Thus the initial effect of marginal-cost price control would be a sharp cut in retail markups. If new investment in fixed retail facilities were properly limited, in accordance with the theory of optimum investment, this excess capacity would rapidly disappear, and the gap between average and marginal costs would narrow, but marginal cost would probably remain below average cost because retailing is subject to decreasing costs (see pp. 213–16 above). In other words, there would be continuing deficits as well as large initial deficits. Hence, full application of marginal-cost price control and optimum investment is not practical under Capitalism. But several partial applications which would not create any deficits are feasible. The use of nonideal service charges, moreover, would permit the achievement of most of the gains promised by those applications which would otherwise create deficits.

The first corollary of marginal-cost control, equal prices for all, outlaws price discrimination. Retail price discrimination is of minor importance, but it does exist. For instance, new styles are often sold at high prices at the start of each style period and at lower prices later on. Legitimate markdowns to move unexpected surpluses are economic, but planned markdowns to sell planned stocks after those who can pay more have done so are uneconomic under Socialism. Under Capitalism, price discrimination may be desirable because it permits prices to be closer to marginal costs some of the time than they would otherwise be.

The application of the second corollary, separate charges for optional services, to retail prices is especially important. Retail stores often provide free of charge optional services which have significant costs. Among these services are alterations, credit sales, approval sales, gift wrapping, delivery, pickup, installation, and repairs. Customers who do not use these services are required to pay the same price as those who do use them. This means that prices to nonusers are increased still further above marginal costs while at the same time those who demand these optional services are not required to pay extra for them and are thus encouraged to consume more of these services than they would be willing to pay for. Hence, retail stores should charge separately for all optional services. This is one easy way of bringing prices closer to marginal costs without any state subsidy.

The third corollary, multi-marginal pricing, suggests the advisability of charging separately for the time given to each customer by each clerk. A customer who takes an hour of a clerk's time should be required to pay for that service whether or not she buys anything. A charge of five cents a minute would be reasonable. Many customers consistently take far more time than the average customer, and others, mostly men, consistently take far less than the average customer. Charging a separate price for the time of salesclerks would reduce the number of salesclerks required, and would also permit prices closer to marginal costs. The chief argument against this application of multi-marginal pricing is that the cost and inconvenience of applying it are greater than the probable benefits. The force of this argument depends upon the type of store and/or merchandise sold. It would seem a conclusive argument against special charges for the salesclerks' time in five and ten-cent stores, but not in women's clothing stores. Considerable research will be necessary to decide when this form of multi-marginal pricing should be adopted.

The fourth corollary, quantity pricing, has more important applications to retailing than to any other industry. It requires the reduction of the price of the second and subsequent units of the same article sold to the same customer at the same time to the marginal cost of selling that additional unit.

The sale of gasoline in service stations may be used to illustrate this principle. The price charged for the first gallon sold should be high enough to cover all the necessary marginal costs involved in the sale of one gallon only. It should be ten to twenty cents above tank-wagon cost and nine to nineteen cents above the price of each subsequent gallon sold in one sale. The general principle, of course, is that the price of each unit should equal marginal costs allocatable to that unit, but since the differences between the marginal costs of the second and subsequent units are probably negligible, they may be ignored.

The application of quantity pricing to gas stations would notably increase the size of the average gasoline sale because it would pass the economy of large purchases on to the consumer and thus persuade him to participate in an important rationalization of gasoline retailing. It might eventually reduce the number of gas stations and personnel required by as much as 30 percent, and it would reduce equally the amount of time spent by the consumer in going to, waiting in, and returning from gas stations.

The same system is, of course, desirable in all retail stores. When a man has taken an hour to find a shirt he desires to purchase, and the clerk has devoted ten minutes to the sale, the customer ought to be offered a substantial price inducement to buy one or two more identical shirts. Since it costs the store much less to sell the second and third shirts, there should be a price difference equal to this cost difference. In the case of a man's shirt, the price might be three dollars for the first one and two dollars for each subsequent identical shirt sold at the same time.

Under quantity pricing, both the high price for the first unit and the low price for the second should equal marginal cost. This would often result in losses. However, a compromise form of quantity pricing which would create no deficit is possible under Capitalism. The cost of the first unit could be set high enough to cover both marginal and non-marginal costs, and the price of the subsequent units could then be made equal to marginal costs without causing any loss. This would not be as sound as reducing the price of all units to marginal cost, but it would be much preferable to present practice. Since this compromise would increase economic welfare without causing private losses, its adoption should be required by a Capitalist state.

Cyclical pricing, the fifth corollary of marginal-cost control, means that prices should vary with marginal costs when these costs go through regular cycles. Since there are marked daily, weekly, and seasonal cycles in retail sales, the application of cyclical pricing to retail prices is especially important. Retail prices should vary cyclically with, but not necessarily in close proportion to, retail demand during demand cycles in which marginal cost varies enough to justify price changes.

Since variations in marginal retail costs are relatively small during periods when ample excess retail facilities exist, and since the inconvenience to customers and the cost to the store of changing prices is significant,[5] the application of cyclical pricing to retail prices should probably not involve price changes during these periods. On the other hand, marginal retail costs may rise suddenly and substantially when sales press upon the limits set by physical capacity. Moreover, it is often essential at such times to raise retail prices merely to reduce congestion and waiting for service by customers. Retail prices should always be high enough to reduce the number of customers until they can all be served without undue waiting or crowding.

Cyclical pricing plus optimum investment would achieve a much more even volume of sales throughout the day, week, and year than now exists and would justify longer hours of store operation. Reduc-

[5] To vary retail prices from peak to off-peak periods during the day or week, it would not be necessary to change all the price tags. It would only be necessary to announce a schedule of discounts during off-peak periods.

ing prices to marginal costs during off-peak hours would increase sales at such times, and raising them during peak hours would decrease sales. The result might well be a 50 percent reduction in the amount of capital required for retail facilities. These facilities should be expanded only if the markup over marginal cost during hours of peak demand is high enough to promise a net gain on new retail capacity. In other words, the markup during peak hours should be far above the markup during off-peak hours before retail stores are expanded, and this would be a strong inducement to consumers to buy during off-peak hours.

Cyclical price fluctuations should not be the same for all classes of goods. In the case of high-price items, fluctuations should be smaller than for low-price items. A 1 percent reduction in fur coat prices might increase daily off-peak sales as much as a 10 percent reduction in cigarette prices.

As the number of hours of demand high enough to justify prices above marginal cost increased, it would become necessary to vary the amount of the markup over marginal costs in order to maintain a stable volume of sales during peak hours of varying peak demand. Variations in demand during periods when prices above marginal cost are proper should result in price variations, not in fluctuations in sales volume. The eventual result of optimum investment under Socialism might be a situation in some stores in which prices were never equal to either marginal or average costs, but were always just high enough to result in capacity sales.

We have noted that certain applications of marginal-cost control to retail markups are not feasible under Capitalism because they would result in deficits. Such deficits may be avoided, without giving up the major part of the benefits of marginal-cost price control, by using nonideal service charges, i.e., by charging admission to all retail stores. If admission fees were high enough, all goods could be sold at marginal costs without resulting in any deficit. Department stores might charge admission to each large department or group of small departments. There are many intriguing problems here which we have not the time to analyze. Store admission fees would prevent or delay some desirable sales, but not nearly as many as so-called average-cost pricing prevents. Moreover, they would induce people to enter stores less often, thus reducing the need for floor space and clerks, and would persuade them to make more and larger purchases on each visit to a store. Although appearing to be an additional charge, they would actually reduce retail costs and total retail charges.

The Factory Prices of Manufactured Articles

Nearly all manufacturing firms have marginal costs which are normally well below both their average costs and their selling prices because of surplus capacity, optional variable costs, multi-unit sales, and free optional services. On the average, marginal manufacturing costs are probably 20 to 30 percent below average costs and current prices.

The application of the first corollary of marginal-cost price-output control, equal prices for all customers, to the factory prices of manufactured articles is clear. It means, among other things, that manufacturers should not charge different prices for equal quantities sold at the same time and place to different buyers and should not offer free service to some buyers and not to others.

The second corollary, separate charges for optional services, means that manufacturers should make separate charges for credit, delivery, pickup, consignment, alteration, repair, and other optional services. The first corollary requires that these services shall be available to all buyers at the same price.

The third corollary, multi-marginal pricing, does not have any obvious application to the pricing of manufactured goods.

The fourth corollary, quantity pricing, means that different prices shall be charged for the first and for subsequent units of an article sold in one sale. The price of the first unit should cover all the marginal costs of selling this unit, assuming that only one unit is sold, and the price for additional units should cover only the much lower marginal costs of selling one more unit in the same sale. Quantity pricing should replace quantity discounts, and should be applied to every sale. However, it would affect factory prices much less than retail markups.

Cyclical pricing, the fifth corollary, means that the prices of manufactured articles should go through seasonal cycles. The prices of new automobiles, for instance, should be high in the spring and low in the fall. The demand for cars is higher in the spring than in the fall. Hence, both output and marginal costs should be higher in the spring. Moreover, some cars produced in the fall should be stored for sale in the spring, which would add storage costs to marginal production costs. The cost of storing a $2,000 car for one year is perhaps $200.00, including interest, and the maximum seasonal variation in the prices of such cars should not exceed a year's storage costs. Car output in the spring should be increased up to, but not beyond, the level which results in a $200.00 increase in marginal production costs. Because of the possibility of storage, seasonal price variations should be relatively less for manufactured articles than for services, which cannot be stored. For instance, they should be much less than the seasonal variation in retail store markups and utility rates.

The seventh corollary, on joint products, has more applications in manufacturing than in any other industry. There are many industrial joint products, which include all by-products. In such cases, it is the sum of the prices of the joint products which should equal the marginal costs of producing them.

The eighth corollary that piece rates should equal marginal value productivity, applies when piece rates are paid, and such rates are more widely used in manufacturing than in other industries. Therefore, this corollary should be applied most widely in manufacturing. It would make price equal the marginal cost of producing the last unit each day.

The application of the basic principle of marginal-cost price-output control and its corollaries to manufactured articles would normally result in deficits. Under Socialism the number of manufacturing trusts would be so small and the rewards of the managers would be so determined that it would be feasible to subsidize these trusts so that they could practice marginal-cost output control. Under Capitalism both the number of manufacturing firms and the motives of their managers make subsidies impractical except perhaps in a few industries dominated by large firms. Nevertheless, most of the benefits of marginal-cost control could be achieved by means of various compromises with marginal-cost control.

We have noted that quantity pricing requires different prices for the first and subsequent units of any article sold in one sale. Full marginal-cost output control makes the price for the first unit, as well as the price for subsequent units, equal to marginal cost. But the price of the first unit could be raised high enough to cover sufficient of the non-marginal costs of manufacturing to avoid any deficit. Nearly all sales by manufacturers run to more than one unit. In such cases the major benefits from marginal-cost control, including quantity pricing, result from selling additional units at marginal cost. Raising the price of the first unit high enough to avoid deficits would prevent some sales that ought to be made because it would allocate non-marginal costs to buyers, but the volume of sales would be larger than under so-called average-cost pricing, probably much closer to the ideal level than to the present level.

Other possible compromises are the use of nonideal work-place rents (see pp. 193, 224 above) and the application of those corollaries which would not result in any deficit.

Real-Estate Commissions

Real-estate firms bring buyers and sellers of real estate together and help them to buy or sell. For this service they receive a commission of 5 percent of the value of the property, which is paid by the seller and is paid only when a sale is made. This is a very bad method of pricing the services of real-estate firms because it results in prices which have no relation to the marginal cost of the service rendered. A realtor may sell a $20,000 house and earn a $1,000 commission for one day's work, and he may spend a month in selling a $1,000 lot and earn a commission of $50.00. Overpriced houses are much harder to sell than under-priced houses, and some buyers require many times as much service as others, but the commission paid has no relation to these factors.

The only way to apply marginal-cost control to the price paid for the service of a realtor is to require realtors to charge by the hour for all time spent in selling each property. It is the number of hours devoted to a sale, not the value of the property sold, which varies with and determines marginal cost. It is entirely feasible to adopt this method of pricing the services of realtors under Capitalism because it need not involve any deficits. It is true that prices per hour of service equal only to marginal cost would involve some losses. Such losses could be avoided under Capitalism, and most of the benefits of the proposed pricing system could be obtained, by raising the hourly price for realtor's services high enough to cover their average costs, which are mostly variable costs.

The problem of who should pay the hourly price of a realtor's services is not covered by the theory of marginal-cost price control. Probably the potential or actual buyer should pay part of it so that he will not take an undue amount of the realtor's time, and probably also the would-be seller should pay part of it in order to induce him to fix a reasonable price for his property. We suggest that the buyer pay two thirds and the seller one third on the ground that buyers are more apt to waste the time of realtors than are sellers.

If this allocation of realtors' costs were adopted, marginal-cost price control would probably result in a sharp decrease in the amount of time required to make real-estate sales. Buyers would do less shopping around and would reach a decision more quickly since they would have to pay for all time spent with a relator. Moreover, they would have more trust in the realtor since there would remain no incentive for him to misinform the buyer.

Taking salesmen off a commission basis would reduce their incentive to keep busy, but this is a minor loss in comparison with the gains from the proposed system of payment. Even today many firms pay their salesmen on a salary basis in order to assure better service to customers and more stable earnings for their salesmen.

The same analysis is, of course, applicable to the remuneration of all other brokers now working on a commission basis.

REFORMS WHICH WOULD BRING PRICES CLOSER TO MARGINAL COSTS IN MANY INDUSTRIES

So far in this chapter we have confined ourselves largely to the problem of how marginal-cost price-output control should be applied to individual goods by those who produce them. We have occasionally suggested that measures which would help to solve this problem should be made compulsory, but we have not discussed any economic reforms whose adoption by the state would indirectly help to bring prices in many or all industries closer to marginal cost. To this subject we shall now devote a few pages. To save space, we shall limit ourselves to brief comments on the most important reforms.

In the first place, a drastic restriction of advertising would bring nearly all prices closer to marginal costs. The case against advertising is so strong and so well known that it requires no summary here. It has frequently been noted that in addition to improving the content of newspapers, magazines, radio programs, etc., the elimination or drastic restriction of advertising would save up to six billion dollars a year in the United States. However, so far as we are aware, no one has ever gone on to point out that such measures would also bring nearly all prices closer to marginal costs. This in turn would redistribute the factors among industries and increase their marginal productivity in all industries.

In the second place, government restriction of the frequency of style changes would increase output and bring prices down closer to marginal costs because it would result in the very substantial costs of model changes being spread over a larger output. Such costs are fixed costs, and the more they can be reduced per unit of output, the closer average costs will be to marginal costs. Most style and model changes are made to stimulate sales, not to improve the product, and desirable changes need only be briefly postponed.

Standardization, defined as reduction in the number of styles and sizes produced at the same time, also spreads fixed costs over a larger output and thus brings prices closer to marginal costs. The American federal government has been aiding voluntary standardization in peacetime and requiring it in periods of war or rearmament for thirty years, but it has never pushed standardization nearly as hard as it should. In addition to reducing fixed costs per unit of output, standardization often achieves a sharp cut in marginal costs.

A fourth reform which would bring prices closer to marginal money costs is state conduct of or subsidies for industrial research. Research costs are a money cost which never enters marginal cost but must be covered by prices in private industry. If the state agreed to pay half of all such research costs, prices could be lowered and this would usually bring them closer to marginal cost. The development of a giant synthetic rubber industry by the American federal government illustrates another method of achieving industrial research at public expense. If the synthetic rubber plants are sold to private investors, they should be sold at a price which does not cover any of the research and development costs, thus permitting prices closer to marginal costs.

All protective tariff duties raise marginal money costs above marginal real costs and should be abolished. This would be a correction of marginal money costs, not an application of the rule that prices should equal marginal money cost. It would also correct average money costs, and is highly desirable for that reason under average-cost pricing. We have consistently avoided or limited discussion of the many problems involved in making money costs measure real costs better because we believe this subject deserves a separate monograph and would unduly enlarge and complicate this study. Hence, we merely mention the need for abolishing protective tariffs as an intro-

duction to a less important reform affecting foreign trade, the legaliza-
tion and encouragement of mutual dumping.

Private producers who cannot afford to sell to domestic consumers
at prices below average costs can often afford to sell in foreign markets
at prices well below their domestic prices. This form of price discrimination is called dumping, and is naturally disliked by those firms who
suffer from it, but it may be very beneficial to both the importing and
the exporting country. The theory of marginal-cost control makes
clear why prices below average costs are desirable when marginal costs
are below average costs. Dumping is one method of bringing prices
closer to marginal costs which is entirely feasible under Capitalism,
for it does not involve losses to the producer. It would, of course, be
better to reduce both domestic and foreign prices all the way to marginal costs in all cases, but, until this is achieved, dumping will be
beneficial because it will reduce some prices part of the way to marginal costs.

Dumping usually makes possible a reduction in domestic as well
as in foreign prices of the dumped commodity. The price to foreigners
is kept above the bare marginal costs and foreign sales contribute towards payment of the overhead costs on the domestic sales, thus permitting sale of the domestic supply at a lower price without a reduction in profit. If monopoly prevents this reduction in domestic prices,
it is a fault of monopoly, not a fault of dumping.

It is true, of course, that dumping has at times been practiced
temporarily in order to destroy competitors, create a monopoly, and
permit high subsequent prices. Moreover, legitimate dumping is unpopular because of old mercantilistic beliefs. Both of these reasons for
opposing dumping could be minimized by agreements permitting and
guaranteeing two-way legitimate dumping for a period of years. For
instance, the United States and Switzerland might sign an agreement
that the United States should dump in Switzerland each year ten million dollars worth of automobiles at prices 10 percent below United
States levels and that Switzerland should dump in the United States
ten million dollars worth of watches at similar price reductions. An
agreement of this sort would reduce the price of watches in the United
States and the price of cars in Switzerland. It might also reduce the
price of cars in the United States and the prices of watches in Switzerland. In any case, it would benefit both states because it would bring
some prices nearer to marginal costs in both countries.

All state measures which increase the use of existing capital facilities bring prices closer to marginal costs, not by lowering prices, but by raising marginal costs. Most measures which raise prices and employment in periods of depression have this effect, though it may seem paradoxical to claim that measures which raise prices already well above marginal cost also bring them closer to marginal cost. The explanation is that they raise marginal costs faster than prices. Marginal costs rise very fast when output approaches capacity.

All laws which limit or prohibit price competition—for instance, American retail price maintenance laws—prevent some firms from reducing some prices closer to both their average and their marginal costs. Private trust or cartel agreements to maintain prices have the same effect.

It may seem to the reader that all laws which limit monopoly and promote competition bring prices closer to average and marginal cost by eliminating monopoly profits. This is not true, however. Pure monopoly achieves important economies of scale and reduces the need for advertising, style changes, aggressive selling, etc. These savings may be larger than the resulting monopoly profit. Monopolistic competition increases selling costs, product differentiation costs, and other non-marginal costs until monopoly profits disappear, but this does not mean prices are closer to marginal costs. Most, if not all of the increased costs are non-marginal, and they widen the gap between price and marginal cost.

XI

THE GENERAL ECONOMIC EFFECTS
OF IDEAL PRICE-OUTPUT CONTROL
AND INVESTMENT

IN THE PREVIOUS CHAPTER we explained the application of ideal (marginal-cost) price-output control to those industries whose prices and outputs would be directly affected to the greatest degree by such pricing. We noted that, in the absence of new investment the initial effect of such control upon price and output would often be temporary. The adoption of optimum investment, however, would turn a large part of these initial effects into permanent effects. These price and output changes would have significant overall or general economic consequences which are not as obvious as the direct effects upon the industry concerned. In this chapter, we shall note and briefly discuss the major general economic effects of optimum price-output control and optimum investment.

The most significant general consequence, of course, would be a notable increase in economic welfare. We have already made this clear in our demonstrations of the advantages of optimum price-output control and investment. Therefore, we shall not directly elaborate this point in the present chapter, except to note the effect upon real income. We shall devote our space to less obvious and more specific general effects of ideal price-output control and investment. We begin with the effects upon the physical structure of the economy.

ON THE STRUCTURE OF THE ECONOMY

The general adoption of optimum price-output control and investment would change: (1) the geographical location of nonextractive industry and therefore of population; (2) the scale of production of decreasing-cost firms; (3) the relative size of different industries; and (4) the volume of saving and investment in fixed capital.

The Relocation of Industry

Optimum price-output control and investment would drastically alter the geographical location of industry because: (1) it would eliminate present differences between freight rates on raw materials and end products, and (2) it would sharply reduce nearly all freight rates.

Railroad freight rates on end products are now several times, often more than ten times, as high as on the raw materials and supplies used to make them. This is a strong force tending to persuade all firms to locate new plants near the markets for end products rather than near the sources of raw materials and supplies. With optimum pricing, freight rates on end products would be the same as rates on materials and supplies. The weight of the materials and supplies consumed is ordinarily much more than the weight of finished articles shipped out. Coal and other fuels are completely consumed in the plant, and there is considerable loss of weight in the raw materials used. Hence, if freight rates on finished products were as low as rates on materials and supplies, the most economic plant location, other factors being equal, would be as near as possible to the sources of the materials and supplies.

If freight rates equaled marginal cost, most of the remaining textile plants in the Northeast would be moved to the Southwest and to California to be near the sources of cotton and wool. Most of the clothing factories would be moved from the Northeastern and Middle Atlantic states to the South and Southwest to be near the textile mills. The rubber plants in Ohio would be moved to the South and Southwest to be nearer the synthetic rubber plants and the ports of entry for crude rubber. Many other illustrations of the eventual effect of uniform freight rates on plant location might be given.

Such a relocation of manufacturing plants would notably reduce the total number of ton-miles of freight haulage necessary to produce all manufactured goods. It would substitute hauling of end products for hauling of much heavier materials and supplies.

Increase in the Scale of Production

The second major effect of ideal price-output control and investment upon the structure of industry would be a great increase in the scale of production in decreasing-cost industries due to: (1) lower freight rates on manufactured goods, and (2) the creation of monopolies in decreasing-cost industries.

As we have noted, ideal price and investment policies would sharply reduce freight rates on manufactured goods, probably by 50 to 90 percent. This would greatly expand the market area for each manufacturing plant. Since nearly all such plants have decreasing costs, broadening their markets would enable them to increase their scale of output and lower their costs. Both the reduction in freight rates and the lowering of manufacturing costs would tend to extend their market, increase their sales, and reduce the total number of plants. Existing freight rates on manufactured goods operate, like protective tariffs, to narrow markets, reduce competition, and restrict the scale of production.

Even if freight rates were left unchanged, the application of ideal price-output and investment policies to nontransport industries with decreasing costs would have notable effects upon the scale of production. Nearly all nonextractive industries have indefinitely decreasing costs. If the largest plants in each market area reduced their prices to marginal-cost levels and expanded their investment in durable capital to the ideal degree, they would eventually drive their competitors out of business.

A general tendency towards monopoly already exists, since the average as well as the marginal costs of large plants are usually lower than those of small plants, but it is restrained by legal, political, and ideological forces. Antitrust laws, fear of nationalization or increased government regulation, and fear of price competition all prevent managers of the largest plants from exploiting the advantages of large-scale production to the full.

Greater Relative Expansion of Decreasing-Cost Industries

The third major effect of ideal price-output and investment policies on the physical structure of industry would be a notable increase in the absolute and relative size of decreasing-cost industries and a decrease in the relative, and perhaps in the absolute, size of increasing-cost industries. Marginal-cost price-output control would immediately reduce the prices of all goods produced in plants having excess capacity, and nearly all decreasing-cost plants have excess capacity. The prices of goods produced by increasing-cost industries, now close to marginal cost, would fall when and if demand fell. The sales of nearly all decreasing-cost goods would increase, and the sales of many, perhaps most, increasing-cost goods would fall. This would result in a notable immediate shift of labor, materials, and variable capital from increasing-cost to decreasing-cost industries. Moreover, in time, optimum investment would increase the physical capacity of decreasing-cost industries much faster than the capacity of increasing-cost industries.

In each industry the degree of both the immediate and the long-run effects would depend upon, (1) the rate at which costs decrease or increase, (2) the elasticity of demand, and (3) the effect of increasing national real income upon demand. Other factors being equal, the greatest changes in size would occur in industries with the most rapidly decreasing or increasing long-run average-cost curves, the most elastic demand curves, and demand curves most affected by an increase in average real income.

The industries whose output would expand the most are probably the public utilities and the durable goods industries. They have costs which decrease relatively fast and have relatively elastic demand curves which would be shifted upwards relatively far by an increase in national real income. The chief exception is freight transportation, the demand for which would be sharply reduced by relocation of industry. Book publishing, the production of synthetic raw materials, and moving-picture exhibition would also expand greatly. We shall say no more on the expansion of decreasing-cost industries because we covered this in the previous chapter. However, we have not previously discussed in any detail the effect of ideal price-output and investment policies on the size of increasing-cost (extractive) industries.

The effect of these ideal policies on such industries would also depend upon the same three factors—rate of cost increase, elasticity of demand, and income effects. The over-all effect would be a marked fall in relative size, but the effect would vary widely from industry to industry. The greatest declines in output would occur in extractive industries producing natural raw materials for which synthetic and/or manufactured substitute materials are now available (wool, cotton, lumber, leather, crude rubber, etc.) and in industries producing cheap, low-grade foods for which more desired and expensive substitutes are available. In the case of both foods and natural raw materials, highly processed types would tend to replace less processed types. For instance, plywood would tend to replace lumber because the cost of processing would fall and the cost of the raw wood at the mill might rise. For the same reason, aluminum, glass, and plastics would replace copper, steel, nickel, tin, etc., in many uses. Glass and paper containers would probably tend to replace tin cans, steel drums, and wooden boxes. Aluminum would replace more copper in electric wires. In the construction industry, there would be a widespread substitution of paper, glass, clay products, plastics and other highly processed synthetic materials for wood, stone, and marble. Moreover, the use of prefabricated components would be greatly increased because prefabrication is subject to rapidly decreasing costs.

An increase in real national income would raise the value of food consumed, even though farm products are subject to increasing costs. But ideal price-output and investment policies would result in a notable change in the type of food consumed. The output of cheap, little-processed foods (potatoes, beans, etc.) might actually fall, while there would be a marked increase in the output of expensive, highly processed foods (meat, cheese, salad oils, etc.). The use of frozen foods would grow. The output of expensive foods like beefsteak would increase simply because of the rise in real income. The output of highly processed foods would grow because of the reduction in processing costs and the rise in the costs of many raw foods.

Greater Production of Manufactured Capital Goods

The fourth major effect of ideal price-output and investment policies upon the structure of industry would be a substantial increase in the use of tools, machines, and factory-made equipment in both increasing-cost and decreasing-cost industries. These policies would: (1)

sharply reduce the prices of such goods, all produced in industries with decreasing costs; (2) increase the real wages of workers whose labor would be saved by the use of such capital goods; and (3) expand the supply of capital funds available for investment. The increase in capital funds would result from higher personal real incomes.

ON THE SO-CALLED BUSINESS CYCLE

Under Capitalism, widespread marginal-cost control would greatly reduce the severity of so-called business cycles (irregular fluctuations in output). One of the chief causes of booms and depressions is the relative inflexibility or stickiness of some prices, notably in nonextractive industries. Marginal-cost control would make prices in these industries far more flexible. When the output of a nonextractive industry is above capacity, short-run marginal costs are usually well above average cost, but a small decline in output will reduce marginal costs very sharply because it will reduce plant congestion, overtime work, and the use of high-cost machinery. Hence, marginal-cost control would usually result in a sharp price decline when output fell from above to below capacity.

A business recession reduces marginal costs not only by reducing output but also by lowering money wages and the cost of materials and supplies. The products of one plant are often the materials and supplies of another. Thus, when a depression begins, marginal-cost control would lower prices even in industries previously operating well below capacity.

In addition to reducing prices quickly and generally, marginal-cost control might help to increase the quantity of money and effective demand when a recession begins. The general fall in prices would make necessary larger subsidies to individual firms in order to cover the difference between average and marginal costs. In order to pay these subsidies, the state should create new money, for more money is needed whenever the value of money starts to rise.

Under so-called average-cost pricing there is a universal reluctance to reduce prices when demand falls. Some industries, notably the railroads and public utilities, even try to raise their prices on the plausible ground that the decline in output has increased their fixed costs per unit of output. Fortunately, the force of events usually defeats the logic of orthodox average-cost price-output theory at such times, and many businessmen are compelled to lower their prices below average costs, thus making an unwilling and partial concession to the logic of marginal-cost control.

We have not claimed that marginal-cost price-output control would reduce or prevent large fluctuations in output under Socialism because there are several other features of such an economy which should prevent such fluctuations—for instance, giving workers the right to demand work, central control of saving and investment, and central control of the quantity of money. However, if none of these alternative methods of preventing large irregular fluctuations in total output were used, marginal-cost price-output control would prevent such fluctuations.

ON THE PRICE LEVEL

The sudden general adoption of marginal-cost control today would initially reduce the retail price level by perhaps 10 to 20 percent, assuming an average level of production. (It would be less in a boom, much more in a depression.) Optimum investment would make most of the initial effect permanent.

The price level would fall initially for two reasons. As we have explained, marginal costs are normally below average costs in nearly all nonextractive industries for a variety of reasons. In some—for instance, in most public utilities—marginal costs are usually far below so-called average costs. Optimum investment would tend to maintain most of the initial fall in prices because it would direct new capital into decreasing-cost industries. Moreover, the combination of ideal price-output control and investment would probably lower the demand curves for some goods produced by increasing-cost industries. Their supply curves also might be shifted lower because the cost of materials and supplies might fall enough to offset the effect of higher wages and interest. Thus ideal price-output control and investment would reduce the prices of some products of many extractive industries.

All of the structural changes previously described would increase the total real output of goods by increasing the productivity of existing factors. For instance, plant relocation would sharply reduce real transport costs. Assuming no compensating increase in the quantity or turnover rate of money, this increase in real output would lower the price level proportionately.

ON INTEREST, RENT, AND WAGES

The effect of marginal-cost price-output control on interest rates cannot be determined in advance because such control would create several unmeasurable counteracting forces which would affect these rates. The shift in existing capital from less to more productive marginal uses and the allocation of more new capital to decreasing-cost industries would tend to increase the marginal productivity of capital and, hence, interest rates. On the other hand, the fuller use of both old and new capital facilities, due to the smoothing out of daily, weekly, and seasonal production cycles and irregular fluctuations in output and to longer hours of plant operation, would tend to reduce the marginal productivity of capital. Moreover, any increase in saving due to the growth of real national income would tend to depress interest rates.

The effect on total land rent is also unpredictable for the same reasons. Marginal-cost control would reduce output and rent in extractive industries producing raw materials and supplies with synthetic substitutes and, hence, a very elastic demand. It would increase the output of luxury materials and foods without close synthetic substitutes. The expansion of nonextractive industries due to ideal price-output and investment control would also increase rent, but very slightly.

Since rent might fall, and interest rates would rise little, if any, almost the entire increase in national income made possible by optimum price-output control and investment would take the form of higher real wages. The rise in real wages might easily amount to 20 to 30 percent in normal years, and would be much higher if figured on a depression year base. Assuming no increase in the quantity of money, this rise in real wages would be due to a fall in the retail price level rather than to a rise in money wages. Fundamentally, of course, it would be due to an increase in the marginal productivity of labor caused by a large shift of labor from uses in which the marginal productivity of labor is relatively low to uses in which it is greater.

ON REAL NATIONAL INCOME

As previously noted, the most significant effect of the general adoption of marginal-cost control would be a substantial increase in the real national income. This would result from: (1) a transfer of some existing labor and variable capital from less productive marginal uses in industries operating at capacity to more productive uses in industries with surplus capacity; (2) the allocation for a number of years of nearly all new variable capital and labor to relatively productive marginal uses in firms whose marginal costs are below their average costs; (3) the extension of the hours of plant operation whenever marginal costs during the additional hours are below market prices; (4) variation of retail prices during the hours of the day and days of the week so as to achieve a larger volume of business with existing facilities; (5) variation of all prices from week to week to help achieve this goal and to give steady and full employment to labor; (6) the increased output of workers paid piece rates fully reflecting the value of their marginal output: and (7) the more rapid introduction and acceptance of newly patented capital and consumers' goods and copyrighted text and reference books; etc. This list could be greatly expanded. Every application of optimum price-output control and investment which we have discussed in this monograph would increase the real national income or the leisure enjoyed by workers.

It is extremely difficult to estimate the magnitude of this increase in national income. First, an estimate depends upon whether one credits marginal-cost price-output control with the power to end so-called business cycles. Secondly, it depends to a considerable degree upon how far business leaders and the state are willing to go in increasing the hours of operation of stores and plants. Thirdly, a good estimate requires a study of the demand and marginal cost curves in all large industries.

In making our own crude estimate, we assume no effect upon the business cycle. There are so many other effective ways of preventing depressions that we can scarcely give full credit for this to marginal-cost control, and, also, we wish our estimate to be conservative.

On this basis, we estimate that the general application of marginal-cost control would, over a period of years, increase the real national income by 10 to 20 percent, in addition to any normal secular growth. A large part of this increase would be due to a fuller use of capital equipment rather than to a shift in factors from increasing-cost to decreasing-cost industries and/or an accelerated development of the latter. Ideal piece rates alone might increase the output of most piece-rate workers by 20 percent without any increase in plant capacity.

BIBLIOGRAPHY

* Designates most important

Arrow, K. J. "Little's Critique of Welfare Economics," *American Economic Review*, XLI (Dec., 1951), 922–34. See pp. 933–34.

Bain, Joe S. "The Normative Problem in Industrial Regulation," *American Economic Review*, XXXIII, Supplement (March, 1943), 54–70.

Baldwin, C. D. Economic Planning. Urbana, University of Illinois Press, 1942. See pp. 132–35, 147–51.

Barnes, Irston R. The Economics of Public Utility Regulation. New York, Crofts, 1942. See pp. 586–88.

*Beckwith, Burnham P. The Economic Theory of a Socialist Economy. Palo Alto, Calif. Stanford University Press, 1949. See pp. 22, 67–86, 151–88, 355–62, 373–76, 406–10.

Bergson, Abram. "Socialist Economics," in H. S. Ellis (ed.), A Survey of Contemporary Economics. Philadelphia, Blakiston, 1948. See pp. 424–28.

*Bonbright, James C. "Major Controversies as to the Criteria of Reasonable Public Utility Rates," *American Economic Review*, XXX, Supplement (Feb., 1940), 379–89. See p. 385.

Bowen, Howard R. "The Interpretation of Voting in the Allocation of Economic Resources," *Quarterly Journal of Economics*, XLVIII (Nov., 1943), 27–48. See p. 28.

—— Toward Social Economy. New York, Rinehart, 1948. See pp. 164–71.

*Buchanan, James M. "Knut Wicksell on Marginal-Cost Pricing," *Southern Economic Journal*, XVIII (Oct., 1951), 173–78.

*Clark, John M. Studies in the Economics of Overhead Costs. Chicago, University of Chicago Press, 1923. See pp. 17–32, 323–26, 448–49.

Clemens, E. W. Economics and Public Utilities. Appleton, New York, 1950. See pp. 260–62.

—— "The Marginal Revenue Curve under Price Discrimination," *American Economic Review*, XXXVIII (June, 1948), 388–90.

—— "Price Discrimination in Decreasing Cost Industries," *American Economic Review*, XXXI (Dec., 1941), 794–802.

*Coase, R. H. "The Marginal Cost Controversy," *Economica*, XIII (Aug., 1946), 168–82.

*Coase, R. H. "The Marginal Cost Controversy: Some Further Comments," *Economica,* XIV (May, 1947), 150–53.

—— "Price and Output Policy of State Enterprise: A Comment," *Economic Journal,* LV (April, 1945), 112–13.

Dickinson, H. D. Economics of Socialism. London, Oxford University Press, 1939. See pp. 105–8, 151–54.

—— "Price Formation in a Socialist Economy," *Economic Journal,* XLIII (June, 1933), 237–50.

Dobb, Maurice. "Economic Theory and Socialist Economy: A Reply," *Review of Economic Studies,* II (1934–35), 144–51.

—— Political Economy and Capitalism. London, Routledge, 1937. See pp. 308–9.

—— "Problems of a Socialist Economy," *Economic Journal,* XLIII (1933), 588–98.

Durbin, E. F. "Economic Calculus in a Planned Economy," *Economic Journal,* XLVI (Dec., 1936), 676–90.

—— "Note on Mr. Lerner's 'Dynamical Propositions,' " *Economic Journal* XLVII (Sept., 1937), 577–92.

—— Problems of Economic Planning. London, Routledge, 1949. See pp. 84–90, 150–55.

Ellis, Howard S., and William Fellner. "External Economies and Diseconomies," *American Economic Review,* XXXIII (Sept., 1943), 493–511.

*Fleming, J. M. "Price and Output Policy of State Enterprise," *Economic Journal,* LV (Dec., 1945), 328–37.

*—— "Production and Price Policy in Public Enterprise," *Economica,* XVII (Feb., 1950), 1–22.

Fraser, L. M. "Rejoinder," *Review of Economic Studies,* I (Feb., 1934), 141–43.

—— "Taxation and Returns," *Review of Economic Studies,* I (Oct., 1933), 45–59.

Frisch, Ragnar. "The Dupuit Taxation Theorem," *Econometrica,* VIII (April, 1939), 145–50, 156–57.

Graham, Frank. "Some Aspects of Protection Further Considered," *Quarterly Journal of Economics,* XXXVII (Feb., 1923), 199–227.

Hayek, F. A. von (ed.). Collectivist Economic Planning. London, Routledge, 1935. See pp. 226–27, 274, 289.

—— "Socialist Calculation: The Competitive Solution," *Economica,* VIII (May, 1940), 125–49. See pp. 138–39.

Hazelwood, A. "Optimum Pricing as Applied to Telephone Service," *Review of Economic Studies,* XVIII (1950–51), 67–78.

*Henderson, A. M. "Prices and Profits in State Enterprises," *Review of Economic Studies,* XVI (1948–49), 13–24.

—— "The Pricing of Public Utility Undertakings," *Manchester School,* XV (Sept., 1947), 223–50.

Hicks, J. R. "The Rehabilitation of Consumers' Surplus," *Review of Economic Studies,* VIII (Feb., 1941), 108–16.

Hoff, T. J. B. Economic Calculation in the Socialist Society. London, Hodge, 1949. Translated from the Norwegian edition of 1938. See pp. 144–52.

*Hotelling, Harold. "The General Welfare in Relation to Problems of Taxation and of Railway and Utility Rates," Econometrica, VI (July, 1938), 242–69.

—— "The Relation of Prices to Marginal Costs in an Optimum System," Econometrica, VII (April, 1939), 151–55, 158–60.

Houthakker, H. S. "Electricity Tariffs in Theory and Practice," Economic Journal, LXI (March, 1951), 1–25.

Johnston, Kenneth H. British Railways and Economic Recovery. London, Clerke and Cockeran, 1949.

Kahn, R. F. "Some Notes on Ideal Output," Economic Journal, XLV (March, 1935), 1–36.

Knight, F. H. "Some Fallacies in the Interpretation of Social Cost," Quarterly Journal of Economics, XXXVIII (1923–24), 582–606.

*Krishnamurti, B. V. Pricing in Planned Economy. Bombay, Oxford University Press, 1949.

Lange, Oskar. "On the Economic Theory of Socialism," Review of Economic Studies, IV (1936–37), 53–71, 123–42, 143–44.

Launhardt, W. Mathematische Begrundung der Volkswirtschaftslehre. 1885. See pp. 201–4.

*—— Theorie der Tarifbildiung der Eisenbahnen. Berlin, 1890. See pp. 1–43, especially p. 5.

*Lerner, Abba P. The Economics of Control. New York, Macmillan, 1944. See pp. 98–105.

*—— "Statics and Dynamics in Socialist Economics," Economic Journal, XLVII (June, 1937), 255–70.

*—— "Theory and Practice in Socialist Economics," Review of Economic Studies, VI (Oct., 1938), 71–75.

Lewis, W. A. "Fixed Costs," Economica, XIII (Nov., 1946), 231–58.

—— Overhead Costs. London, G. Allen, 1949. See pp. 9–69.

—— "The Two-Part Tariff," Economica, VIII (1941), 249–70, 399–408.

*Lindahl, Erik. Die Gerechtigkeit der Besteurung. Lund, Sweden, 1919. See pp. 158–63.

*Lippincott, Benjamin E., Fred M. Taylor, and Oskar Lange. On the Economic Theory of Socialism. Minneapolis, University of Minnesota Press, 1938. See pp. 76–78, 92.

*Little, I. M. D. A Critique of Welfare Economics. Oxford, Clarendon Press, 1950. See pp. 148–210, 255–66.

Locklin, D. P. "The Literature on Railway Rate Theory," Quarterly Journal of Economics, XXXXVII (Feb., 1933).

McKenzie, L. W. "Ideal Output and the Interdependence of Firms," Economic Journal, LXI (Dec., 1951), 785–804.

Marshall, Alfred. Principles of Economics. 8th ed. New York, Macmillan, 1948. See pp. 470–90.

*Meade, J. E. An Introduction to Economic Analysis and Policy. Oxford, Clarendon Press, 1936 (New York, Oxford University Press, 1938). See Chap. 8 of Part II.

—— Planning and the Price Mechanism: the Liberal-Socialist Solution. London, G. Allen, 1948.

Meade, J. E., and J. M. Fleming. "Mr. Lerner on 'The Economics of Control,' " Economic Journal, LV (April, 1945), 47–69.

*—— "Price and Output Policy of State Enterprise," Economic Journal, LIV (Dec., 1944), 321–28, 337–39.

*Montgomery, R. H. "Government Ownership and Operation of Railroads," in American Academy, Annals, CCI (Jan., 1939), 137–45.

Myint, Hla. Theories of Welfare Economics. Cambridge, Mass., Harvard University Press, 1948. See pp. 166–72, 181–83.

*Nordin, J. A. "The Marginal Cost Controversy: A Reply," Economica, XIV (May, 1947), 134–49.

Norris, Harry. "State Enterprise and Output Policy and the Problems of Cost Imputation," Economica, XIV (Feb., 1947), 54–62.

Paine, C. L. "Rationalization and the Theory of Excess Capacity," Economica, III (Feb., 1936), 46–60. See p. 52.

—— "Some Aspects of Discrimination by Public Utilities," Economica, IV (Nov., 1937), 425–39.

Pareto, V. Manuel d'Economie Politique. Paris, V. Giard and E. Briere, 1909. See pp. 363–64.

Pegrum, D. F. "Incremental Cost Pricing: A Comment," Journal of Land and Public Utility Economics, XX (Feb., 1944), 58–60.

Pigou, Arthur C. The Economics of Welfare. 4th ed. London, Macmillan, 1948. See pp. 221–24, 313–15, 365, 802–10.

—— "Empty Economic Boxes: A Reply," Economic Journal, XXXII (1922), 458–65.

—— Socialism versus Capitalism. London, Macmillan, 1937. See pp. 109–15.

—— Wealth and Welfare. London, Macmillan, 1912. See pp. 176–78.

Putnam, John. The Modern Case for Socialism. Boston, Meador, 1943. See pp. 146–47.

Reder, Melvin W. Studies in the Theory of Welfare Economics. New York, Columbia University Press, 1947. See pp. 48–60.

Robertson, D. H. "Those Empty Boxes," Economic Journal, XXXIV (March, 1924), 16–41.

Robinson, Joan. The Economics of Imperfect Competition. London, Macmillan, 1933. See pp. 204–8, 283–84, 316–18.

—— "Mr. Fraser on Taxation and Returns," Review of Economic Studies, I (Feb., 1934), 137–40.

Rowson, R. B. "The Two-Part Tariff, Further Notes by an Electrical Engineer," Economica, VIII (Nov., 1941), 392–98.

Ruggles, Nancy. "Recent Developments in the Theory of Marginal Cost Pricing," Review of Economic Studies, XVII (1949–50), 107–26.

—— "The Welfare Basis of the Marginal Cost Pricing Principle," *ibid.*,
XVII (1949–50), 29–46.

Samuelson, P. A. Economics. New York, McGraw, 1948. See pp. 515, 601.

—— Foundations of Economic Analysis. Cambridge, Mass., Harvard University Press, 1948. See pp. 207–8.

Schumpeter, J. A. Capitalism, Socialism, and Democracy. New York, Harper, 1942. See pp. 175–76.

—— "Vilfredo Pareto (1849–1923)," *Quarterly Journal of Economics*, LXIII (May, 1949), 147–73. See p. 164.

Shove, G. F. "Varying Costs and Marginal Net Products," *Economic Journal*, XXXVIII (June, 1928), 258–66.

Sweezy, A. R. "The Economist's Place under Socialism," in *Explorations in Economics*. New York, McGraw, 1936. See pp. 424–25.

Thirlby, G. F. "The Marginal Cost Controversy: A Note on Mr. Coase's Model," *Economica*, XLV (Feb., 1947), 458–67.

Thompson, C. W., and W. R. Smith. Public Utility Economics. New York, McGraw, 1941. See pp. 272–74.

*Troxel, C. Emery. Economics of Public Utilities. Rinehart, New York, 1947. See Chap. 20 and pp. 755–61.

*—— "I. Incremental Cost Determination of Utility Prices," *Journal of Land and Public Utility Economics*, XVIII (Nov., 1942), 458–67.

*—— "II. Limitations of the Incremental Cost Pattern of Pricing," *ibid.*, XIX (Feb., 1943), 28–39.

*—— "III. Incremental Cost Control under Public Ownership," *ibid.*, XIX (Aug., 1943), 292–99.

Tyndall, D. G. "Incremental Cost Pricing: A Further Comment," *Journal of Land and Public Utility Economics*, XX (Feb., 1944), 60–63.

—— "The Relative Merits of Average Cost Pricing, Marginal Cost Pricing, and Price Discrimination," *Quarterly Journal of Economics*, LXV (Aug., 1951), 342–72.

Uhr, C. G. "Knut Wicksell—A Centennial Evaluation," *American Economic Review*, XLI (Dec., 1951), 829–61. See pp. 834–35.

*Vickrey, William. "Some Objections to Marginal-Cost Pricing," *Journal of Political Economy*, LVI (June, 1948), 218–38.

Wallace, Donald. "A Critical Review of Some Instances of Government Price Control," in Temporary National Economic Committee Monograph No. 32, *Economic Standards of Government Price Control*. Washington, Government Printing Office, 1941. See p. 214.

—— "Kinds of Public Control to Replace or Supplement Antitrust Laws," *American Economic Review*, XXX Supplement (March, 1940), 194–212.

*Wicksell, Knut. Finanztheoretische Untersuchungen. Jena, Gustav Fischer, 1896. See pp. 126–38.

Wilson, T. "Price and Output Policy of State Enterprise," *Economic Journal*, LV (Dec., 1945), 454–60.

Young, Allyn. "Pigou's Wealth and Welfare," *Quarterly Journal of Economics*, XXVII (Aug., 1913), 672–86.

INDEX